Revealing the Hidden Hope:
Entering in at the Strait Gate, Through The Doorway to an Already Decided Destiny

Matthew 7:13

BY

Dr. Xavier T. Carter Sr.
Educator, Author, Pastor, and Teacher

authorHOUSE®

AuthorHouse™ LLC
1663 Liberty Drive
Bloomington, IN 47403
www.authorhouse.com
Phone: 1-800-839-8640

Published by AuthorHouse   04/28/2014

ISBN: 978-1-4918-4635-3 (sc)
ISBN: 978-1-4918-4633-9 (hc)
ISBN: 978-1-4918-4634-6 (e)

Library of Congress Control Number: 2013923516

AN ABSTRACT OF THE BOOK

"Revealing the Hidden Hope:
Entering in at the Strait Gate, Through
the Doorway to an Already Decided Destiny"
By
Xavier Trone Carter Sr., Ed. D.

"Revealing the Hidden Hope" is about making a decisive-decision to enter into life at the 'Strait Gate:' [going] through the doorway into an already decided destiny. Hereinafter I shall call it *Entering* for it is a work in progress.

Over time we've been led to believe that Salvation is synonymous with dying and going to heaven. While I respect what happened yesterday, I am more focused on today and the future—one that's innovative, positive, productive, and progressive. I believe that Salvation should no longer be defined by 'what we have always done' but rather what should be done. The full complement of Salvation begins now, while we yet live. It includes apprehending and adhering to the Divine Order of Authority in this world. Stated succinctly, it is the perfect combination of trust and belief—which means doing the right thing, the right way.

While some may still be convinced that history is the way to go, we—the Holy Spirit speaking to me and through me—invite you to come to your own conclusion. ***"Revealing the Hidden Hope: Entering in at the Strait Gate through the doorway to an already decided destiny"*** is about the calling of the Church-of-God-in-Christ together, defining, describing, and delineating the path of righteousness from earth's sorrow to heaven's joy for the people whom God created as one body in Christ. Simply stated this book is a virtual 'how-to' manual for those who have an ear to hear what the Spirit of God is saying to the people of God, both within and without the organized Church.

In what I believe to be one of the most salient of all of His revelations, Jesus identified and compared "good" and "evil" without leaving a stone unturned. In St. John 10:10, He called

Satan a thief, and labeled him a criminal with undetermined limitations. He stated with certainty that Satan came to steal, kill, and destroy. By labeling him a thief, Jesus makes it known that by using thoughts, ideas, and suggestions (TIS's), Satan will steal, kill and destroy without provocation or exception. As a matter of fact, his provident purpose for coming into this world is to deprive every one of their life, liberty, and pursuit of happiness. The unfortunate circumstance with which we live is that many if not most people, do not know him and are unaware of his dastardly deeds. In comparison, Jesus omitted the specificity but in a very stunning and striking contrast, identified Himself, his role and his function. He said, *"I am come that they might have life and that they might have it more abundantly"* (John 10:10b).

That statement raised two questions for this writer. The first is "When?" Jesus made this statement more than two-thousand years ago; so my question is "when can we have it?" My next question is "How?" Jesus told us what to expect now that He has come; but He stopped short of telling us "How" to access the "abundant life." That said dotting the "i's" "crossing the "t's" and filling in the blanks is the focus of *'Entering.'*

A diligent and protracted study of the scriptures has informed this writer that there are answers to both of those questions, and that they are readily available to those who have an ear, and who wish to hear what the Spirit of God (SOG) is saying to the Churches (Revelation 2:11, 17, 29; 3:6, 13, and 22). Further, in *Entering* I argue that there is an overarching need to develop strategies that are paramount, and will ultimately overcome traditional barriers to spiritual growth and development. What I have found is "the hidden hope"—which has been there, in plain sight, all the time. That 'Hidden Hope' is quite possibly the focus of the 'profitability' to which Paul was referring in his second letter to Timothy, Chapter 3 Verse 16. There we read,

> *"All scripture is given by inspiration of God, and is profitable for doctrine, for reproof, for correction, for instruction in righteousness: that the man of God may be perfect, thoroughly furnished unto all good works."*

So it is that I believe I can say with certainty to those who are concerned, your search is over for the answers to both questions are presented in this book.

What you are reading here is an abstract of a book for which almost all of Christendom has been waiting. What makes that so? You might ask. No doubt you have heard or read the cliché which says, "In the battles of life, you win some and you lose some." While that cliché might be true for most people much of the time, my question is "Does it have to be? And if so, are there any options?" In response to several inquiries, my response was 'No it does not have to be, and yes, there are options. Since Jesus did not put any contingencies on His claim, I have found it to be meaningless to go through life placing question marks where He arbitrarily placed periods. In the last six years, prayer and supplication have given me access to the "Hidden Hope" that has been there all the time; and the authority to reveal it to the world.

SEMANTICS

Unless otherwise indicated, all scripture references herein are taken from the King James Version (KJV) of the Bible, copyright 1997. For clarity and conciseness, and in an effort to keep with the gender specifics of the Bible, all concerns, comments, conclusions and directives in *Entering* are addressed primarily to the man, unless they are clearly feminine. Thus, the hero in this book is designated as "he," but without prejudice, since the same situation, unless otherwise indicated, could just as easily be outlined with "she," *mutatis* mutandis—that is to say, the necessary changes have been made. If on occasion, however, the woman's role differs significantly from the man's, it is treated separately. The preacher and teacher, similarly without prejudice, is designated as "he" and the vocabulary and viewpoints are primarily oriented towards the pastor as the primary teacher. However, the laity, regardless of his or her station in life, will find this book extremely challenging, equally as helpful, interesting, and user-friendly.

As a matter of personal perception, I don't believe history can really be understood unless and until it is lived (Ecclesiastes 1:9, TEV). Therefore, suffice it to say—let it be enough to say—that the information contained herein is part of my ever-present past. I have either lived it, or I am in the process of living it. That said I have written primarily in the first person. However, there are times when I fluctuate between the second and third person to avoid the appearance of excessive repetition. Finally, somewhere I read that "repetition is the mother of retention;" so it is that you will find that in *Entering,* repetition of certain scriptures and selected pre-suppositions, will be prevalent.

VITAL STATISTICS

TITLE
"Revealing the Hidden Hope: Entering in at the Strait Gate, Through the Doorway into an Already Decided Destiny"

AUTHOR
Xavier Trone Carter, Sr., Ed. D.

TO WHOM WRITTEN
To the people of God everywhere

PURPOSE
THE overall purpose of *Entering* is to enlighten, enhance, and encourage participants-in-the-process to develop a mental state of readiness that equates to their desire for the abundant life to which Jesus referred in St John 10:10b, thereby revealing the wondrous grace of God, line upon line, precept upon precept.

AIMS AND OBJECTIVES
THE aims and objectives of this work are to paint and present a literal portrait of success, and the procedural process which leads to it. The end result is the enjoyment of the full complement of salvation. Traditionally speaking, the act of going to heaven when we die is believed to be the end-all and the crowning glory for the Christian man or woman. It is my intent to introduce to some and present to others a divinely-disseminated pattern for godly living—the end of which will enable and empower all participants-in-the-process to enter in at the Strait Gate (Matthew 7:13) and to experience and be exposed to heaven on earth in real time. Simply stated, it will assist them in doing the right thing the right way, thereby enjoying the blessings of heaven while he or she yet lives.

SETTING
IN the Great Commission (Matthew 28:18-20, KJV), Jesus used the verbs "Teach" and "Teaching." For reasons known only to them, preachers today—believing, I suppose, that in all preaching there is some teaching—have substituted "preach" for "teach" and "preaching" for "teaching." However effective their brand of preaching may be—in this case—it is lacking in learning. Thus, their hearers are left to bathe in the innocence of ignorance, riding a merry-go-round of madness on an exercise in futility.

KEY PEOPLE
GOD in all three persons: the Father, the Son, and the Holy Spirit; my mother—who in me, prepared the soil for the seed to be planted in the fullness of time—and the people of God over whom the Spirit of God has given me charge for more than three decades.

KEY PLACES
Richmond, California; Los Angeles, CA, and Birmingham, AL

KEY WORDS
"Who," "What," "When," "Where," "Why," "How," and "Now What"

SPECIAL FEATURES
THIS writer believes God has invested in him a modicum of His wisdom, a complimentary amount of knowledge, and the holy boldness to call a spade a spade and sin by its right name without fear of contradiction or condemnation. It is because of God's investment and my voluntary but deliberate follow-up that I am currently being, showered with blessings-unlimited and all good things without end for my obedience (1 Corinthians 2:9). That having been said it is my heart's desire and my prayer to God on a daily basis that the context and content of *"Entering"* will uncover

and delineate truth in a language that my readers will receive and believe. Further, that by believing they will have life through the name of Jesus; and with their lives they will edify themselves and glorify God.

CONTENTS

PART FOUR

PART ONE

INTRODUCTION

IN GOD'S OWN TIME

NOTHING happens for naught. Everything was designed to be manifested in God's Kairos—God's own time. Thus, what you will read in this book has come into being in God's own time. In the opening lines of Book One of Charles Dickens' 'A tale of two Cities (1859), we find these words written:

> "It was the best of times, it was the worst of times, it was the age of wisdom, it was the age of foolishness, it was the epoch of belief, it was the epoch of incredulity, it was the season of Light, it was the season of Darkness, it was the spring of hope, it was the winter of despair, we had everything before us, we had nothing before us, we were all going direct to Heaven, we were all going direct the other way . . ."

What Dickens was describing was life as directed by the Spirit of God and life when we strive to live it void of the Lordship and leadership of the Holy Spirit. Dickens wrote in 1859. This is 2013. The scene that Dickens described a hundred and fifty years ago is still prevalent today. The only things that have changed are the players and the fact that we are not left alone to make this journey from earth's sorrow to heaven's joy.

Paul wrote:

> *Likewise the Spirit also helpeth our infirmities: for we know not what we should pray for as we ought: but the Spirit itself maketh intercession for us with groanings which cannot be uttered. And He that searcheth the hearts knoweth what is the mind of the Spirit, because He maketh intercession for us with groanings which cannot be uttered. And He that searcheth the hearts knoweth what is the mind of the Spirit because He*

> *maketh intercession for the saints according to the will of God.*

Paul's focus is on God-the-Holy-Spirit, the third person in the blessed Trinity. And for the record, each of the three persons in the Trinity has three facets: person, presence, and power; and it's important to be able to distinguish between each facet. In this passage, emphasis is on the person and the power of the Spirit of God. For example, Jesus identified Him as the Comforter—which, said He, making reference to His power—is the Holy Ghost—this time to Him as a person—who will teach you all things, and bring all things to your remembrance whatsoever I have said to you." Many, if not most believers have not stopped to see each of those three facets at work. And personally, I have only been aware of them for the last six years.

However, because each of them are active in our lives all day, every day, I believe it is paramount for us to discern the differences.

In the opening pages of the New Testament, we read that John the Baptist came to prepare the way for the Messiah as prophesied by the prophet Isaiah in Chapter 53. John arrived and established his role-and-function as the fore-runner, of Christ—who is our hidden hope. He described himself as "the voice of one crying in the wilderness," 'make straight the path of the Lord.''

When his time was fulfilled, scripture says John had been put in prison and Jesus came into Galilee preaching the gospel of the kingdom of God. The Spirit of God (SOG) directed John Mark—his given name—to highlight Jesus' arrival in Galilee in the first chapter of his Gospel. Verse fifteen (15) reads, ***"The time is fulfilled, and the kingdom of God is at hand. Repent, and believe in the gospel"*** (Mark 1:15, NKJV). Those words revealed our hidden hope and launched Jesus' ministry in Galilee. After reading them they not only became my marching orders, they gave me the inspiration to write from my experiences and exposure. By way of explanation it was as if all of a sudden I was transformed; my mind was renewed, my ears were opened to hear the voice of the Spirit of God, and I was made able to receive and believe what thus saith the Lord, verbatim and without exception.

For the first time in more than thirty-five years of preaching, I not only took those words of Jesus verbatim and without exception, I was empowered to read between the lines, connecting man to God and God to man. Simply stated, I can now see clearly what I have not been able to see since I began preaching in 1976. The only explanation I have is that everything began happening in God's own time. Whereas I have struggled to interpret the scriptures in a positive and meaningful way from the outset of my preaching ministry; since January, 2007, the SOG has enabled and empowered me to use the scriptures to manifest the "Incarnate Word by the spoken word, from the written word," in a more positive, productive, progressive manner. In addition, my insight has been deepened, my motivation has been enhanced, and as a result I have been blessed and inspired to write three books: *Entering* is the third of the trilogy.

IN GOD'S OWN TIME

UNTIL now, pastors and preachers in the organized church have endeavored to share the gospel by a curious form of 'story-telling'—for lack of a better way to describe contemporary preaching. They interpret selected scriptures and then sermon-by-sermon they strive to fit the lives of their people into those scriptures. Perhaps there is nothing wrong with that form of sharing the gospel. However, in these last seven years I have been moved to take exception to that methodology, and to develop and delineate an alternative. Such is the focus of this book.

It is not my intent to re-invent the wheel, but rather to start the wheel to roll in a different direction. Why? Someone asked. My answer is, "it's time." Everyone has an opinion, and rightfully so, they are entitled to it whether we agree with it or not. Suffice it to say *"Entering"* is my opinion. The major difference between any of my opinions and the opinions of those from whom I have heard is that my preaching is limited to making my hearers able, accessible, and accountable. Instead of being satisfied with leaving them to 'bathe in the innocence of ignorance' and to remain members of 'Pastor said' club, I strive to make them able to see for themselves; to develop their spiritual growth and development by enlightening, enhancing, and encouraging them to use what God gave each of us: "the Spirit of power, and of love, and of a sound mind" (2 Timothy 1:7). Close observation will reveal that most practicing Christians are scripturally ignorant, and will respond to questions by saying, "I don't know, but the pastor said."

Along with enhancing their abilities, thereby making them able, lessons in humility are attached to help keep them accessible. My experiences and exposure have been encouraged by the apostle Paul when he urged all of his readers to "study to show themselves approved unto God . . ." His encouragement caused me to put the Spirit of my sound mind to work. I ultimately ascended to the top rung of the academic ladder in the public school system. However, I have learned And as a result, I learned by experience that it is very easy to allow your academic altitude to ruin your spiritual attitude. Thus, I took all available steps to help my students / hearers remain accessible.

Accountability is evasive for many, if not most people. I think that exists because of the lack of connectivity to the Spirit of God. Therefore in my efforts to impart the necessity of being accountable, and using the old adage that 'people would do better, if they knew better;' I strive to impress upon the minds of those who have an ear to hear that God will hold everyone accountable. Those things said and done I began the task of writing this manual as a testimony to the goodness and the grace of God.

THE GATEWAY TO ETERNAL LIFE

THE editors of the Life Application Study Bible (Tyndale House Publishers, 1996) were correct when they said,

> *"the gateway to eternal life (John 10:7-9) is called "strait"—an old word for "narrow." This does not mean that it is impossible to become a Christian; but it does mean that there is only one way to live eternally in the presence of God; and that only a few will decide to*

walk that road. Stated succinctly, I thank God there is
only one way.

This book is a literal road map of that way: it reveals the hidden hope. In *Entering* I have addressed three very relevant and salient issues. First of all, without fear of contradiction or condemnation, I have exhibited the unmitigated gall to call a spade a spade and sin by its right name. Frankly speaking I believe authors of non-fictional books designate too much print-space responding to the pros and cons of what others believe to be worthy of mention, without examining that which has been overlooked for years.

Secondly, I have also done away with the need for parishioners to continue to bathe in the 'innocence of ignorance' and remain members in "the pastor said" club, counting on him (or her) to inform them, and to validate what they have come to believe. This was done by removing the presumptuousness of preaching and the precariousness of perception, leaving the final interpretation and interpolation of Scripture to the discretion of the reader, under the leadership of the Holy Spirit.

The validity in this is undergirded by the supreme wisdom of God, who endowed every man with the Spirit of Power, Love, and a Sound-mind. Third and finally, this writer has dared to pull the covers off the traditional Christian practices of the "Church of God in Christ"—not to be confused with the local denominational body by the same name—thereby leaving the "cognitive grunt-work" to each member, and the teaching to the Spirit of God. Dr. Carter's overall terminal objective is to provide an answer the question, "What, in this world, is the church supposed to be?" That having been said and because there is much ground to cover, I have decided to stop here and go to work.

As a child in elementary school I was taught to search for and answer the "5W's of Journalism" in any literary piece, in order to better understand what a writer meant by what he said. My teacher, Mrs. Shaw, would say, "Trone—that's my middle name—if you answer those questions completely, you will better understand the passage; and with the help of a Dictionary-thesaurus, you will be able to re-tell the story in your own words." That lesson has followed me for more than sixty-five years. For the benefit of those who will read this writ and discover that they can profit by using it, I have included a review and overview of what she meant by what she said, along with selected answers from the content of this book.

WHO? Who is a Pronoun which answers the question, "Who is the person (s) involved in the passage in question.

SPECIFICALLY, this book centers on the person, the presence, and the power of God the Father, God the Son, God the Holy Spirit, and those who have an ear and are willing the hear what the Spirit is saying to the Churches.

WHAT? What—when unstressed—is a Pronoun which answers the question, "Which thing or which particular one of many?"

SPECIFICALLY, the title and the subject matter of *Entering* is about what God the Father has already done, what He is doing right now, and what He will yet do throughout this day and the rest of our tomorrows.

WHEN? When is an Adverb which answers the question, "At what time or at which time?"

SPECIFICALLY, with God time is relative. On the one hand mankind measures time chronologically and clockwise: from left to right. On the other hand with God the operative word is "KAIROS," a Greek term which speaks of a space in time. A working example of that perception is found in the prophecy of Isaiah, Chapter 6 Verse 1:

> **"In the year that King Uzziah died" I saw also the Lord sitting upon a throne, high and lifted up, and his train filled the temple.**

WHERE? Where is also an Adverb which answers the question "At or in which place?"

SPECIFICALLY, we are asking "In what situation or position are we?" Continuing in specifics, when it comes to God, location, like time, is also relative. For example, God is Omnipresent, which translates to: everywhere present at the same time equally. Therefore, wherever you are you will find Him there; which makes anywhere the best place to get started. Additionally, you will find that He is involved in all situations.

WHY? Why is an Adverb which answers the question, "For what purpose, reason, or cause?"

SPECIFICALLY, the answer to this question is also found in *Entering.* Because God is the same yesterday, today, and forever, His reasons for doing what He has done are both, specific and open-ended. A good guess would be because He loves unconditionally, and He is always "working things out." Besides being open-ended, we can also say that all answers end in glorifying God.

HOW? How is an Adverb which answers the question, "In what manner or what way?"

SPECIFICALLY, How calls for a description. The answer to this question is answered in *Entering,* straight-forward and unabridged. For example,

> This is the word of the Lord unto Zerubbabel, saying, *"Not by might, nor by power, but by my Spirit, saith the Lord of hosts" (Zechariah 4:6).*

NOW, WHAT? "Now, what" is a combination of an Adverb which answers the combination-question: "At What time" or "At Which time?" *and a Pronoun which answers the question:* "Which thing or which particular one of many? Collectively, they respond to the questions, "WHAT shall we do, and HOW shall we do it?"

Again, the answers you will find in *Entering* are straight-forward and unabridged. As a matter of fact, it is the primary focus of this book. Much has been written on the subject of what should be done, and how it should be done." *Entering* is focused primarily on "HOW;" and when stated succinctly, it reads: "When all else fails, it's time to give the word of God a chance." HOW? You simply *"Do the Right Thing, the Right Way by entering in at the Strait Gate."*

Six years ago I set out on a journey of research and discovery (R&D) in an effort to locate, develop and delineate the answers to

7

those two questions; answers that would be both, acceptable and workable. What follows is what I found. Read it carefully and use it wisely for this is the key. A very wise man once said, *"As a man thinks in his heart, so is he."* So, for our purposes here, my first step was to make certain that all that I write would be positive, productive, and progressive; consistent, continuous, and conducive; and that the content would be flanked by scriptural validation.

For the record, the above six attributes—which appear in a previous publication entitled, "In His Own Image" (Carter, 2011)—were used to partially describe and delineate the nature of God, in whose image man was created. Using those attributes as a guide, I came to the conclusion that there are only two ways to think; and subsequently, only two ways to live our lives. The way God intends for us to live is what I am calling 'God's way;' and the way we chose to live our lives is what I am calling 'Man's way.'

The way God intends for us to live can be found in the contents of the Bible (2 Timothy 3:16). However, I must hasten to say that if one chooses to think and to live-life God's way, care must be taken not to try to force-feed our lives into what we read in the Bible. No. No. The truth is found in the reverse: when necessity dictates, we are to insert portions of the Bible into our lives. Translated, we must keep in mind that what we read in the Bible happened to those people who lived in Bible days. It is their history, their heritage, and their culture. On the one hand, unless the identically same thing happens in our lives—contextually, culturally, and contemporarily—it would be an exercise in futility for any of us to try to fit any part of our lives into any of the biblical passages we read—sometimes disguised as 'biblical interpretation.' On the other hand, this is the key to success when using the scriptures. We are to study the Scriptures, extracting from the stories we read, facts that when placed in the proper context, will enlighten, enhance, and encourage us in our spiritual growth and development.

Stated succinctly, what we take from the Bible should enable us to straighten out the crooked places in our lives; elevate lower-order thinking, and level off the high places in our cognitive constructs, as opposed to striving to restructure our lives to fit the circumstances we find in those stories. In addition and designed to make our job easier, there is a verified truth which must not be overlooked or obliterated. The voice of God said to the prophet Zechariah, ***"It is not by might, not by power, but by the Spirit of God, says the voice of God."*** Stated another way, under the Lordship and leadership of the Holy Spirit, the answers to those questions will become clear and understandable; and His instructions will enable and empower [almost] anyone to dot all of the "i's", cross all of the "t's", fill in the blanks, and ultimately produce a fool-proof, fail-safe formula for successfully living.

Finally, there is an old axiom which says, "If you don't know where you are going, any road will take you there." This book is a portion of a literal road map from "earth's sorrow to heaven's joy." If you read it and follow the instructions contained within, 'blessings unlimited' and 'all good things without end' await you and everyone who has the holy boldness to hear the word, receive it and believe it. Once internalized we must make the decisive-decision to "become doers of the word and not hearers only" (James 1:22); and then commit to serving a true and living God (1 Corinthians 2:9). And for the record, serving a true and a living God pre-supposes that the reader knows who God is, and what He is in him. To make certain that there is no confusion, I shall pause right here and introduce to some and present to others the Divine Order of Authority in this world.

CHAPTER ONE

An Introduction to the Divine Order of Authority (DOA) in This World

PROLOGUE

THE prologue is a preview before the presentation. In this case the Divine Order of Authority (DOA) is about God, who is the ultimate authority. It is He who made the world and everything that's in it, which makes Him sovereign and ultimately in charge. Thus we can say with certainty that the proper place to start is with the spoken and written word of God, which we call the Bible. There are two things about the Bible that must capture and hold your attention. First, there must be no doubt in your mind that the Bible is the unadulterated word of God. Many books have been written but none start at the 'unbegun-beginning.' Nothing has been changed in over two-thousand years, and nothing is to be added because of technological advances. Newer and different translations in which the wording has been changed to accommodate cultural differences have been printed. Regardless of those differences, the editors have succeeded only in opening wider the door to the Omniscience of God. Secondly, the Bible is the voice of God speaking to the world that He created. What He said more than two thousand years ago is still relevant today. Whether we accept it or reject it doesn't alter its position in the world. It is still the word of God, and it's still sacred to those who believe.

PRESENTATION

JUST as the United States of America has a Federal Constitution which is designed to regulate all fifty states; and each State has a State Constitution designed to provide equal protection under the law for the citizens and residents of each state, God the Father saw to it that the world would be the recipient of segment number one, the Divine Order of Authority (DOA) in this World. Stated succinctly, we are talking about the written word of God—A.K.A the Holy Bible.

Because history informs us that God made His covenant with Noah in Genesis Chapter 6, and that it was drafted 4004 B.C.— four thousand and four years before Jesus and the Christian Church were born—I believe I am on safe ground when I say that God used the Bible as His medium of choice to introduce Himself to His world, and to provide mankind with a standard on which to build a regulatory system that would be in line with His will and His way. Further, that it would wind up in the hands of the Church as the rule and guide to her faith and practice. That is understandable when you consider that mankind was created in God's own image. Stated another way, the two Constitutions are man-made but the Bible—the beginning of the DOA—is the inspired word of God (2 Timothy 3:16). The difference between the two Constitutions and the DOA is that unlike the two constitutions—which carry with them their own consequences for violations—the people of God have free-will which carries with it both, the authority and the power to make choices; and those choices depend on whether or not they have decided to hear the word of God, receive it and believe it. That decision manifests the willingness to apprehend and adhere to the dictates of the DOA, with no implied punishment for choosing to do otherwise.

We must keep in mind that the Spirit of God will not make choices for you. The words spoken by God the Father contain options that, when placed in the proper context, enable a man to make good decisions. In other words, contrary to the opinions of modern man, God the Father does not dictate how to live your life. However, considering the stories that appear in the Bible—the Spirit of God inspired man to write using examples that suggest guidelines which will work for you without fail. The Image of God in which men were created contains "free-will," and you— as an individual—can use it to accept or reject the word of God at will. The only thing the Bible says on the subject is, ***"Be not deceived; God is not mocked; whatsoever a man sows, that shall*** *he also reap"* (Galatians 6:7). When it comes to either of the two Constitutions, obedience is mandatory. However, make no mistake about it all three documents have rewards and consequences for obedience, rejection, and / or rebellion.

For information purposes only, be aware that our relationship with God—which is blood-bought—is synonymous with our relationship with His Word. Stated succinctly, the way we handle the Word of God manifests the way we feel about its Creator. Similarly, what we know about the written word is also what we know about the person, the presence and the power of God. In other words, without the Bible we would know nothing about the Creator God. Therefore, it is incumbent upon those who desire a fellowship with God—once their relationship with Him has been re-established—to follow the precepts of Paul as stated in (2 Timothy 2:15), to wit:

> **"Study to show yourself approved, unto God, a workman who needs not to be ashamed; rightly dividing the word of truth."**

FROM THE BEGINNING

SOMEWHERE I read the following:

> "A vase shatters, brushed by a careless elbow; a toy breaks, handled roughly by young fingers; and fabric rips, pulled by strong and angry hands. Spills and rips take time to clean up, effort to repair, and money to replace, but far more costly are shattered relationships. Unfaithfulness, untruths, hateful words, and forsaken vows tear delicate personal bonds; and wounds are inflicted that are not easily healed. Most tragic, however, is a broken relationship with God" (Author Unknown).

I include that verse of poetry to say this: "Healing the broken relationship that exists between mankind and the God of creation is paramount and primary." It is paramount because of God's supremacy in rank, power and authority. It is primary because nothing can be accomplished as long as the relationship is fractured. The first question that came to my mind was, "What do I do after I have done all that I know to do? Stated another way, after all of the known, positive, productive and progressive steps have been taken to build on that re-established relationship with God, "now what do I do?" In other words "Now what?"

Answering that question in detail is the primary focus of this book. However, the simplest answer would be: "rightly divided the word of truth and the answer becomes self-evident: you do the right thing, the right way, for God is not through with any of us yet." What makes that so? I was asked. Simply this: it is by doing the right thing, the right way, that the Hidden Hope will be revealed; and then as an individual, any of us will be enabled and empowered to "Enter *in at the Strait Gate"(Matthew 7:13).* In addition, once you enter you will find that *the Strait Gate* will take you through the doorway to an already decided destiny.

All of that sounds good, I know. But the question is still "HOW?" How do you do the right thing, if you don't know what the right thing is; to say nothing about doing it the right way. That's what this book is all about. *Entering* will confine itself to providing you with the needed assistance to re-establish your broken relationship, and then to mend your broken fellowship with God. It begins with apprehending and adhering to the written word of God.

Almost everyone has heard the story; but for the sake of clarity and conciseness—and for the profitability of those who are out of the loop—this writer will strive to not leave a stone unturned. The last population release that I heard states that there are more than seven (7) billion people in this world—and counting. That suggests that if everyone would speak, at least seven billion stories would be told. *Entering* is just one of those stories—it is my story. All of our stories are different, but all of them will start and end at the same junction. Jesus said,

> *"Enter ye in at the strait gate: for wide is the gate, and*
> *broad is the way, that leads to destruction, and many*
> *there be which go in there at: because strait is the gate,*

and narrow is the way, which leads unto life, and few
there be that find it: (Matthew 7:13-14).

In *Entering* I am telling my story because I believe it is time.
Stephen Covey (1989) was correct when he suggested that to keep
doing the same thing, the same way, hoping to somehow get some
different results is a working definition of insanity. For many years
I walked in insanity. But things have changed. Everybody knows
that you cannot teach what you do not know, nor can you lead
where you cannot go. I am convinced that my experiences and
exposure constitute my learning and my burning. Thus, it is my
time.

A few years ago I began to do some things differently and
this book is the manifestation that they are working. To get us
started, let me be one of the first to say that enough lies have been
told. Stated succinctly, the absence of truth is a lie. There is no
wiggle-room in truth. It can be a half-truth, but a half-truth is a
whole lie. You can elect to not tell the whole story, but if the part
you don't tell alters the bigger picture, that's a lie, and you might
as well admit it. Here is a working example. The absence of a
working knowledge of "who God is" has forced a goodly number
of people to make up stories—lies—that fit a given circumstance.
I was one of them until the Spirit of God opened my eyes so that I
could see, and my mind so that I could receive. Then He wrought
a change in my heart so that I can now believe. Let me make that
clearer.

The power of the Spirit of God literally and figuratively
took me by my heels, turned me up-side-down—as it were—
and commenced shaking me until He shook 'all of the junk' out
of my pockets. He then turned me right-side-up and placed my
feet on solid ground. It was then that He demonstrated to my
understanding that I am a soul worth saving; that I have a song
worth singing and a story worth telling. He then put it in my
heart to "run and tell that." That started in January, 1974, and I've
been running ever since. *Entering* is about my journey thus far,
from earth's sorrow to heaven's joy. This project will start at the
beginning of creation and hopscotch through the developmental

15

process of God's pre-planned world, using the precision and power that I have been given.

Everybody knows about God, but few actually know Him in the pre-pardon of their sins: that is, with a re-established relationship that's up-close and personal. Why is it that so few actually know Him? I was asked. The answer is because they refuse to submit and surrender which will force them to 'think, face the truth, and change; which starts on the road to repentance. Instead, they have become satisfied with bathing in the innocence of ignorance and relying on "the pastor said syndrome." You know the story. What we don't know, we say, "Well, the pastor said . . ."

Therefore, we—the Spirit of God speaking to me and through me—will begin with what is known about God and move forward. That said and taking for granted that we all know that God loves unconditionally, we will introduce to some and present to others a description and delineation of who God is; His person, presence and power. And finally, in as many words as I find to be necessary, I will share with the reader what I believe the voice of God meant by what He said, from the beginning to the present.

For the sake of clarity and conciseness, there are two questions which must be asked and answered by every believer: Who is God? And what is He in us? Following those two questions, I have included a literary connection between Reality and Actuality. Why? You might ask. Isn't everything real? The answer is found in the words of Solomon, who once said, ***"Wisdom is the principal thing; therefore get wisdom. And in all your getting, get an understanding"*** (Proverbs 4:7). On that note we are going to pause and expand on "The joy of understanding" as an answer to that question. The Apostle Paul said "follow the dictates of scripture in 2 Timothy 2:15; and then follow it up with 2 Timothy 3:16.

Those scriptures read:

> ***"Study to show thyself approved unto God, a workman that needeth not to be ashamed rightly dividing the word of truth." All Scripture is given by inspiration of God, and is profitable for doctrine, for reproof, for correction, for instruction in righteousness, that the***

man of God may be complete, thoroughly equipped for
every good work."

TOWARDS A GOOD UNDERSTANDING

TO better understand the word of God—including His purpose and
His plan, His will and His way—the Bible can safely be divided
into four major themes: **Principles, Promises, Prophecy and**
Procedures. By way of definition and explanation, **Principles** are
sometimes called Commandments, Laws, Statutes, Testimonies,
Ordinances and Decrees in the Bible. They depict a portion of the
"Purposeful Will" of God. They are non-negotiable and not subject
to change. His **promises** may be called divine incentives, and may
be positive or negative, depending on the context in which they
appear.

On the one hand for example, in the fifth Commandment in
Exodus 20:12, there is a principle and a promise that's written as a
positive incentive. On the other hand, the principle and the promise
of God in Galatians Chapter 6, verse 7, is an example which can
be either positive or negative, depending on the context in which
it is used. In most cases, the promises of God follow one of His
Principles, and "there is always a one-to-one correlation between
the adherence to a Principle and the enjoyment of the promise."
That correlation is an example of the changeless character of God.
Once God makes a promise, you can believe it because He will
fulfill it, complete with examples of the cause and effect of sin,
when the people are inclined to be disobedient. It should be noted
that Prophecy—because it comes from God—is both, reality and
actuality.

Prophecy—while it was still in the mind of God was Reality—
and would come under the heading of the "I Will's" of God. But
when God spoke and prophecy manifested itself in the lives of men
that Reality became Actuality in real time. An example of that is in
Genesis 3:15.

Hear the word of God about the Prophet: he who delivered
prophecy and was ordained a prophet to the nations by God before
he was formed in his mother's womb (Jeremiah 1:4). The Prophet

came forward in the fullness of time to deliver the word of God. As a matter of record, Prophets were not permitted to interpret or explain what God said. They could only speak the mouth of God. The prophet was under the protection of God, and appears to be invincible in the Bible.

That may well be because God had David the King to get the word out that's recorded in Psalm 105:15. There, David could be heard saying, ***"Touch not mine anointed, and do my prophets no harm."*** Prophecy is a restatement of one or more of God's Principles in real time, to real people.

Prophecy is the substance of a vision given by God to one of His chosen. Prophecy is usually preceded by one of the following leads: "The angel of the Lord said unto me;" or "The word of the Lord came unto me saying . . . ." God's Principles were designed to prevent sin. ***Procedures*** provide a way of escape (1 Corinthians 10:14), but leave the decision-making up to you. His procedures are sure, and designed expressly for mankind, enabling him to deal with sin.

Those procedures are usually linked to a promise, and in this book are sometimes referred to as "Procedural-promises." Found mainly in the New Testament, they are restatements of the principles and the promises found in the Old Testament. They are real-time procedures for accurately applying the word of God to our lives (2 Timothy 3:16). That said, the reader is now free to accept or reject the word of God. As a word of caution, the reader is encouraged not to "mix and match;" that has not worked for the last two thousand years. The Bible gives you an alternative: ***"Choose you this day whom you will serve"*** (Joshua 24:15), whether it will be God or Satan. Those are the choices. If you choose to take God at His word without exception, your journey from earth's sorrow to heaven's joy will begin, and your faith will lead you to heaven on earth. Meanwhile back at the beginning of the DOA.

THE DOA ENUMERATED

1. The Bible is the spoken and written word of God. It was designed to be the Rule and Guide to the faith and practice of all members of Christendom.
2. God the Father: The Creator of the heaven and the earth: "His Person, His Presence and Power;"
3. God the Son is the Christ of Redemption and Sacrificial Lamb: "His Person, His Presence and His Power." His name is Jesus, but His mission is Messianic. [And]
4. God the Holy Spirit is the Veritable Power of Almighty God. It is "His Person, His Presence and His Power." The Prophet delivered the message to King Zerubbabel, saying, "not by might, nor by power, but by my Spirit, saith the Lord of hosts" (Zechariah 4:6).

These four segments undergird the Kingdom of God, sometimes called the Kingdom of Heaven. The Kingdom of God is the realm in which God in all three persons, reigns and rules without exception, and without any input from us. In 1 Corinthians 14: 40 Paul wrote: ***"Let everything be done decently and in order."*** Using that verse as both, our inspiration and a spring-board from which to launch this literary project, the first order of business is to spell out the tenets of the "DOA" in this world—which must be apprehended, and to which everybody—according to the prophecy of Isaiah (45:23)—will adhere in the fullness of time.

TO EVERY MAN A PURPOSE

I BELIEVE there is a general agreement that God has a purpose for every man born of a woman. Suffice it to say–whether he is conscious of it or not—every man is living out a purpose-driven life. The direction his life takes is purely up to him. At any time in his life, a close observation will reveal that he is in the midst of doing what he wants to do, and the results that are manifested are in accordance with the choices he has made. Simply stated, what happens in life is either by commission or omission. The works of this writer are no exception. On that note and given the fact that the Bible confirms that God has invested in every man the Spirit of Power and of Love and of a Sound Mind (2 Timothy 1:7), I believe my experiences and exposures have prepared me to be a literary conduit through which biblical truth—what the Bible means by what it says—will flow without exception. Let me pull over and park, and help somebody right here.

In the Great Commission (Matthew 28:18-20, KJV), Jesus used the English word "Teach" which—in the original language—meant to have perspective students enrolled as scholars; and the English word "Teaching" which meant to have those students' learn at a rate that would be emblematic of building a Super-structure on the foundation that He had laid (1Corinthians 3:11). Not to unfairly criticize positive preaching, but for reasons known only to themselves, contemporary preachers—believing that in all preaching there is some teaching—have substituted the words "preach" and "preaching" for the words "teach" and "teaching." As a result, their preaching, however effective, is void of the learning necessary *"For equipping of the saints for the work of ministry, for the edifying of the body of Christ . . ."* (Ephesians 4:12-13, NKJV).

That's it in a nutshell. In many, if not most cases, contemporary of teaching the people of God "How" to think and how to live life the way God would have them to be taught, so that they can "live" rather than merely "exist." That is not meant to be an indictment; it is meant to be truth without exception. What makes me so sure? The voice of God informed us and keeps on reminding us:

My people are destroyed for lack of knowledge: because you have rejected knowledge, I also will reject you from being priest for Me; Because you have forgotten the law of your God, I also will forget your children."

In that declaration the voice of God comes through the prophet Hosea, Chapter 4 Verse 6 (NKJV), and I am a living example of its far-reaching impact. I practiced preaching as a pastor—in-preparation for more than twenty-five years before my change came. After undergoing what I call 'a real conversion experience,' during which time my people didn't have to worry about their preacher getting lost in the shuffle, because I was busy shuffling along with the lost. However, since my spiritual eyes have been opened, through the recall of God's word the Spirit of God has enabled me; and by the indwelling of God's Holy Spirit He has empowered me to do what I like to call "the extra-ordinary." I have learned how to think, face the truth, and make positive change when necessity dictates.

Stated succinctly, "through the recall of the word of God I have been enabled;" and "by the indwelling of His Holy Spirit I am being empowered;" and between the two I have been subjected to the beginning stages of transformation by the renewing of my mind (Romans 12:2). Stated another way, I have been made able to utilize my Spirit of a "Sound-mind," a feat from which most people shy away in favor of using their instincts. And as a result my life has begun to be transformed. Simply stated, the Spirit of God has begun to bring about transformation in my life by the renewing of my mind.

Why me? You might ask. Am I special or an exception to the rule? The answer is a resounding no. This same opportunity is extended to everyone (Romans 2:11). I am simply one who has begun to take advantage of it. Stated succinctly, I am 'E Pluribus Unum—out of many one.' What will I do with this golden opportunity? Again, simply stated, I will endeavor to enlighten, enhance and encourage those who have an ear and are willing to hear what the Spirit is saying to the Church (Revelation 2: 11, 17, 29; 3:6, 13 and 22). Exactly what does that mean?

Speaking to me and then through me, the Spirit of God— through this medium and others—will (a) turn on the light where many are yet walking in darkness; (b) build a super-structure on the already laid foundation which is Jesus, who is called the Christ; and (c) encourage believers to use what God has given them to rise above mediocrity and access the abundant life to which Jesus alluded in John 10:10b.

How will these things be accomplished, and what will be the methodology used? In a few words, participants in the process will be urged to concentrate on "doing the right thing the right way." The context and content of this book is designed to help any and all committed Christians who have an ear to hear, to locate and "enter in at the strait gate" through the doorway to an already decided destiny (Matthew 7:13).

For what purpose will these things be done? That is the central question? The ultimate purpose is to answer the question, "What—in this world—is the Church supposed to be?" The question is **not** what the Church is supposed to be **doing**; the question is, "What, in this world, is the Church **supposed to be?**" As simple as it may sound, rest assured that the answer to that question is not obvious. As a matter of fact, I have not found a specific or definitive answer recorded in scripture. Therefore, to discover an answer that is both, acceptable and workable, it was necessary for me to put the Spirit of a Sound-mind with which God has endowed me to work. After much prayer and supplication, I had to sit down and reason with God (Isaiah 1:18) and let the Spirit of God teach me an alternate meaning of a bridge over troubled water. That brings to an end this introduction and dictates that it's time to get to work.

CHAPTER TWO

An Introduction to the Old Testament

THE PROLOGUE

I DARE not take anything for granted. Instead, we will start at the beginning, introduce to some and present to others the Holy Bible. THE Old Testament is the initial, foundation covenant that was struck between God and man. The question was once asked, "What is the difference between a contract and a covenant?" Generally speaking, the difference between a covenant and a contract is found in the absence of contractual contingencies. For example, whereas a contract is based on a set of agreements between two or more individuals, in Scripture a covenant is generally made by God and has no such agreement. God's covenant is His word and stipulates what He will do without exception.

The Old Testament is comprised of thirty-nine books which contain God's Law—sometimes called Commands, Ordinances, Statutes and Testimonies—and which records His creation of the heaven and the earth" (Genesis 1:1). In it is also the record of His creation of man in his own image; the fall of man from grace, and God's prophetic declaration—in Genesis 3:15—that He would save him from self-destruction.

Chapter one of Genesis will introduce the foundation of the creation story. Following the introduction two questions are asked and answered: Who is God? And what is He in us?

THE PRESENTATION

GENESIS: Genesis is the book of beginnings—the Creation, Mankind, Sin, Redemption, and God's Nation.

EXODUS: In Exodus, God delivers His people out of Egypt and gives them the Law.

LEVITICUS: Leviticus contains Priestly laws on holiness and worship, through sacrifice and purification.

NUMBERS: The book of Numbers tells the story of the Israelites during the nearly forty years from the time they left Mount Sinai until they reached the eastern border of the land that God had promised to give them.

DEUTERONOMY: The book of Deuteronomy is organized as a series of addresses given by Moses to the people of Israel in the land of Moab, where they had stopped at the end of the long wilderness journey, and were about to enter into and occupy the land of Canaan.

The next 12 books in the Old Testament are historical. They were written between 1100—600 B.C. and describe God's dealings with His chosen people, Israel—the Hebrew nation.

6) JOSHUA   10) 2 SAMUEL   14) 2 CHRONICLES
7) JUDGES   11) 1 KINGS   15) EZRA
8) RUTH   12) 2 KINGS   16) NEHEMIAH
9) 1 SAMUEL   13) 1 CHRONICLES   17) ESTHER

The next five books are poetic, describing in poetry and song, God's greatness and His dealings with man.

JOB: In Job, we have the suffering and trust of a man who loved God.

PSALMS:	In Psalms we have songs of prayer, praise and instruction.
PROVERBS:	Proverbs is a portrait of practical wisdom for successful living.
ECCLESIASTES:	In Ecclesiastes, we have a verbal portrait of the emptiness of earthly life without God.
SONG OF SOLOMON:	In the Song of Solomon, we have a portrait of God's Love for His people.

THE OLD TESTAMENT Continued

The five books of the Major Prophets follow. The Prophet was commissioned by God to deliver His message verbatim—i.e. "word for word" and without interpretation—to all mankind, more especially the children of Israel. These books are called "Major prophets" because they are generally longer than the writings of the "Minor prophets." These five books were written in the two-hundred years between 750 — 550 B.C.

1) ISAIAH   4) EZEKIEL

2) JEREMIAH   5) DANIEL

3) LAMENTATIONS of JEREMIAH—a verbal portrait of Jeremiah's grief

The last 12 books of the Old Testament are called "Minor prophets." These books were written between 800 – 400 B.C.

1) HOSEA   7) NAHUM

2) JOEL   8) HABAKKUK

3) AMOS   9) ZEPHANIAH

4) OBADIAH   10) HAGGAI

5) JONAH   11) ZECHARIAH

6) MICAH   12) MALACHI

Those are the 39 books which make up the Old Testament. By ways of reminder they house the creation story and formulate the foundation of all life in this world.

THE CREATION EPIC

BEGINNING with Genesis 1:1 and proceeding through verse 25, Moses recorded the spoken word of God. Prior to Him speaking everything into existence, everything was REALITY in the mind of God. Once He spoke, Reality became Actuality in real time. Chapter one of Genesis gives us an account of "What" God did. Chapter two provides us with a brief description of "How" He did it; and Chapters 3 and 4 tells us "Why" He did what He did and introduced Satan to the first family, in real time.

In Verse twenty-six (26) of chapter one, the voice of God the Father—the Chief Justice of the Supreme Court of Heaven—spoke to the other two members on the Court—God the Son, and God the Holy Spirit—proposing that they make man in their image. In Verse twenty-seven (27), God spoke not another word but went straight to His work. You might say, God was in a creative mode. Scripture says, "So God created man "In His Own Image.""

The difference between Verse twenty-six (26) and twenty-seven (27) is understandable if you study the scriptures and let them speak to you. Let me make that plain. Had God followed through with His proposition as stated in verse twenty-six (26), by including the other two members on the Court in the initial creative process—that is, making man in "their" image, the first man would have been body, soul, and spirit. However, scripture says "God made the man in His Own Image." That made him "Soul and Spirit" because God is Spirit and does not have a body— notwithstanding (Genesis 2:7) made God's creation "a living soul."

Close observation will reveal that man remained in that creative mode until the Bible informs us in Chapter 3 that "***God made coats of skin and clothed them* and sent them forth from the garden of Eden, to till the ground from whence he was taken"** *(Genesis 3:21, 23).* That, I believe, is when they were made fully human.

THE FIRST COMMANDMENT

MUCH has been said about what appears in the Old Testament, and no doubt much more will be said. However, to satisfy our purpose we will begin with an overview of the first commandment. Although it is often overlooked, the first Commandment of God to be violated—which is, in my opinion, the most important—is recorded for us in Genesis 2:16. Scripture says:

> *"And the Lord God commanded the man, saying, "Of every tree of the garden you may freely eat; but of the tree of the knowledge of good and evil you shall not eat, for in the day that you eat of it you shall surely die."*

As we approach the story, keep two things in mind: (1) that God does not change, and (2) God does not repeat Himself. If you let your consecrated imagination go to work, you can join me as we pick up the story in Genesis 2:15. Scripture says God took the man that He had made and placed him in the Garden of Eden to dress and keep it. FYI: the Garden of Eden is emblematic of a portion of the world that God had created. Thus, Adam's work in the world was cut out for him.

To arrive at what I believe is the best understanding of that verse, we must preface it with the reminder of what the voice of God, speaking in Malachi 3:6, said: *"I am the Lord, I do not change; therefore you are not consumed, O sons of Jacob."* The reference here is to Genesis 1:27, and the making of man "In God's Own Image." In other words, the way God made the man is the way man was destined to remain, and the way we are today. That conclusion is validated in God's declaration in Genesis 3:15. For the sake of clarity, look closely and see the prophecy of Salvation as we know it, in that verse.

As we approach this foundational treatise on the Old Testament, the reader is also reminded that the Bible means everything that it says, but it does not say everything that it means. For that reason what might appear to be vacillations are really oscillations. Stated succinctly, as we have already said, God does not repeat Himself. In Scripture He said what He wanted to say one time, to one person, in one place. However, what He said was meant for everyone, everywhere, and for all eternity. Let me hasten to also say that when you read prophetic utterances which contain repetition in real time; those messages were delivered to the prophet by Angels of God, not God Himself. There is a difference.

What God said directly to Adam in that first commandment pre-empted the need, and was actually designed to avoid the first transgression. However, as we all know, that is not the way things worked out in the end. This is where we pause and come face-to-face with Satan, the arch-enemy of God. Like as with God, not much is known about Satan; but we will attempt to fix that as well. Simply stated, let me hurry up and say that if we believe that God exists, we must also believe that the Devil exists as well. The Scriptures make it clear.

> **"We know that whosoever is born of God does not sin; but he who has been born of God keeps himself, and the wicked one does not touch him. We know that we are of God, and the whole world lies under the sway of the wicked one. And we know that the Son of God has come and has given us an understanding, that we may know Him who is true; and we are in Him who is true, in His son Jesus Christ. This is the true God and eternal life" (1 John 5:18-20, NKJV).**

Again, we say that in the Bible are guidelines. They are herein printed to keep us aware of truth without exception. The writer said, *"We must become aware that as believers we are of God, and the whole world lieth in wickedness."* That we are of God speaks to creation, and pre-supposes that we have submitted and surrendered to bring us back in line with God. Meanwhile back at the beginning.

BACK AT THE BEGINNING

GIVEN the context of the story, I believe I am on safe ground to suggest that it was a bright, bright sunshiny day. The Voice of God was speaking to Adam, and as fore stated God gave Adam this specific Commandment:

> *"And the Lord God commanded the man, saying, "Of every tree of the garden you may freely eat; but of the tree of the knowledge of good and evil you shall not eat, for in the day that you eat of it you shall surely die."*

When this story was told in one of my classes, a member asked, "didn't God know that Adam would be disobedient?" The answer is a resounding yes. However, keep in mind that I have also said that the Bible is a set of guidelines to serve as the rule and guide to our faith and practice, not necessarily as a chronological story of what happened. That must be kept in mind.

Nevertheless, to further remove the appearance of presumptuousness, let me insert what I believe might have happened. Look ahead at Genesis 1:31 which reads,

> *"And God saw everything that He had made, and behold it was very good. And the evening and the morning were the sixth day."*

It doesn't take a rocket scientist to see that several things happened between Verses 29 and 30, among them God made provisions for the first family and for every other beast that lived on the earth. Then prior to speaking Verse 31 into existence, I believe God the Father had God the Holy Spirit—to rewind back to verse twenty-five (25)—stretch all of creation out on a specially-prepared drawing board and dot every "i" and cross every "t". Then after He had perused what He had purposed to create, He set the man in the midst of His creation and permitted him to exercise his free-will. It was there that Moses inserted Verse 31.

Now, I could be wrong, but I don't think so. I believe that after placing man in the midst of His creation and allowing him to exercise his free will, God then extended His 'Purposeful will' to allow for the tenets of His 'Permissive will' and the rewards and consequences that went with it. Once mankind had done all that he desired to do, the fullness of verse thirty-one (31) came into view making way for Chapter 2 Verse 1 which reads:

> *"Thus the heavens and the earth were finished, and all the host of them. And on the seventh day God ended His work which He had made, and He rested on the seventh day from all His work which He had made. And God blessed the seventh day, and sanctified it: because that in it He had rested from all His work which God created and made. making way or Chapter 2, Verses 1-3"*

Fast-forwarding to Chapter three (3) as the story goes, Satan accosted Eve (Genesis 3:1-7) and engaged her in a rhetorical conversation that was designed to catch her off guard and subsequently deceive her. Scripture says Satan, disguised as the serpent, said to Eve,

> *"Yea, has God said you shall not eat of every tree of the garden?"* **To which Eve replied, "We may eat of the fruit of the trees in the garden: but of the fruit of the tree which is in the midst of the garden, God has said, "You shall not eat of it, neither shall you touch it, lest you die"**

Close observation will reveal the error of Eve's ways. She did two things that must be avoided by everyone today. First of all she allowed Satan to engage her in a conversation. But how can we know when Satan is speaking? One of my students asked. The answer to that question is found in Isaiah 55:8-9:

*"as the heavens are higher than the earth, so are my
ways higher than your ways, and my thoughts than
your thoughts."*

Suffice it to say, Point #1, "Never dance with the devil if you
want to avoid self-destruction. Point #2, "Keep your mind on the
word of God." Why? Simply because as Solomon once said, **"as a
man thinks in his heart, so is he" (Proverbs 23:7a)** And by the
way, if you know that you aren't as aware of the word of God as
you should be, rather than guess and be in error or wade out into
uncharted waters, it would be better to heed the word of God as
spoken by David in Psalm 46:10: *"Be still and know that I am
God: I will be exalted among the heathen, I will be exalted in the
earth."* In other words, just wait. It won't be long. The answer is
just around the corner. After all, today is that tomorrow that you
talked about yesterday.

Scripture says, *"She took the fruit thereof, and did eat, and
gave also unto her husband with her; and he did eat."* While it
is true that Eve sinned first; look closely and you will see that God
charged Adam with the responsibility of "dressing and keeping
the garden." Therefore, for failing to adhere to His words in that
first Command Adam died, spiritually (Genesis 3:17). In other
words, his relationship with God was severed, but their fellowship
lingered on. So it is that we can say with certainty that the
condition of the world today is because of what Adam did, not Eve.
But that's not how the story ends.

Adam's rebellion brought spiritual death on himself and on his
posterity. That factor is seen in the attitude and actions of his first
son, Cain: who committed the first recorded murder when he slew
his brother, Abel. Beginning with Adam, mankind has been under
the influence of the evil one; and Eve—because she was one with
her husband—is under the same curse. But that's not how the story
ends either. Genesis 3:15 informs us that God didn't waste any
time ushering in Salvation for fallen mankind.

Although His name is not mentioned, it is clear from the
context and the content that when God said, *"He would put enmity
between Satan and the woman, and between his seed and hers,"*
He was setting up divinely designated boundaries. Simply stated,

He was talking about the Christ of God whose name is Jesus. God the Father did exactly what He said He would do.

THE BELIEF FACTOR

IN John 3:16-18, the Scripture says,

> *"For God so loved the world that He gave His only begotten Son, that whosoever believeth in Him should not perish, but have everlasting life. For God sent not His Son into the world to condemn the world, but that the world through Him might be saved. He that believeth on Him is not condemned: but he that believeth not is condemned already, because he has not believed in the name of the only begotten Son of God."*

What we have here is a failure to communicate. That God loved this world unconditionally is without a doubt. That He gave the world His only begotten Son as a contingency for salvation is equally without doubt. It's the "Belief Factor" that causes man to stumble. The fact is, we really don't have a clear understanding of the concept of belief; and that is at the heart of the problem with life today.

In order to believe, one must trust; and then one's trust must be activated before it can be called belief. The definition of trust—according to Webster—is "having complete confidence in the ability, the integrity, and the character of another." In this case we are talking about the Lord God who has all power in heaven and in earth. We can know this because it was God to whom Solomon was referring in Proverbs 3:5-6 when he said,

> *"Trust in the Lord with all thine heart; and lean not unto thine own understanding. In all thy ways acknowledge Him, and He shall direct thy paths."*

We know that's true because, after all, Jesus had not been born. Nevertheless, if we fast-forward to the New Testament for just a moment, and consider the fact that God does not change, we can also see that this same level of confidence and trust also belonged to Jesus. The validation is in His statement after His resurrection. It was then and there that Jesus declared that all power in heaven and in earth had been given to Him. Therefore being in possession of the power of God the Father, made Jesus Omnipotent; which speaks volumes about His ability.

Secondly, because God does not change, we can be sure that Jesus would hold fast to His own value system, which validates His integrity. Lastly and characteristically speaking, the fact that He is Omniscient, Omnipotent and Omnipresent assures us that we could find no better candidate in which to place our complete confidence. The only thing that remains is for us to let our walk match our talk. In other words, we must go far beyond mouthing platitudes to impress others, live like we trust Him, and let our lives be a testimony to our belief. Meanwhile, back at the beginning, the failure of Adam to keep God's Command rendered his offspring helpless when it comes to living life like God would have him to live it, and makes it necessary for him to participate in the salvation process.

SUMMARY

IF we look closely at the context and the content of the First Commandment, we can see that the foundation of life was spelled out for us. Notwithstanding, Adam messed up what God set up; but God didn't leave man in that fallen condition. He set salvation in motion in the fifteenth (15) verse of that 3rd Chapter. Nothing remains but for us to "wrap our heads around the concept of salvation that God spelled out in that verse, and move forward. For that we move to the New Testament.

CHAPTER THREE

An Introduction to the New Testament

THE PROLOGUE

THE New Testament—sometimes called the New Covenant or the New Dispensation—is God's "present agreement" with mankind. It restates portions of the Old Testament and presents us with an overview of Christ the Redeemer of mankind, whose name is JESUS—the only begotten Son of God—who was also the Sacrificial Lamb. The New Testament has within its boundaries, five stipulations that beg to be clarified, understood and committed to memory: (1) a portrayal of Jesus' primary, perpetual purpose for coming; (2) his death, burial, and the power of His resurrection, and (3) the Prophecy of his second coming for His Bride—which is His Church without spot or blemish, (4) the Wedding feast—which is by invitation only—and the Rewards for those who overcome; and (5) the only Command that Jesus made of His disciples. We call it the Great Commission. It reads:

> *"Go ye therefore, and teach all nations, baptizing them in the name of the Father, and of the Son, and of the Holy Ghost: teaching them to observe all things whatsoever I have commanded you: and lo, I am with you always, even unto the end of the world.* Amen.

The importance of that scripture will become self-evident once the deeper meaning of what Jesus meant by what He said is made clear. The English word "Teach" translates the Greek word, *Matheteuo* (math-ayt—yoo-o) which means to enroll prospective disciples as scholars.

The English word "Name" translates the Greek word *Onoma (o-no-ma) which means power and or authority.*

The English word "Teaching" translates the Greek word, *Didasko* (did-as-ko) which comes from the Greek root *Didache* (Did-a-kay) which means to build a super-structure on an already laid foundation. The remainder of the reasoning is seen when you re-read that scripture using the original language for clarity and conciseness. It reads:

> *"Because I have all power in heaven and earth, you go and make disciples of all nations"(NKJV). "Enroll them as scholars and put them under the authority and power of God the Father who created; God the Son who redeems; and God the Holy Spirit who will seal them and keep them for all eternity. And lo—used only to call attention to—I will be with you always, even to the end of the world."*

I am sure you will agree that the original meaning surpasses the surface meaning, which makes the substitution of the words "preach and preaching" for "teach and teaching" toxic. Again, I say, this is my opinion; I am entitled to it and opinions are never open to argument.

THE PRESENTATION

MATTHEW | is a portrayal of the life of Jesus, written especially for the Jews. It reveals Jesus the Christ, as their long awaited Savior-King.

MARK | is a portrayal of the life of Jesus, revealing Him as the obedient Servant of God.

LUKE | is a portrayal of the life of Jesus, revealing Him as the Savior, while at the same time emphasizing his humanity.

JOHN | is a portrayal of the life of Christ, revealing Jesus as both, the human Son of God, and the altogether Spiritual Christ of God. John emphasizes the Deity of Jesus.

This is a good place to insert what I like to call "a trash fact." A trash-fact is a fact, but it must be used in the proper context, to equate to the truth. Let's be clear on that. However, if you can't use that fact right away, put it in the trash-can of your mind. It will still be a fact, but you need not let it clutter your active mind. When you need it, the Spirit of God will "bring it and all things to your remembrance" just like Jesus said He would in John 14:26. Here is the trash-fact.

The gospel recorded by Matthew, Mark, Luke, and John comprise what is known as the Synoptic Gospels. They are called synoptic because all four of them are about the life and times of Jesus, the Christ. The first three Gospels form what is theologically described as "the synoptic problem." When compared to each other, they look the same. And that's the problem: without garnering a complete understanding before moving on, Christians today assume that because they are about the life of Jesus, they are the same. That is a fact, but it is not truth. Read on.

On the one hand, Matthew, Mark and Luke wrote what Jesus said and did. But on the other hand, partly because he was the only one to live long enough to see the end, John was anointed and appointed to write "What Jesus meant by what he said and did." Thus, John's Gospel is sometimes described as "The solution to the synoptic problem."

ACTS   [of the Apostles] is a portrayal of the beginning and the spread of the Christian Church. Luke's book could well have been called the "Acts of the Holy Spirit."

The next 21 books are Epistles, which means "letters." They were written to individuals, to Churches, and to believers in general. These letters deal with every aspect of the Christian faith and responsibility. Relatively speaking, they contain the Procedures (or guidelines) for Christian living.

Paul's Letters are sometimes called "The Pauline" or "Pastoral letters."

1) ROMANS	8) 1 THESSALONIANS
2) 1 CORINTHIANS	9) 2 THESSALONIANS
3) 2 CORINTHIANS	10) 1 TIMOTHY
4) GALATIANS	11) 2 TIMOTHY
5) EPHESIANS	12) TITUS
6) PHILIPPIANS	13) PHILEMON
7) COLOSSIANS	

The New Testament Continued

General Letters

14) HEBREWS	18) 1 JOHN
15) JAMES	19) 2 JOHN
16) 1 PETER	20) 3 JOHN
17) 2 PETER	21) JUDE

The last book of the New Testament is a book of prophecy and promise. It tells of future events—including the return, the reign, and the glory of the Lord Jesus who is our Christ; and the future-state of believers and unbelievers. This book is known as **Revelation.** Because Revelation is apocalyptic—a prophecy of end-times—and the mind of man is naturally curious, the reader is cautioned against putting a "final" interpretation on the book of Revelation. Revelation, while absolutely factual, is a chapter left un-finished by the Creator of the world. However, Revelation does give all who read it a preview of things to come.

THE NEW TESTAMENT FOUNDATION

IN the New Testament, we also find a comprehensive view of (1) the life of Jesus who is called the Christ, (2) the founding of the Church and the beginning of Christianity; (3) the procedural process leading to Salvation, (4) God's principles and procedural promises for dealing with sin and Christian living; and (5) God's plan for the future of His world, and all that dwells therein.

In a collective sense, the first five books of the New Testament—like the first five in the Old Testament—are historical. They provide us with the "setting" or the genre. This writer uses them to completely convey his message. I call it the "big picture." What follows is the procedural process that leads to the full complement of salvation. It is my firm belief that when you hear members of the organized Church speak of salvation, and you read what I have written in this book, the conclusion is, we are not talking about the same thing. What is the difference? One of my members asked. I am so glad you asked was my reply; because I want so badly to tell you. My answer begins with the reminder prophesied by Hosea in Chapter 4 Verse 6 (NKJV). It is there that you hear the voice of God saying,

> *"My people are destroyed for lack of knowledge: because thou has rejected knowledge, I will also will reject you from being priest for Me. Because you have forgotten the law of your God, I also will forget your children."*

The problem with which I had to wrestle is described by the apostle, Paul, to the Church at Ephesus (6:12). Paul said,

> *"We wrestle not against flesh and blood, but against principalities, against powers, against the rulers of the darkness of this world, against spiritual wickedness in high places."*

I am not sure how or when it all started, but what I am sure of is that the damage that has been done is deep and abiding and it borders on being irreparable.

But all is not lost. The voice of God inserted the prophecy of Salvation in Genesis 3:15. For the sake of clarity I am going to revisit that scene and delineate the deeper meaning of what I believe God meant by what He said—that which is written between the lines. Mankind was relationally separated from God because he chose to think in opposition to God and rebel. Therein is the beginning of sin. To right that wrong, mankind will need to accept the gift that God gave (John 3:16), and then meet the criteria attached to it to validate their acceptance. Three people laid the foundation on which the New Testament is built.

John the Baptist was the first to speak. John said, *"Repent, for the kingdom of Heaven is at hand" (Matthew 3:2).* John was saying, "The rule and the reign of God is near unto you. God's people in the world have lived according to their own pleasure ever since creation. But now the promise of God is near unto them. Jesus was the second person to make that declaration. Jesus said, *"The time is fulfilled, and the Kingdom of God is at hand: repent ye, and believe the gospel"* (Mark 1:15). He delivered the same message using a different set of words.

When the voice of God said, *"You shall bruise his heel and it shall bruise your head,"* He was making reference to the coming of the Messiah—who would bring salvation to a sin-sick soul— and the person and power of the Holy Spirit which would make all things possible. Jesus was His name, Salvation was His mission.

Peter was the third man to echo that same declaration; however, Peter included the reward for obedience. On the day of Pentecost, Peter said, *"Repent, and be baptized every one of you in the name of Jesus Christ for the remissions of sins, and you shall receive the gift of the Holy Ghost"* (Acts 2:38). The declaration uttered by those three men satisfies the "what" factor. They told us "What" was required to meet the criteria for salvation. The question that still remained unasked and unanswered is, "How?" The writer to the Church at Rome said it this way: *"If thou shalt confess with thy mouth the Lord Jesus, and shalt believe in thine heart that God hath raised Him from the dead,*

thou shalt be saved (Romans 10:9). *Again, we have the "what" but without the "how."*

As previously stated, if there had been a deeper understanding of the meaning of the Great Commission; that is to say if the wording had not been substituted, perhaps we would not have the problem we have today. But it is what it is. We have already said that the Bible means everything that it says, but it doesn't say everything that it means. In this case, the spotlight is on a lack of misunderstanding when it comes to the word, "shall," which has served to promote a false sense of security within the body of Christ and left many, if not most of them believing that by verbally confessing Christ, they have a gift of entitlement.

It is the absence of a clear understanding of the word "shall" that I believe contemporary preachers use to lead their people, allowing them to believe that all they have to do is "confess" Christ and they are saved. Stated another way, all they have to do is wait on the Lord and He's going to work it out. All of that may be factual, but none of it is true because the context is clearly missing. The point to raise and remember is, "to arrive at the truth content must always be wrapped in the context."

If we hone in on Peter's prognosis and delineate it, line upon line and precept upon precept, the context will reveal the true meaning of the content. Peter said, "Repent . . ." Here is the catch: "True repentance" as contrasted with "mouthing platitudes" comes only by the word of God. The foundational scripture which carries the word of God concerning repentance is found in 2 Chronicles 7:14. This is my perception. In answer to Solomon's prayer concerning sin, the voice of God had this to say:

> *"If my people, which are called by my name, shall (1) humble themselves, and (2) pray; and (3) seek my face, and (4) turn from their wicked ways; THEN will I hear from heaven and will forgive their sin, and will heal their land."*

To make this clearer, please allow me to personalize it. In this verse there are four steps to God's forgiveness before the adverb "then" is inserted. I realize that this conclusion will not set well with some, but I didn't write the scripture. I merely had the opportunity to hear it and heed it, and I did.

To humble myself meant I had to "come down off my high horse." Translated, I had climbed to the top of the academic ladder, and had been given all the accolades that come with an earned Ph.D. That meant, in spite of what my circle of friends, family, and colleagues had to say about my lofty perch, I didn't know it all, after all. Thus, I had to assume a posture of meekness. The next step is to pray. That called for me to approach the throne of Grace in the spirit of humility, acknowledge my weaknesses—that it wasn't all about me, mine, and ours—and talk to God about who He is, what He is doing, and what He expects of his people.

The third step required me to consult step number two of the procedural process (2 Timothy 2:15), in search for the face—the purposeful will—of God. Perhaps I should mention that the third step alone took me the better part of five years to reasonably complete a diligent and protracted study of the scriptures; and make sufficient notes as I went. The fourth and final step validates the other three, because implementation was next in line Scripture said, *"Turn from my wicked ways."* For ease of understanding, let me say it this way. For every step towards the way of God I took, I had to take the same step away from my former way of thinking.

It took a great deal of time for me to complete what I started. But all of that comes with true repentance. First comes repentance then comes submission and surrender. Simply stated, with my eyes opened and my mind in a renewal mode, God heard my prayer, forgave my sin, and caused me to once-again be prosperous. That is true repentance. But that's not how the scenario ends.

Peter said, "Repent. But he didn't stop there; he said: *"And be baptized every one of you in the name of Jesus Christ for the remission of your sins."* Translated and as previously stated, that part of the passage would read "put these perspective disciples under the power and the authority of God the Father, God the Son, and God the Holy Ghost for the remission of their sins. Anything short of those four (4) contingencies is an exercise in futility. I am a living witness because it was only after I made those four steps did God hear my prayer, forgive my sin, and once again made me prosperous. the re-establishment of my relationship with God becomes self-evident as the Spirit of God caused blessings without number and all good things without end to become a staple in my life.

THE TRUTH OF THE MATTER

HOWEVER else tradition may choose to identify it, "True repentance" is first and foremost, and it must follow the dictates of God the Father. Let's be clear about that. Again, that is not how the scenario ends. When I completed the four steps to true repentance, my reward—according to scripture—was **"The gift of the Holy Spirit."**

Make no mistake about it the Holy Spirit did not "just" come on the scene. He has always been here (Genesis 1:2), and He has always been active in our lives. The completion of the requirements for "true repentance" gave the Holy Spirit the Lordship and the leadership in my life. That is validated for us in Genesis 2:7. Let's be clear about that as well. The very breath of life that God the Father had God the Holy Spirit to breathe into the nostrils of the man He had created—causing him to become a living soul—was the Holy Spirit. He has been there all along keeping us alive, but He will not transgress your free-will—or mine—and He will not take over your life. That comes only by submission and surrender.

The difference between then and now lies in submission and surrender. I had to submit to the sovereignty of God over my life. I had to cognitively and consciously recognize who God is and His authority over all things living. Then I had to surrender to the Lordship and leadership of the Holy Spirit in my life. That gave Him—at my request—charge over me. Thus, when God said *"Not by might nor by power, but by my Spirit, says the Lord of Hosts;"* full recognition and adherence to His power became the mode of the day.

Needless to say, God knew me before I knew myself. If we rewind back to the part where I perceived that God perused all that He had made—before he placed man in the middle of His creation—He not only knew when and if I would become submissive and obedient, He knows all of us. Therefore it can be said with certainty that we need not bother to try to deceive Him (Galatians 6:7). Without a doubt we are living in the midst of spiritual warfare. That said there is a need to be clear on the two sides who are engaged in warfare.

THE OFF-SPRING OF SATAN

AT this point we are going to pause and rewind back to the third chapter of Genesis, beginning at Verse 4, and having already met Satan, we are going to witness the introduction of four of Satan's sons. The first two were "Doubt and Denial." Once Doubt took up residence in the mind of Eve, she not only began to question the goodness and the grace of God. Her actions suggest that she gave way to his twin brother, "Denial."

Stated succinctly, Satan used Doubt and Denial to tempt her. Being tempted is not a sin; it's only when we yield to the temptation that we transgress God's will. *James said, "Submit yourself to the Lord; resist the devil and he will flee from you" (James 4:7)* Eve did not resist the temptation. Instead she allowed the voice of Satan to set **Doubt** and **Denial** in motion in her mind, concerning what God meant by what He said. When Satan asked the question, Eve repeated what God had told Adam—the best she could—to which Satan, still disguised as the serpent, said,

> *"You shall not surely die: for God doth know that in the day you eat there, then your eyes shall be opened, and you shall be as gods, knowing good and evil. And when the woman saw that the tree was good for food, and that it was pleasant to the eyes, and a tree to be desired to make one wise, she took of the fruit thereof, and did eat, and gave also unto her husband with her; and he did eat."*

Look closely at Genesis 1 Verses twenty-nine (29) and thirty (30), and you will see that God had pre-empted what Satan would use in Chapter 3, Verse 6. Like Adam, Eve had been created "In God's

Own Image" (Genesis 1:27) which gave her the propensity—the inclination or tendency—to be wise should the need arise, but leaving her blind to her own nakedness. In addition God had prepared food for both of them, negating the need to fall into Satan's trap concerning whether the fruit was good for food (3:6). Nevertheless, she yielded to temptation, and her husband followed suit. Scripture says:

> *"They heard the voice of God walking in the garden in the cool of the day; and Adam and his wife hid themselves from the presence of the Lord among the trees of the garden. And the Lord God called unto Adam, and said unto him, "Where are you?" And Adam said, I heard thy voice in the garden, and I was afraid, because I was naked; and I hid myself"* **(Genesis 3:8-10).**

What we have there is an introduction to the second set of twins belonging to Satan: **Fear** and **Insecurity.** That makes a total of four (4) spirits to which I have given personalities; and I did it because they are so prominent in the lives of each of us today. In other words, each of them is alive and well and has his being in the lives of the people of God. We dare not denigrate either of their spirits, because my ever-present past keeps reminding me that many men and women have lost their lives because they thought less of themselves than what God thought of them and subsequently instilled in them. I cannot emphasize too much that "Fear and Insecurity" are alive and well in the lives of the people of God today, making them worthy opponents, and about whom we should be acutely aware.

Ever since the introduction of those four boys, mankind has been trapped by the terrible tragedy of our cultural tradition. **Doubt** and **Denial, Fear** and **Insecurity** first took up residence in our fore parents, and as a result they cause us to live in constant self-abnegation. That said we now have insight into the foundation that was laid during the creation.

The truth is "Sin" entered the picture and distorted it, but it cannot destroy it. That distortion causes us to hold fast to a tradition which has eclipsed truth. What's needed to right the wrongs that have been done is a deeper understanding of what the Bible means by what it says. And that will not come about until we make up our minds to do the right thing, the right way. What we say we believe must be validated by active trust. And active trust comes through complete confidence in the Ability, the Integrity, and the Character of the Lord God. And none of that is possible without the person, the presence, and the power of the Holy Spirit.

THE CONCLUSION

"What Christians believe about the Bible"

WE BELIEVE   The Bible consists of 66 books, and that it is a mini-library unto itself, divided into the Old and New Testaments.

WE BELIEVE   The Bible is the inspired word of God, and is inerrant on its face.

WE BELIEVE   The Bible is the final authority for Christian faith and practice (2 Timothy 3:16, 17; 2 Peter 1:19 – 21).

WE BELIEVE   That there is one true God who exists in three persons: God the Father who Created; God the Son who redeemed us, and God the Holy Spirit who resides with us and in us as the Person and the Power of the Eternal God.

WE BELIEVE   Distinct in relationship, Each of the three persons of the tri-unity of God is fully God, and One in essence, existence, evidence, plan and purpose.

WE BELIEVE   God has revealed Himself to be the infinite, personal Creator, who is sovereign and over all things. (Deuteronomy 6:4; Mark 1:9-11)

WE BELIEVE Jesus the Christ is God's eternal Son. Being both, fully God and fully man, He was born of a virgin, lived a sinless life, died as an atoning-sacrifice for the sin of all mankind; that He rose bodily from the dead and ascended into heaven where he sits at the right hand of God the Father making intercession on behalf of all believers (Matthew 1:18-23;1Corinthians 15:1-8; and Acts 1:9-11).

WE BELIEVE Mankind was originally created "In God's Own Image." But having been tempted, the first Adam chose to rebel against God, bringing sin into the world and causing mankind to fall from Grace. As a result of this fallen condition, God's image has been distorted and all of mankind was separated—by sin—from God, and in need of salvation. Through true repentance—as stated in 2 Chronicles 7:14—and faith in Jesus' finished work on the Cross, we can be reborn by the Holy Spirit and restored to fellowship with God (Genesis 3: 9-13; Romans 5:8-12).

WE BELIEVE the Holy Spirit encourages us to repent of our sins and accept Jesus, the Christ, as Lord of this life, and Savior in the world to come.

WE BELIEVE The Holy Spirit equips men and women with spiritual gifts for effective ministry, and empowers us to live, go and grow, and serve in obedience to God (John 14:26, 16:8-10; Acts 1:8; Corinthians 12:4-9).

WE BELIEVE The Church is an Organism—the living Body of Christ on earth—which is comprised of all true believers in Jesus as our Christ.

WE BELIEVE Jesus is the head and the source of all power in the Church's life, which exists only to glorify God.

WE BELIEVE   The Church fulfills its mission by cultivating personal growth in the knowledge and the fullness of the stature of Jesus, by caring about one another in the Christian community, communicating the gospel by word and by deed to the world, and by celebrating the goodness and the Glory of God (Matthew 16:15-19; Ephesians 4:14-16; Acts 2:41-47). Finally,

WE BELIEVE   Jesus is the Christ, and will physically return to earth to establish His eternal kingdom; that He will judge the world—which includes the quick and the dead—and that He will reward the saints and rule for all eternity.

THE HIDDEN HOPE

CONTAINED in the foundation of the New Testament is the blessed hope of the Church of God in Christ—wherever it may be located and by whatever name they have chosen for local identity. Those who have been reborn of the water and of the Spirit of Christ will live with Him forever (John 14:1-3; Matthew 24:29-31; and Revelation 19:11-21). With all things considered, if our belief-system is intact, we can now speak of things to come with faith—as if they are already here. And this we will do as we move towards apprehension and adherence to the DOA in this world. The only thing that will hinder any of us is our relationship with God—a relationship that must be re-established and kept in an up-close and personal position.

CHAPTER FOUR

What does the Bible Say?

THE PROLOGUE

WHAT does the Bible have to say about other world religions? Simply stated, the Bible does not sit in judgment, nor does it criticize. However, the Bible does have much to say on the topic of "Spiritual Warfare" which separates the people of God. It states with certainty that there is a spiritual war going on between God and Satan, between the annals of good and the impact of evil. The purpose and the plan of Satan, the sultan of sin and the arch-enemy of God, along with his host of demonic spirits—are to divert mankind away from the truth. John the Revelator wrote: *"the whole world lies under the sway of the wicked one" (1 John 5:19 NKJV)"*, and the apostle Paul warned us that people will *"follow deceiving spirits and things taught by demons" (1Timothy 4:1, NIV)*. Therefore, with respect to every man's opinion, I will stop right here.

It is common knowledge in all of Christendom that from the beginning Satan, using the disease of deception, has been deceiving humanity. In the Garden of God, he told Eve, *"ye shall be as gods, knowing good and evil."* At the risk of sounding like I am "mud-slinging" or "belief-bashing," I find it interesting that some of America's best-known preachers, unknowingly, have taken the essence of the phrase, *"In His Own Image"* in Genesis 1:27, merged it with the mention of faith in Romans 10:8-10, and fashioned a whole new Movement called "Word of Faith" (WOF). Using that phrase as a launching pad, they have made "being divine" or being "as god" a common thread. While I believe that there are sincere Christians within the WOF movement, my prayer is that they will take a serious look at the questionable doctrines of their leadership that are conducive to leading people into spiritual pride.

Literally speaking the leaders in this movement proclaim that "we are god manifested in the flesh"—which is heresy—but they also teach the practice of (1) "being slain in the spirit;" (2) that Jesus was tormented by Satan in hell for three days;" (3) "that if you are truly filled with the spirit, you will speak in tongues;" (4) "that you can receive a second separate baptism of the Spirit long after conversion, instead of baptism of the Spirit being the linchpin which brings on conversion, and (5) the bizarre practice of "holy laughter," and other unscriptural and dangerous doctrines. Many WOF teachers have also made false prophecies; and some have even predicted doom and gloom for Christians who would dare to challenge their teachings. For a more thorough expose of the *Word of Faith* heresies, visit www.BibleFacts.org on the internet.

I will stop here but that's not how the story ends. The Bible teaches that Satan and his servants will masquerade as ministers of righteousness (2 Corinthians 11:13-14). Satan's servants and the hoisting of false religious practices have been a very effective lie, since it mixes in some truth. The reader should keep in mind that "a half truth" is "a whole lie." In other words, a lie mixed in with truth is much like taking in 99% good food, and 1% poison. It's that 1% of poison that will eventually kill you.

THE PRESENTATION:
Judaism and the Old Testament

JUDAISM in the Old Testament looked forward to the coming of the Messiah. Chronologically, the New Testament celebrated His arrival and looks forward, unequivocally, to His return. Therefore, regardless of what men say, it's not "either/or," it's "both/and." The Old Testament is the foundation, and the New Testament is the Super-structure that was built on that foundation. In comparison, just as the Pharisees denigrated the Ten Commandments by developing more than six-hundred laws from them, the contemporary preacher denigrates the power of God by down-playing the full complement of Salvation, making it a one-time event which gives credence to the prophecy of

49

Hosea in Chapter 4, verse 6: "My people are destroyed for lack of knowledge."

In point of fact, modern-man in the Western Hemisphere, by calling themselves Christians, are playing the role of "The pot which called the skillet black," by slamming Judaism and denigrating Islam, while they, themselves, are bathing in the innocence of ignorance and leading the people astray. For example, men have said that Islam is based on the writings of Muhammad and not on the word of God. The question to be asked and answered is how is that any different than Christianity? Let's be clear. If Muhammad was the prophet whom God anointed and appointed to write the Koran—and all of Islam says he is—how is that any different than Christianity being based on the writings of thirty-five to forty men who wrote the Bible—and all of Christendom say they were. I am of the opinion that those critics are not teaching what the Koran says, they are advancing what they believe Muhammad meant by what he said, which is no less than what preachers and teachers have done with the Bible and Christianity. Instead of preaching and teaching what Jesus said, they are advancing what they believe Jesus meant by what He said.

Since Islam is fast gaining prominence in America, a word about the lie that has been perpetrated is in order. Today, the writings of men would have you to believe that the religion of Islam worships a single, impersonal god, rather than the one true God. That is simply not true. Every man is entitled to his own opinion, and opinions are never open to argument. But here is another view on the matter.

The word "Allah" is a title, not a name. It is used by Muslims as the Arabic identification of God. However, the word Allah is not specific to Islam; Arabic-speaking Christians and Jews, and the Catholic Maltese, also use it to refer to the monotheistic deity. For instance, in Arabic translations of the Bible, although the title "Allah" is most commonly associated with Islam, it was also used in pre-Islamic times. It was used by Arab Christians in the pre-Islamic *Umm al-Jimal* inscription in the 6th century. Similarly, God is His title not His name (Exodus 2:7). That is the word of God for the people of God from a Christian perspective. Now look with me at a paraphrase of what another sacred text has to say about Islam.

The father of Muhammad, Islam's Prophet, had the name Abdullah, which when translated, means "slave of Allah." The Hebrew word for deity, "EL" or "Eloh," was used as an Old Testament synonym for Yahweh. The Aramaic word for God is Aloh-o (Syriac dialect), which comes from the same Proto-Semitic word (Ilah) as the Arabic and Hebrew terms. In Matthew 27:46 and Mark 15:34 respectively, Jesus is described and as having used this word on the cross (in the form el-i and elo-i) respectively. One of the earliest surviving translations of the word into a foreign language is in the Greek translation of the Shahada, from 86-96 AH (705-715 AD), which translates it as *"ho theos monos,"* literally "the one God." (Aisha Y. Musa, Jews in the Quran)

I could go on from there, but that is not the specific aim of this project. My aim is to comment on the writings of men who have committed travesties of spiritual justice by their propensity to continually perpetuate the status quo, putting down the beliefs of others in an effort to add credence to their own. That is not to say that there are not those who passionately and deliberately create these travesties. I would be remiss if I didn't include a comment on the writings of those men and women who endeavor to lead the people of God astray. For example, Mormonism is based on the writings of Joseph Smith, who had the Bible re-written to support his claims. The Church of "The Latter Day Saints" denies the divinity of Jesus, believe in many gods, and believe men can attain godhood and rule over their own planet." That, in the opinion of this writer, is a travesty and simply another rendition of what man has said. But they have every right to believe as they wish, even if it is with the end thereof being self-aggrandizement.

There are some Eastern religions such as Hinduism, Buddhism, and a few other Western New-age religions which are questionable. For instance, there is Christian Science—the writings of Mary Baker Eddy—who does not teach from the Bible, but substitutes the "Science and Health" key, which teaches Pantheism or that everything is god. Those advocates will say, "May the force be with you." Others teach a form of reincarnation that's also curious, to say the least. They believe that the spirit continues to succeed itself in another individual until it reaches a level of "enlightenment and oneness" with god, or "the gods."

COMPARATIVE RELIGION

IN comparison, Christianity teaches one death and one judgment (Hebrews 9:27). Christianity is also the only religion that recognizes the hopeless gap between sinful man and a Holy and Righteous God. Christianity teaches that Salvation can only be obtained by grace alone, through faith alone, in Christ alone. All the other religions teach that salvation—or reconciliation—can be achieved through human effort. At this point we should be able to agree that these two major religions are different, but with men producing conflicting and contradictory views, wrong will forever sit on the throne. However, with the proper insight and understanding, those mountains can be moved. To foster a belief comes under the heading of one's own prerogative. And since prerogatives lead to opinions; and since we all have them and we are all entitled to them, one's opinion does not negate the opinion of another.

However and on any subject that comes under discussion, opinions are never open to argument. To accept the word of God without exception is a noble feat, but extremely difficult to do. Nevertheless, according to the Bible, [since] *"We can do all things through Christ which strengthens us"* (Philippians 4:13); the only solution to the problem is to partner with Solomon in Proverbs 4:7 and get an understanding.

Getting an understanding requires at least three things from which most of us will shy away. Rather than "think, face the truth, and change, we will do almost anything to "fit in" and "be accepted." Stated another way and in conclusion, what you think of you is your self-perception; but what you think others think of you controls your self-esteem, and we will do almost anything to remain in their good graces and keep our self-esteem spiraling upward.

CHAPTER FIVE

The Bible on Sin and Salvation

PROLOGUE

SCRIPTURE says:

> *But He was wounded for our transgressions. He was bruised for our iniquities; the chastisement of our peace was upon Him, and by His stripes we are healed. All we like sheep have gone astray. We have turned everyone to his own way. And the Lord has laid on Him the iniquities of us all (Isaiah 53:5-6).*

The Bible states very plainly and very clearly that the only way to the Father is through Jesus, the Christ. The Apostle Peter said, *"This is the stone which was rejected by you builders, which has become the chief cornerstone" (Acts 4:11-12, NKJV). Neither is there salvation in any other: for there is none other name under heaven given among men whereby we must be saved"* (Acts 4:12, NKJV). Jesus Himself said, *"I am the way and the truth and the life, no one comes to the Father except through me"* (John 14:6, KJV). The Bible teaches that sin has separated us from God, and that the only way to be reconciled is for us to confess our sin (Proverbs 18:21) and accept God's gracious gift—the ransom paid on the cross of Calvary by His Son Jesus, who is called the Christ. The Bible also makes it very clear that if you do not accept Jesus as your Savior, when you die you will be judged by God, according to the Law, *"for all have sinned and come short of the glory of God"* (Romans 3:23).

PRESENTATION

FURTHER validation can be found in 1 Kings 8: 22-53; Ecclesiastes 7:20 and Isaiah 53:6. Since God will not force Himself on anyone, His Holy nature leaves no other option but to separate the un-repentant from Him forever, even though it means they will suffer eternally. That may seem harsh and intolerant, without judgment and punishment, but God would not remain true to His character, if He was not true to His word. But that's not how the scenario ends, either. In what I call the "design-phase," God included with His purposeful will, His permissive will and a procedural process for redemption.

Peter gave us His procedural process in Acts 2:38 when he said, **"Repent, and be baptized in the name of Jesus Christ for the remission of sins and you shall receive the gift of the Holy Ghost."** By repenting and being baptized in the name of Jesus Christ, our sin-debt would be wiped away through the shedding of the blood of the Son of God on Calvary. It is a gift of such magnitude that there is only one way to look at it. While this gift is free, "There is a high cost to that free gift." It is so costly, it cannot be earned, nor is it deserved (Romans 6:23). The plan of Salvation is a testimony to the grace and the goodness of God who is also loving and compassionate. The scriptures say that *"while we were still sinners, He sent His Son to die for us* (Romans 5:8). At the risk of sounding biased in light of the attributes of God that we all know about, "True Christianity," in the mind of this writer, is the only religion that makes complete sense.

A diligent and protracted study of World History will reveal that even though the Bible is reputedly the rule and guide to the faith and practice of the Christian Church, God actually had the Bible written and delivered to the world more than four thousand years before Jesus was born and the Christian Church was founded. We can be certain of that because Bible history informs us that the covenant which God made with Noah was made sometime between 4004 and 2500 B.C., depending on which historical document you are reading. The word of God found in Romans 15: 4, states very clearly that *"The Bible was written for our learning, [and] that we, through patience and comfort of the scriptures, might have hope."*

Another school of thought suggests that in addition, the Bible was given to the world for the primary purpose of teaching mankind how to discern the difference between good and evil; and thereby learn how to properly use his "free-will" to make good choices. Be that as it may, the context and the content of the Bible have something to say about every subject that pertains to life: "the good, the bad, and the ugly." Translated, the word of God addresses all topics concerning life, whether they are good, evil, right, wrong, acceptable or unacceptable; they all fall under the grace and the goodness of God. Look close enough, and you will find everything there. Collectively, the writers of the Bible gave us what I like to call "a fool-proof, fail-safe formula for successful living. Stated very simply, it is a God-inspired, disciplined lifestyle (2 Timothy 3:16). The formula contained therein was developed primarily for the edification of mankind, and the glorification of God. To accept it is man's prerogative. Among the many promises of God that are found in the Bible, there is one that stands out and is applicable to all people, everywhere: *"Man will reap what he sows"* (Galatians 6:7b). Metaphorically speaking, the Bible paints a verbal portrait of "the Cause and Effect of sin, the Salvation process, Faith as the Antidote for fear, and the written word of God as the Rule and Guide to the faith and practice of all who will believe."

Natural progression dictates that I remove the presumptuousness in our perception as we move forward. Stated another way, I would be in error if I gave my readers the impression, or inadvertently caused them to believe that everybody who calls him or herself a Christian, is, in fact, a Christian. In addition, that perception would only be exacerbated if I allowed them to think that 'saying they are Christian' guarantees that they know who God is; when, at best, it can only be said that they only know about God. Stated succinctly and when the final bell is toll, I have come to believe that very few of the people of God actually know Him well enough to say that they have a re-established a relationship with Him that's up-close and personal.

So it is that in *Entering* we will include a discussion on all four segments of the DOA. Thus, in company with the Holy Spirit in the lead, we will describe and delineate a concept of God that is both rational and reasonable. Stated another way, we will literally profile God.

PART TWO

CHAPTER SIX

Profiling God

PROLOGUE

THE voice of God still says, *"My people are destroyed for lack of knowledge."* Very little has changed. There is, however, a tendency to pick up and insert the name of the **person,** the **presence** or the **power** of "GOD" whenever necessity dictates, with or without any concrete knowledge of who God really is. It is my intent to put an end to that brand of folly.

Needless to say, the concept of God means different things to different people. The following is my opinion and I am entitled to it. Suffice it to say what I think does not negate what you think, or vice-versa. I believe there is general agreement that there are not enough words in the English language to define God. However, I have selected fifteen attributes that I believe will adequately describe God.

PRESENTATION

THESE fifteen attributes will set forth a clear description of the **character** and the **nature** of God. They are: *Essence, Existence and Evidence; Omniscience, Omnipotence and Omnipresence; Positive, Productive and Progressive; Consistent, Continuous and Conducive; Able, Accessible, and Accountable.*

Characteristically speaking, the first six attributes: Essence, Existence and Evidence; Omniscience, Omnipotence and Omnipresence; speak only of God for only He is in possession of them. In God there are three persons: The Father, The Son, and the Holy Spirit. Each of them performs their own role and function, even though they work in tandem. The next six: Positive, Productive and Progressive; Consistent, Continuous and

Conducive are validated in the creation epic and are contributors to our well-being as well. Even though they mirror the Nature of God, they were inherently instilled in each of us as an integral part of "His Own Image" (Genesis 1:27). In other words, they are inseparably bound to each of us. With them comes the "propensity"—the tendency or inclination—to manifest either of them at will. However, we must keep in mind that those six attributes are restricted by the impact of sin in our lives.

The last three attributes: Able, Accessible, and Accountable, identify a select group who will successfully make the decisive-decision to walk in the ways of God, in spite of and regardless of the roadblocks that appear along the way. That group—according to Jesus—will find the strait gate and walk through it into an already decided destiny (Matthew 7:13). Each of these attributes will be delineated as we proceed. We began with the Foundation. His name is Jesus, His mission was Messianic. We move now to a delineation of all three.

THE HOLY TRINITY

AS previously stated the DOA began with a formal introduction to the written word of God—also known as the Bible. We then move to a definition and delineation of the Holy or Blessed Trinity: the Father, the Son, and the Holy Spirit. Each segment of the Trinity—although not commonly known—has three facets by which He is herein identified, and His role-specification is clarified. Although not typically identified, those facets are: person, presence and power.

Again and as previously stated, all four segments work in tandem to carry out the Kingdom of God, but each one carries out His own individual role and function. At the risk of sounding repetitious, the second, third, and fourth segments make up the Holy Trinity. They are: God the Father, God the Son, and God the Holy Spirit. These four come to rest rule and abide in the Kingdom of God, sometimes called the Kingdom of Heaven. The Kingdom of God is the realm in which God the Father reigns and rules exclusively. Contrary to any opinion which may say differently, the

Kingdom of God reigns in the earth—in the hearts of mankind—as well as in heaven" (Matthew 6:10). Simply stated, "The Kingdom of God" is alive and well and in force, right here and right now; and awaits the opportunity to come alive in each of our hearts and minds. As the reader will soon see, living in the Kingdom of God is an individual preference today, but will become mandatory when the time is fulfilled.

THE CHARACTER OF GOD the FATHER

CHARACTERISTICALLY speaking, after reading the order of creation in Chapter 1 Verses 3, 6, 9, 11, 14, 20, 22, 24, 26 and 29, we come away knowing that *"God is" and that "He is a rewarder of those who diligently seek Him"* (Hebrews 11: 6). God is what? Someone asked. In His Character, God the Father is the Essence, the Existence and the Evidence of everything and everybody. The terms we use to describe His Essence include, but are not limited to His Omniscience, Omnipotence and Omnipresence. Translated, in creation God took out of Himself just enough to re-produce Himself, thereby allowing Him to be absent from Himself, while yet remaining with Himself. He spoke, and His word went forth turning chaos into creation. His word was, *"A child is born; a Son is given" (Isaiah 9:6).*

In His creative posture, the person of God is Positive, Productive and Progressive; Consistent, Continuous and Conducive just to name a few. When properly understood, we can say with certainty that the presence of God is in everybody. And because "God is," we can also say with the same amount of certainty, that His Character is absolute. Stated succinctly and collectively, God is the Essence, the Existence and the Evidence of everything that was ever made, and everybody who was created. In the order of creation, Essence always precedes existence; and existence is always followed by the evidence.

A cursory look at the order of creation will reveal that each time God spoke, something—which **was "REALITY"** in the mind of God **became "ACTUALITY"** real time existence. All that became actuality became physical evidence. Along with the evidence came God's purpose and His intended role and function for all that was created.

THE CONCEPT OF GOD:
The Blessed Trinity continued

AGAIN as previously stated, the Bible presents us with the concept of God in three persons. We have seen God the Father in action, now let's look together at God the Son who is Christ the Redeemer. In the fullness of time He was presented as the only begotten Son of God. Paul called Him "All the fullness of the Godhead, bodily" (Colossians 2:9). His name is Jesus, but His mission was and still is Messianic. Because of a lack of knowledge, the believer today will link all three together, and will become annoyed if you attempt to differentiate between them. Suffice it to say that as it relates to salvation, "Jesus died, Christ didn't." Add the following and the picture becomes clearer.

It was Jesus who said, **"All power is given unto me in heaven and in earth,"** not Christ. As it relates to Christ in the interim while Jesus is away in heaven, consider the following. **"It is in Christ that we live and move and have our being"** (Acts 17:28), not Jesus. Keep in mind that it was Jesus who was crucified dead and buried, and on the third-day was resurrected, not Christ. It is Jesus whom the Bible says ascended into heaven and took his seat at the right hand of power, not Christ. It is Jesus who makes intercession for us with God the Father, not Christ.

Lastly, in answer to a question concerning His identity, it was Jesus who said,

> *"I go to prepare a place for you. And if I go and prepare a place for you, I will come again, and receive you unto myself; that where I am, there you may be also."*

It was Jesus, not Christ (John 14:2-3). It was also Jesus, not Christ, who said, *"I am the way, the truth, and the life: no man cometh unto the Father but by me,"* not Christ (John 14:6). There is more, but I believe my point concerning the second person in the Trinity has been made.

The third person in the concept is God the Holy Spirit—readily accepted by everyone, but seldom understood by many. It was the Holy Spirit who came in person presence and power on the day of Pentecost, and who functions as our Teacher and our Keeper (John 14:26). Collectively speaking it is the Holy Spirit by whom all things happen at the will of God the Father. Because He works at the behest of both, the Father and the Son, what He does is either by commission or omission. All three persons make up "The fullness of the Godhead," which is also known and accepted in all of Christendom, more especially the organized Church, as the "Holy or Blessed Trinity." For the record, the word "Trinity" does not appear in the Bible. By all available sources, it first appeared in the U.S. in a song by Reginald Heber and John Dykes, entitled "Holy! Holy! Holy! Lord God Almighty." In that song, the Godhead was referred to as "The Blessed Trinity."

As we have endeavored to demonstrate, each of these segments is unique and carries out His individual role and function. The Bible is the voice of God the Father, speaking through His prophets, priests and scribes, delivering his message to His people. For example, the voice of God can be heard speaking through the prophet Isaiah in Chapter 45 Verse 23, saying,

> *"I have sworn by myself, the word is gone out of my mouth in righteousness, and shall not return; that unto me every knee shall bow, every tongue shall swear."*

Then in Chapter 46 verses 9-11, the voice of God said:

> *"Remember the former things of old for I am God, and there is none else; I am God and there is none like me, declaring the end from the beginning, and from ancient times the things that are not yet done, saying, "My counsel shall stand, and I will do all my pleasure."*

The prophecy of Isaiah was Reality in the mind of God long before it was communicated to the Prophet. Reality became an Actuality

63

in real time when Isaiah wrote it. We saw the evidence when what God promised was made manifest in the New Testament. For instance, fast-forwarding we hear the voice of Jesus summarizing and restating the Ten Commandments of God in Matthew 22:37-40. There, He not only summarized and replicated Old Testament Law, He also assigned individual responsibility. In that passage Jesus was speaking to the young lawyer, but because God doesn't repeat himself, and with God there is no respect of person, what He said was applicable to all mankind.

The apostle Paul came along and in Romans 14:11 affirmed individual responsibility by restating what God had said through the prophet Isaiah. At the same time he again confirmed what I like to call "blessings-unlimited and all good-things without end" that await those who love their concept of God enough to subscribe to the DOA without exception (1 Corinthians 2:9).

CHAPTER SEVEN

Growing Up in the Image of God

PROLOGUE

Entering was written for the benefit of all of God's people everywhere; but especially directed to world leaders [everywhere] and leaders of the organized Church who subscribe to the Christian ethos. I believe the time has come for Church leaders to take traditional Christian practices to the next level. What exactly does that mean? The sister asked. Simply this: it's time for God's people to be positioned for growth and development from the elementary things to perfection (Hebrews 6:1-2). Stated another way, it's time for the people of God to grow and go "from good" (Genesis 1:31), to "great" (1 Corinthians 2:9). The growth of which I speak, cannot and will not take place until each person has been subjected to a "real conversion experience;" one that culminates in a deeper understanding of who God is, what He is in each of us, and what the Bible means by what it says about Him.

PRESENTATION

LET me begin by bringing to the forefront my convictions concerning the voice of God speaking His own special truth. That's another way of saying that I believe the Bible is the voice of God speaking to the people that He created. Stated succinctly, in the Bible God is saying to believers: "What I have to say is written in the Book. In addition, He is saying I am the Lord God and I change not" (Malachi3:6). Translated, because I love my creation equally and unconditionally, I have directed My Spirit to place within the covers of the Bible: principles, promises, prophecy and procedures. And furthermore, given the fact that I have used some thirty-five to forty people to write the Bible, the reader can say with certainty that those individuals have said what I want the world to know; and they have written with precision and power as they were given inspiration (2 Timothy 3:16).

For example, our current focus is on the validity of the prophecy of Hosea in Chapter 4 Verse 6, which continues to remind us that *"the people of God are [continually being] destroyed for lack of knowledge."* That, says the voice of God, is clear. The priests of old rejected the knowledge of me and I have promised to reject them and those who came after them from being priests in the future. Finally, because they had also forgotten my laws, I have promised to forget their children—those who will come after them.

SYSTEMATIC GROWTH and DEVELOPMENT

ASSUMING that I am joined in literal agreement, I am convinced that the time has come for preachers and all self-declared "Heralds of Salvation"—regardless of denominational preference or statements of faith—to take seriously the suggestion of Paul to young Timothy in Chapter 2 Verse fifteen (15). Paul urged Timothy to, *"Study to show yourself approved unto God as a workman who needs not to be ashamed, rightly dividing the word of truth."* These leaders must begin studying the Bible, not only as the perceived, written word of God to be used for problem solving, but for clarity and conciseness, and as the best piece of English Literature that has ever been written for successful living; to be used on a 24/7 basis, 365 days a year.

Stated another way, rather than continuing to consign the Bible to worship services on Sunday or their designated Sabbath, they should begin now to encourage their parishioners to fill in the gap between Christ and culture—also on a 24/7, 365 days a year. Modern research has revealed that preachers—by far and large—will select a pivotal scripture, announce a subject and preach from it. In so doing, because of inherent ignorance and a lack of validity, they succeed only in taking a quantum leap of faith in hopes that God will hear their prayers and make a miracle out of the mess that one or more of their parishioners have made for themselves. It is my belief that self-declared believers should be taught who God is, in and of Himself, who they are in Him and what He is in each of them. To be able to do that will enable and empower them to discern truth, about and for themselves.

Why all the fuss about studying the Bible? I was asked. The answer is clear. The people of God profess a belief in God that— judging from the conflict between Christ and culture in their lives—exudes a faith that's only relevant in the worship service on Sunday. The evidence seems to suggest that at best, they know about God; but they do not know God. They know what the Bible says God did, but they do not know who God is in and of Himself, or what they can expect from Him. Who is He, preacher? Tell us if you know, said one of my parishioners. "I do, and I will," was my response.

Let me begin by saying that my research has informed me that all we know about God—beyond what our family members have told us or what we learned in Sunday school—is what the Bible says. For that reason, it is incumbent upon each leader to begin studying the Bible for him or herself, which should lead him to a clear understanding of what the Bible means by what it says in John 14:26; and using it to let the Holy Spirit teach God's people. And for the record, because with God there is no respect of person, the answers to the questions that follow will be stated in plural form. The first question is, "Who is God, in and of Himself?" The answer is found in Exodus 3:13-14. There, the Bible informs us of a conversation between Moses and the voice of God, when God was about to send Moses to Egypt to lead His people out of bondage, into the land of freedom. In that conversation, Moses said to God,

> *"Behold, when I come unto the children of Israel, and shall say unto them, The God of your fathers hath sent me to you; and they shall say to me, "What is His name?" What shall I say unto them? And God said unto Moses:*
>
> *I AM THAT I AM. Thus shalt thou say unto the children of Israel, "I AM hath sent me to you." And*

> *God said unto Moses, moreover, thus shalt thou say unto the children of Israel, The LORD God of your fathers, the God of Abraham, the God of Isaac, and the God of Jacob, hath sent me to you: this is my name forever, and this is my memorial unto all generations.*

That is who God said He is, according to Old Testament Scripture. But who is He in real time? A student asked. Can you be a little more specific? My response was, "As a matter of fact, I can." Given what I have come to understand and believe, the voice of God said "I AM that I AM." Translated, God's response requires us to rewind back to Elementary school when we were taught the laws and the mechanics of English grammar. English language grammar informs us that for a sentence to be complete, only two parts of the sentence are needed: the subject and a predicate.

Thus, in that fourteenth verse "I" is the subject and "AM" is the predicate. Therefore, His name is "I AM." But for those who need a "direct object" to make the sentence clearer, try one of these for size. When the voice of God said **"I AM that I AM;"** He was saying in effect: "I AM the sight in your eyes, the hearing in your ears, and the taste in your tongue." I AM the feeling in your fingers, the walking in your feet, and the clapping in your hands.

In addition, look at the night skies, said He. Who do you think made all that you see? Who is it that marches that army of stars out each night, counts them off, calls each one by name and never overlooks a single one? The answer is, "I AM." So it is that we can say with certainty that God's name is "I AM that I AM." BUT we can go on from there. John, in the prologue to his gospel, makes the picture even clearer. John wrote,

> *"In the beginning was the Word, and the Word was with God, and the Word was God. The same was in the beginning with God. All things were made by Him; and without Him was not anything made that was made. In Him was life; and the life was the light of men. And the light shineth in darkness; and the darkness comprehended it not."*

Those five verses make it very clear who God is. As a matter of fact, those five verses parallel the context and content of Genesis Chapter 1, Verses 1-27, in which Moses recorded the entire creation epic.

It was in the creation epic that we learned what we know; and which states very clearly that God is **in** everything; and if the solemn truth is told, **God is** everything. So what we have thus far is who God is and a literal sketch of what He did. Simply stated, considering the fact that God created the heaven and the earth, and lastly He created man "In His Own Image;" we not only have a clear view of who God is, in and of Himself we know what God did, when and where. And not only that, we also know that we are "the image of God." What that means would require an entire book to delineate. However, as we proceed that question will be answered with specificity.

I cannot emphasize enough the need for the people of God to put a halt to some of the traditions of old which limit them to merely reading the word, selecting and memorizing some of the pivotal scriptures. That practice simply perpetuates the status quo. It's time for the words of the writer to the Hebrews Chapter 6 verses 1-2 to be apprehended. Additionally, it's time for the context and content of that same scripture to become meaningful enough for people to see the need to adhere to it. Stated succinctly, the people of God must be prepared for systematic spiritual growth and development, and for godly living both inside and outside of the Church. We have had two-thousand years of experiences and exposure dealing with the perils of being un-prepared: all of which has left us at various stages of being stumped, stymied and stagnated because of a lack of knowledge (Hosea 4:6).

NOW IS THE TIME

WHEN Jesus began his Galilean ministry, He said, *"The time is fulfilled, and the Kingdom of God is at hand. Repent, and believe in the gospel"* **(Mark 1:15)**. That message was communicated one time to one person (John Mark) and in one place (Galilee); but the message was both, timeless and limitless. That's another way of saying that His message was meant for everybody, everywhere; and that it is valid for all time to come.

When Jesus said that *"the time is fulfilled," He was* saying to the reader that even though we live-and view-time on a chronological plane, in God's Kairos "The time is now."

When Jesus said *"The Kingdom of God is at hand,"* He was literally saying that our time of self-governance was up, if we want to live. He was stating that the realm—in and on which God rules without exception—is near unto each of us. Stated another way, He was saying that "too much time has passed and too many people—having been side-tracked by the sediments of sin—have been lulled into a false sense of security, on the basis of what the preacher and 'mama and papa-nem'(sic) have said, and we have unwittingly believed.

It's time now for those who are suffering from severe cases of spiritual myopia, to wake up and smell the coffee, as it were. None of this is meant to be a negative criticism or a put-down; they are only words to the wise which I hope will be sufficient. Jesus validated this truth for us in John 5:39-40 when He said:

> *"You search the Scriptures, for in them you think you have eternal life; and these are they which testify of Me. But you are not willing to come to Me that you may have life."*

My question is, "How can anyone come to Jesus if the way to Him has not been made clear?" That is one of the questions on which the content of *Entering* will focus. In John 10:10 Jesus also said,

> *"The thief does not come except to steal, and to kill, and to destroy. I have come that they may have life, and that they may have it more abundantly."*

Using Jesus' proclamation as a launching pad and as it relates to living life, a second question is "When?" My answer is "now." Above all else, it is incumbent upon those who claim to be called by God to preach the gospel, to be the first to apprehend and adhere to the words of Paul in 2 Timothy Chapter 4, Verses 2-4, and for all the same reasons that Paul gave in that proclamation. That said there are two ways to understand and apply that proclamation: preaching the word, and preaching from the word.

It is my perception that on the one hand and by definition, "preaching the word" is "The manifestation of the Incarnate Word by the spoken word, from the written word." And for the record, that definition of "preaching the word" is designed primarily for the prevention of sin.

On the other hand, preaching "from" the word has its focus on intervention now that sin has overcome the people of God. But even that presents a bigger problem. Preaching "from" the word permits preachers to express and use their opinions—whether or not they are scripturally sound. Jesus made it clear that for preachers to subsequently lead the people where they themselves cannot go, is an example of blind leaders of the blind; and both will fall into a ditch" (Matthew 15:13-14).

Stated succinctly, there is more to thinking like God would have us to think, and living life the way God would have us to live it, than we would imagine. However, showing due-diligence in *"presenting himself to God as a worker who does not need to be ashamed, rightly dividing the word of truth"* (2 Timothy 2:15 (NKJV), is the only way to get started. Preachers must be the first to get on board this symbolic train to Jordan. Choosing to live life God's way requires more than what meets the eye. Pastors and preachers must be the first to take the word of God literally, thereby demonstrating that they believe that the Bible means everything that it says, even though it does not always say everything that it means. Then they must also be the first to surrender to Lordship and the leadership of the Holy Spirit; and under the unction of the Holy Spirit, take the Bible figuratively in their attempt to use it to rebuke and reprove (2 Timothy 3:16). I call this "working under authority."

THE THEOLOGY OF CHOICE

GROWING up in the image of God is a matter of choice. However, a diligent and protracted study of the Scriptures will reveal that there are really only two choices when it comes to living: "God's way" and "Man's way." On the Spiritual level, the key to God's way is spelled out in Scripture, complete with the cause and effect of thinking and acting in opposition to any part of it. However and metaphorically speaking, "Man's way" is comprised of a curious mixture of both, faith and foolishness. Let me unpack that suitcase.

Man was created "In God's Own Image" (Genesis 1:27), which gave him the propensity—a basic instinct, tendency and inclination—to go either way with both being powered by the Nature of God. However, we must keep in mind that from his predecessor Adam, man inherited a fallen nature—caused by Adam eating from the tree of the knowledge of good and evil—a.k.a. opposition and disobedience. Because our fore-parents violated God's first Command (Genesis 2:17), we readily think in opposition to God as a general rule. As a result, we know just enough "good" to give us perfect 20/20 hindsight, and just enough "evil" to make us perpetually self-destructive. When the two are combined—I call it "mixing and matching"—it's a combination of good and evil: God's way and man's way.

On this conclusion some might say that I am wrong, but I don't think so. The act of eating from the tree of the knowledge of good and evil by Adam was a deliberate and decisive-decision. What Adam did brought on the penalty of spiritual death. Absent anything that speaks to the contrary, scripture says Adam turned a deaf ear to the first command that God gave him (Genesis 2:17); and his actions depicted oppositional thinking. Today we have evolved. We were created with a foundation of good that was inherently instilled in us by God, and He called it "In His own image." But His Image became distorted when Satan and his four sons: Doubt, Denial, Fear and Insecurity (Genesis 3:1-10), were allowed to take up residence in the minds of both of our fore parents.

Since then we have grown in oppositional thinking. And using the twin-concepts of mixing and matching, we mix a little of what the voice of God said with a lot of what has been said by members of our circle of family and friends, and collectively we fashion our own special truth. Call it what you will, but it amounts to tradition.

And I call it that simply because the over-whelming majority of the population lives by it. They have sanctioned it and persist in perpetuating it with equal regularity. As previously stated, I have labeled Adam's original sin as "thinking in opposition to God." But not to worry because the voice of God said He would forgive our sin "When and If" His people would make those four steps on the road to repentance, as recorded in 2 Chronicles 7:14. Rebellion on the part of Adam brought him instant, spiritual death; and it brought spiritual death to all who came after him because they were locked in to using the same strategy.

David—reflecting on his own ruin—explains it this way: ***"Behold I was brought forth in iniquity and in sin my mother conceived me" (Psalm 51:5, NKJV)***. More will be said on this subject as we proceed, but for now, our focus is on the fact that Adam was the first to be charged with the violation of ignoring the voice of God and listening to someone else. Consequence came first to the serpent, then to Satan, followed by Eve. Each of them was recompensed according to the cleanness of their hands (Genesis 3:14-16; Psalm 18:20). But Adam was charged with violating the first command of God: that of failing to listen and adhere to what the voice of God said (Genesis 2:17). Look carefully and you will see that God charged Adam with "Listening to his wife," instead of adhering to His word (Genesis 3:17).

By her own admission, Eve was deceived, but what Adam did was deliberate. I believe I am on safe ground when I say that he didn't bother to use his spirit of a sound mind that God had inherently given him; the same sound mind with which Eve used to think for herself. And he could have because it wasn't until after he had listened to Eve and replicated her resign that the sediment of sin was charged to him. This also validates our claim that God's gifts have become discretionary, and must now be accessed and activated.

In addition, Adam chose to abdicate his leadership-role and followed the lead of his wife (Genesis 3:6), which has since caused a myriad of infractions because sin is degenerate. We simply call those infractions "fruit of the poisonous tree." Again, you may call it what you will, but I see the outcome of what Adam did as tantamount to mixing water with oil; and everybody knows that water and oil, like good and evil, will not mix.

The Bible unequivocally states that everything God made was good" (Genesis 1:4, 10, 12, 18, 21, 25). And when everything is working together in peace and harmony—that is to say, free from the throes of sin and evil—the outcome is guaranteed to be "very good" (Genesis 1:31). This is proven in the Christian Manifesto— the epistle to the Romans—for there, Paul said *"Everything works for the good of them that love God, and who are called according to His purpose"* (Romans 8:28). The problem with which we are currently faced is incorrectly defining and delineating the purpose of God. *Entering* seeks to define, delineate and set forth the purposeful and permissive will of God, using deductive logic; which involves moving from cause to effect.

From the outset and for lack of a better way to say it, there has been for many years "something in the air" (Ephesians 2:2) that prompts men in general to overlook Adam's abdication of his God-given responsibility. For reasons known only to themselves— although I strongly suspect that it equates to limited-learning and mental laziness—pastors today will preface their attempt to heal almost any hurt, by saying "Remember, God loves you." While that is an ongoing perpetual truth, the way it is used casts doubt on that reality, as if to suggest—as did Satan—that the problem in question is directly related to an oversight on the part of God, or an intermittent cessation of the love of God because of what that person may have done.

After a diligent and protracted study of the Scriptures which spanned more than six years, I discovered two very salient issues which, when defined and delineated, raised two equally as important questions. Those questions I believe must be asked and answered by all of God's people, if they are desirous of "having life and having it more abundantly" (John 10:10b). In writing the content of *Entering* I confined myself to thinking out loud with a group of students in college who agreed to act as sounding boards in the preparation of this manuscript. Our aim was to collectively discover, define and delineate the answers to those questions in a consistent continuous and conducive manner.

The **first** issue was we agreed that in scripture there are no questions which deal with life and how to live it, that have been left unanswered. Similarly, there are no problems in life which have not been solved. The knowledge of everything that is, and ever will be, is part and particle of the Omniscience of God. Secondly, we agreed that the ability to know that beyond a reasonable doubt was inherently instilled in the man that God created "In His Own Image. And all that is required for each of us to be able to answer any question or solve any problems, is to adhere to the proclamation of Paul to Timothy in his second letter, Chapter 2 Verse fifteen (15). The boundaries and validation of that Scripture are spelled out in Chapter 3 Verse sixteen (16). In other words, the ability to discover the answers to these questions depend largely on what each person is willing to trust and believe; and that pre-supposes that he (or she) has a clear concept of what it means to trust and then to believe.

The second issue was that the Creator God has a perfect plan which includes, but is not limited to directing His Spirit to factor in the rewards and consequences of the choices that mankind has already made, or will ever make. That conclusion is based on Paul's declaration in Galatians 6:7: ". . . whatsoever a man sows, the same shall he also reap." I also believe God's plan is being worked out on a 24/7 basis, 365 days a year. And as with everything else, these are facts that you can accept or reject. Your choice won't change the will of God, nor will it frustrate the purposeful or the permissive will of God.

CHAPTER EIGHT

The Nature of God in Each of Us

PROLOGUE

THIS chapter brings us to the question: "What is God in each of us?" Stated succinctly, God is the Soul and Spirit in each of us. The Soul and Spirit of God provides each of us with our base-nature—which was all good before sin entered the equation—which includes, but is not limited to having the propensity to think as God thinks. Simply stated, who man is will never change; but what man is will never stop changing. Translated, Christ is eternal (John 8:58), and He is the Word spoken of in John 1:1 and 1:14. In point of fact, we have inherited a portion of God's nature. We have the **propensity**—the tendency or inclination—to think positive; be productive and progressive; to be consistent, continuous, and conducive; able, accessible, and accountable.

Those nine attributes were instilled in all mankind as part of the image of God. However, when sin entered the equation, those attributes became distorted and discretionary. What happened to change what God had purposed in His perfect plan? The answer is in the story of Adam and Eve. Sometimes learning about our ancestors often helps us to understand ourselves. Our first ancestors were the crowning glory of God's creation. But they chose to think in opposition to God and live life 'their way' rather than 'God's way.' The story of Adam and Eve has much to teach us about the nature of sin and the consequences that come with it.

In Genesis Chapter 2, Verse 18, God pulled back the curtain of creation allowing us to see what happens when we make the decision to use our free-will to think in opposition to God. Stated another way, God allowed us to see what happens when we fail to 'do the right thing, the right way.' The voice of God said, "It is not good that the man should be alone; I will make him an help meet for him." Was that a good thing or was it a bad thing? The sister asked. She continued by asking, are we saying that God made a mistake in providing Adam with 'a help meet?' My answer was unequivocally no; God does not make mistakes.

Scripture says God gave Adam a partner who was designed to be 'a help suitable for need.' Satan worked his way into the picture and neutralized the sound mind that God had given Eve, used the disease of deception and caused Eve to think in opposition to God. Had Eve kept the commandment that God had specifically given Adam (Genesis 2:16-17), that is to say, had she done the right thing, the right way, it is a good possibility that Adam would have followed her down that road as well. I could be wrong, but I don't think so. I believe it is safe to say that sin in their lives and ours might not have come into being. However, by allowing sin to enter into the equation that He had purposed to be void of failure, what better way for God to let us see what happens when one-half of the marriage equation pulls against the other?

Because of man's willful choice to engage in sin, God directed His Spirit to expand His purposeful will to include His permissive will. Translated, man's free-will had to be included, along with the rewards and consequences which followed the choices he made. The image of God in man remained the same. It was God's Reality and it would never change. When God spoke His Reality became Actuality in real time. Sin entered the minds of Adam and Eve causing God's image to become distorted. Satan succeeded in changing the mind of man.

God, having created man "In His Own Image," gave the man He created the Spirit of power, of love, and of a sound mind. However, Satan, using the disease of deception, neutralized the mind of man, causing him to become disconnected from the source of his life. The source of man's life is God's Reality. "God's Reality is the life of man; and the life of man is the light of man" (John 1:4). Those attributes—which constitute a portion of the Nature of God—were given to man as part of His image. They are guaranteed but they are not automatic.

Each of us—as part of the procedural process which leads to the full complement of Salvation—must access and activate those gifts. Scripture says *"it's in Christ that we live and move and have our being"* (Acts 17:28). In *Entering* we will strive to enlighten, enhance and encourage our readers to become knowledgeable about how to have life and to have it more abundantly; but we will not do the work for them. All of the gifts of God are left to the discretion of each person; and each of us can accept or reject at will.

In addition, close observation will reveal that almost all of God's gifts contain one or more Principles, which must be apprehended, and to which adherence is required. Those principles are primary, profound and absolutely necessary. They are primary because they are first in importance; profound because they comes from the depths of one's being; and necessary because they are required to bring about the desired results, in accordance with the word of God.

A LESSON TO BE LEARNED

AS part of the lesson to be learned, I have included an in-depth delineation of the principles, the promises, the prophecies, and the procedures which will enable us to develop a mental-state-of-readiness that equates to our desire for the abundant life to which Jesus referred in John 10:10b. These lessons will also help guide the participant-in-the-process as he (or she) moves from where he is to where God would have him to be at this time in his life. Lastly and in addition, it will also assist him in making the necessary decisive-decisions at the proper time.

PRESENTATION

THE theme of *Entering* was inspired by the Holy Spirit, who has propelled and guided me from the beginning of these three projects. That's it; pure and simple. I have no other source. Everything that I have written in these three books encompasses my experiences and exposure. To coin a phrase out of the contemporary language community: "I have been there, done that, and I have a cap, jacket, shoes and anything else they are giving away at the finish line for playing the fool;" that is to say, for doing things my way. Simply put, I have paid my dues, and you, the reader, are being given an opportunity to profit from my mistakes.

The Holy Spirit has been my Comforter, my Teacher, and my Guide ever since I began traveling the road to repentance as specified in 2 Chronicles 7:14, just over six years ago. By way of reminder and for the record, that scripture reads:

> **"If My people who are called by My name will humble themselves, and pray and seek My face, and turn from their wicked ways, then I will hear from heaven, and will forgive their sin and heal their land."**

To be sure, I have had my personal ups-and-downs; and I have encountered opposition from many along the way. In addition, I am not ashamed to admit that much of the opposition that I encountered along the way was because I chose to substitute the traditional definition of repentance for the voice of God. Some have said in part that "repentance doesn't take all of that." They quickly added, "No preacher, 'Salvation' is a free-gift.'" And then they endeavored to goad me into an argument about the tenets. However, with me there is no argument. My convictions are based solely on what Jesus said to Satan in Matthew 4:4, without exception. There, we read: *"It is written, **Man shall not live by bread alone, but by every word that proceeds out of the mouth of God."*** So it is that as I share with you from my experiences and exposure; and where possible I have included the appropriate scripture-citation to validate my conviction.

The fact that the word "Man" in the above-citation is capitalized denotes that Jesus was talking primarily about Himself. However, since He is our perfect model, and **"In God there is no respect of person"** (Romans 2:11), I have concluded that his message was meant for all mankind; after all, Jesus came to seek and to save that which was lost (Matthew 18:11). In addition, I have learned to leave all of my naysayers with these words: "This is your life and the choice is yours." But I have to say that the one thing that all of us can count on is, "all of us will reap what we sow" (Galatians 6:7). That brings us to question number three: "Who are we in God?"

WHO AM I?

SIMPLY stated, God designed us to be His mirror-image. But when sin entered the picture, that image became distorted. Thus and at best, it can only said that each of us is only as much as our self-perception. However, because of the penalty paid by Jesus— His death, burial, and resurrection—when we have submitted and have begun to surrender; that is to say "when we have been born-again of the water and of the Spirit" (John 3:5), we have the power to become "The mirror-image of the righteousness of God in Christ Jesus" (John 1:12). That's who we are in God. Stated another way, the penalty that was paid by Jesus gave us the right of re-entry back into the Garden of God (Genesis 3:23), where we can eat from the tree of life—dine on the word of God on a daily basis—and live eternally in the presence of God. What does that mean in real time? I was asked. Stay with me and I'll explain, was my response.

The voice of the prophet Hosea (4:6) said, "My people are destroyed for lack of knowledge . . ." Today, because of that lack of knowledge, I'm going to use the shorter of two opinions to answer that question. "What you think of you is your self-perception." But "what you think others think of you controls your self-esteem." And because sin has caused our self-perception to be inherently shaky, the opinions of the members of our circle of family and friends inadvertently cause our self-esteem to roll up and down like a window shade. In order to regain control of our self-perception, we must ascertain who we are in God and make certain that our self-perception is on solid ground.

Let me say that another way. Because we were created in the Image of God, what we think about ourselves is what we think about God; and vice-versa. Suffice it to say, because we don't know who God is, in and of Himself, we really don't know who we are. That leaves us open to the influences of Satan, his thoughts, ideas, and suggestions (TIS's). We know what our loved-ones named us, but do we really know who we are? If we say we do, we must be able to explain why we get so upset when someone calls us out of our name, or says something derogatory about us.

I submit that we become shaky because we really don't know who we are. Similarly, we really don't know who God is. We know about Him, but we really don't know Him. To know God requires a relationship established by blood. What we have is a fellowship established by love. Tell us who He is, the sister said. Take out a pen and paper and get ready to write was my response. You won't remember all of what I'm going to tell you, so prepare yourself to write. We will start with who He is. In Exodus 3:14ff, in response to Moses' question about who sent him to them, the voice of God had this to say. He told Moses:

> *"I AM THAT I AM." You tell the Children that "I AM" sent you, and that "I AM" is my name, and it shall be a memorial unto all generations."*

What does all of that mean? She asked. I'm so glad you asked because I want so badly to give you my version. Keep in mind what has been said about the Characteristics and the Nature of God. Now, add to that what the voice of John said in 4:24: *"God is Spirit and they that worship Him must worship Him in spirit an in truth."*

Having been created in God's Own Image, that made you and I "Soul and Spirit" (Genesis 1:27) to begin with. Now move to Genesis 3:20-21, and there read where **"unto Adam also and to his wife did the Lord God make coats of skins, and clothed them."** That's when we became "body, soul and spirit," which was God's proposal to the Supreme Court of Heaven in the first place in Genesis 1:26. We inherited His Nature before Satan came on the scene. That means we were created with the propensity—the inclination and/or the tendency—to function like God, until Satan and sin robbed us by taking up residence in the minds of Adam and Eve, and neutralizing their spirit of power, of love, and of a sound mind.

Now, instead of manifesting those nine gifts that are part of the fifteen (15) attributes that are present in the Character and Nature of God at all times, in order to function as the man or woman who was created in God's Own Image, we have to access and activate each of those gifts. Suffice it to say unless and until you do that, neither you nor I will be the man or woman that God made us to be (Isaiah 1:18-20).

Whether you accept or reject that definition and delineation is your choice. But be reminded that there is a direct correlation between acceptance, adherence and enjoyment, AND rejection, rebellion, and reliance on what you have always done, somehow expecting to get some different results. I trust that all of your questions concerning who you are, have now been answered. The last question is bi-focal. It asks "What has God already done and what will He yet do?" Scripture says, "While we were yet sinners, Jesus, which is called Christ, died for us" (Romans 5:8). Stated succinctly, to demonstrate His love God sent His Son to die for our sins. That is what He has already done.

What will He yet do is too lengthy to summarize. However, we will handle the question as we proceed along the path to our already-decided destiny. As we approach the lessons to be learned in this section, which relates to the last portion of this question, let's line up with the declaration in Hebrews 11:6. It is incumbent upon preachers and teachers to make plain what the Bible means by what it says, separate and apart from the traditional application. That said the Bible informs us that:

> *"Without faith it is impossible to please God; for those who come to Him must believe that "He is" and that "He rewards them that diligently seek Him."*

What follows is a favorite of mine because it gets right to the point. So fond of it am I, it is repeated in two of my previous books. In Shakespeare's Macbeth, Act iii, Scene iii, the Prince raised a searching question when he said, "To be or not to be?" That is the question. In the body of *Entering* I have seized the opportunity to replicate what Shakespeare said, putting my own spin on the question and then on the answer. In my mind it reads: "To be or not to be?" That is the question: whether it would be more noble and profitable to know God and His resurrection-power, thereby being enabled and empowered to enjoy the full complement of Salvation, or to remain unaware and uninformed, thereby forced to continue doing the same thing, the same way, hoping to somehow get some different results."

SUBMISSION AND SURRENDER

NEEDLESS to say, I have concluded that the former would be more profitable; which means I had to *"study to show myself approved unto God, a workman who has no need to be ashamed, rightly dividing the word of truth (2 Timothy 2:15).* In my studies I learned one thing very quickly; and that was, 'even though salvation is free,' I discovered that because of sin, at the end of the day there is actually a high cost to that free gift. Translated, the high cost of that free gift is **submission and surrender**. Submission on the one hand was almost instant. I needed only to make a decisive-decision. Surrender, on the other hand, takes time. Over the last six years I have striven to pay on that high cost to God's free gift." On a daily basis I find myself striving to reach the mark of the prize of the high calling of God in Christ Jesus, which leads to the full complement of Salvation.

THE PROCEDURAL PROCESS

I VERY quickly submitted to the sovereignty of God over my life; and then began a slow, systematic surrender to the Lordship and leadership of the Spirit of God (SOG) in my life. Hence and on a daily basis, at my request the SOG has taught me what I needed to know each day, and at the same time brought all things to my remembrance that God had already said to me over the more than six decades; things that I had arbitrarily set aside or decided to forget. In so doing, He made me usable so that my prayer to be used in Kingdom-building has begun to be made manifest.

Dr. Xavier T. Carter Sr.

Throughout the body of this text, I have striven to define, describe and delineate portions of my personal journey—using the scriptures to identify both, the direct and indirect impact that the presence of God the Father, and the power of God the Holy Spirit, have had on my life, all of my life. It's all a matter of choice. It is my intent to present myself to the world as a clear witness to the faithfulness of God to His word, His greatness and His goodness; even when I wasn't aware of, or didn't understand what He is doing. For instance, in Ecclesiastes 1:9, Solomon, said, ***"That which has been is what will be; that which is done is what will be done, and there is nothing new under the sun***

CHAPTER NINE

In Pursuit of Understanding

PROLOGUE

KING Solomon once said, *"Wisdom is the principal thing; therefore get wisdom. And in all your getting, get understanding"* *(Proverbs 4:7).* That declaration and proclamation caused me to dig deep into the recesses of my mind and the annals of history, to discover the underlying meaning of the two key terms: Wisdom and Understanding. What follows is my conclusion. On the one hand, knowledge is having the ability to do something. On the other hand, wisdom is having the insight and being able to do it well. In any event an equal amount of wisdom and knowledge is required on any subject, before you make a decisive decision and be able to say, "I know that."

For example, many stories have been told about how Satan—the progenitor of sin—came to be the chief-resident-of-evil in our minds and hearts. Which of these stories you choose to believe is your prerogative. However, before you draw your final conclusion, make certain that you know who Satan is, in and of himself, and how he works his magic in the minds of men. Paul makes it clear for us in his letter to the Church at Ephesus in Chapter 6 Verses ten (10) through twenty (20). That said keep in mind that everybody has an opinion. He (or she) is entitled to it, and that opinion is never open to argument. Therefore, what I think does not negate or cancel what you think; nor does what you think negate or cancel what I think. In either case, the doors to our individual minds—whether we know it or not—are propped open, allowing more information to enter.

PRESENTATION

IN response to the brother's request, the first order of business is to have a good understanding of what happened in the beginning before we attempt to reverse the trends. For instance, when I looked at Bible history through my mind's eye and used my consecrated imagination, this is what I believe might have happened, and how I have chosen to believe it could have happened. Stated succinctly, when it comes to living life man's way, "sin is to blame." The definition of "Sin" is "Missing the mark." Whatever else we choose to call it, Sin must be defined without allowing for what I call "wiggle room." On the one hand, acquiring the knowledge of God and all that is good should be our aims and objectives. On the other hand, one must also have a deep and abiding understanding of Satan and Sin—which is all that is evil and a direct contrast. Without making any allowances, Adam and Eve simply missed the mark that God had established (Genesis 2:16-17). Evolution during the last two-thousand years—to include what you, me, I, we, us, and they have said and done—merely exacerbated the situation.

THE CAUSE:
Adam's contribution

EVER so often we hear somebody say, "sin is to blame," seeking to explain the occurrence of an unsavory event in our lives. Why do we say that, and what is the underlying meaning of that statement? The answer goes farther than most folk might have realized. In Genesis 3:10, scripture says the voice of God called out to Adam, saying, *'Adam, where are you?'* Adam answered with this riveting response: ***"I heard Your voice in the garden, and I was afraid because I was naked; and I hid myself."*** Close observation will reveal that the voice of God did not allow for any discussion on the matter. As a matter of fact, He cut right to the chase, establishing the cause and the effect, in reverse order.

For clarity and conciseness it doesn't take a rocket scientist to see that two things stand out in Adam's answer which begs our attention. The first is that Adam said "I was afraid because I was naked;" and secondly, that he would have the audacity to try to hide from an omnipresent God. Cutting to the chase, the apostle Paul referred to a portion of God's image that was inherently instilled in all mankind. 2 Timothy 1:7 states that, *"God did not give us the spirit of fear."* **[Instead]**, *God gave mankind "The Spirit of power, and of love, and of a sound mind."*

Simply stated, **FEAR**—**F**alse **E**vidence **A**ppearing **R**eal—is Satan's most powerful weapon and was not part of God's equation. The fact that Adam admitted to being afraid, sends a message that's loud and clear: "Sin had entered his mind and his heart, and neutralized the soundness of his mind." The result was, "fear replaced faith and doubt replaced certainty." As a result, Adam's answer was neither here nor there. He had rebelled. He had chosen to be disobedient, and now he was in line for the consequence that God had promised. Yes, Adam had sinned. The cause and effect that the voice of God stated, validates the authenticity.

SPIRITUAL MYOPIA

ADAM had chosen to think in opposition to God and as a result, developed a case of spiritual myopia—which means "a visual defect in which a lack of discernment or short-sightedness in thinking" replaced his spirit of a sound mind" (Webster's II New Riverside University Dictionary, 1988). Now, instead of God's image being prominent in his self-perception—distortion had clouded the mirror of his mind (1 Corinthians 13:12), and his spiritual vision had become blurred.

Translated, what Adam had done marked him and all mankind for an eternity. The result was and still is Sin. Doubt and Denial, Fear and Insecurity—the purveyors of sin—are now sitting on the throne of our hearts. Let's be clear about that. In God there is no respect of person (Romans 2:11), so what happened to Adam is prevalent and prominent in all of his offspring. Therefore, before we draw any concrete conclusions let's take a close look at the contribution of *"Eve, the mother of all living"* **(Genesis 3:20)**.

THE CAUSE CONTINUED:
Eve's Contribution

AS we approach this portion of the creation epic, the reader is urged to keep three additional points in mind. The first is that success in any venture requires "a set of instructions and a plan." For example, the first chapter of Genesis sets forth the answers to the 5'W questions, which tell us "Who did What, When, Where and Why" they were done. Collectively, you could say that the first chapter is God's way of educating us; and Chapters two and three reveals God's plan—that is, they tell us "How" those things were done, and how some other things came to be.

The second thing to keep in mind is that contrary to any popular opinion which might say otherwise, there is no such thing as "a coincidence," nor is there really any such thing as "good luck." Why would you say that? A member asked. Working backwards, I am saying it for two reasons. First of all God has a perfect plan—which includes His purposeful and permissive will.

That plan is being carried out on a 24/7 basis, 365 days a year. God's plan also eradicates what we call luck, and replaces it with the assurance that everything that happens is because the Spirit of God either caused it to happen as part of God's purposeful will; or He allowed it to happen as part of God's permissive will. The latter is the result of allowing us to exercise our free-will.

Secondly, a co-incidence is a seemingly planned sequence of accidentally occurring events." That said, nothing happens for naught: everything happens for a reason. And to be totally honest, for it to be any other way the outcome would deny the true character of God; which is another way of saying that God is no longer "Omniscient;" and there are some things that He does not know before it happens.

Adam introduced "Fear and Insecurity," but chronologically speaking, Eve's contribution of Doubt and Denial precede them. Metaphorically speaking, what Eve did allowed Satan's two oldest boys to take up residence in her mind and heart; and collectively, both parents passed those maladies on to their children. There is only one Lucifer—whom we call Satan—but he has a host of demons which come and go at his beck and call. Scripture says, as it relates to God's wrath on unrighteousness (Romans, Chapter one), that there comes a time when God will give his people over to a reprobate mind.

I gave those first four spirits names because they are most prominent in all of us today; and the names I gave them are most familiar. So it is that Satan's four children: Doubt and Denial, Fear and Insecurity are inherently deposited into the psyche of all babies, and they live in each of us until we are delivered—that is, until we are saved from our own self-destruction. The record of their entrance and introductions are found in the conversations between Eve and Satan in Genesis 3:1-6; and between Adam and God in Genesis 3:10. Let me pull over and park and try to help somebody.

In Genesis 3:1-6, there is a conversation between Satan and Eve. Satan began the conversation by doing what Satan does best: deceiving and deriding. Make no mistake about it, if you are not careful Satan will lead you to the slaughter, and then laugh at you for being there. Scripture says, he approached Eve, and using pretentious language raised a rhetorical question. He asked, ***"Has God indeed said, you shall not eat of every tree of the garden?"*** That question was pretentious and rhetorical. It was pretentious because he was scheming: pretending that he didn't know what God has said; and rhetorical, not deserving of an answer. Why? Because, for him to ask the question, Eve, having been created in the image of God, should have known that he already knew the answer. Nevertheless, her first mistake was in striving to answer it anyway.

In verses 2-3 we read:

> ***"And the woman said to the serpent, 'We may eat the fruit of the trees of the garden; but of the fruit of the tree which is in the midst of the garden, God has said, You shall not eat it, nor shall you touch it, lest you die.'"***

Making the decision to answer him was her first mistake. The second mistake was to engage in a frivolous and unnecessary conversation with Satan—who was disguised as a serpent. Verses 4-5 tells us that Satan's response was,

> *"You will not surely die, for God knows that in the day you eat of it your eyes will be opened, and you will be like God, knowing good and evil."*

Verse 6 informs us of Eve's contribution. It reads:

> *"So when the woman saw that the tree was good for food, that it was pleasant to the eyes and a tree desirable to make one wise she took of its fruit and ate. She also gave to her husband with her, and he ate."*

Even though she, too, had been created "In God's Own Image" 'giving her substance and insight' and even though God had already made provisions for their food, she began to doubt and deny. She doubted the relationship that she and Adam had with God, and denied the authenticity of His word. That was the first sign of Satan's deceit. Eve's actions manifested Satan's influence.

The Bible says,

> *"For all that is in the world—the lust of the flesh, the lust of the eyes, and the pride of life—is not of the Father but is of the world"* *(1 John 2:16).*

Satan's deceit caused Eve to open the door to her mind so that his twin boys—Doubt and Denial—could enter and take up residence. Satan's modus-operandi is the use of "Thoughts, Ideas and Suggestions" (TIS). In this case his suggestion caused Eve to rely on the lust of the eye and the pride of life. He entered her mind and worked his way to her heart. This is a good place to insert the fact that what happened to Eve, happened to all of her children. TIS's are still being used by Satan and his demons with uncanny success.

THE CAUSE CONTINUED

PLEASE!!! Make no mistake about it. God does not repeat Himself. Search the Bible for yourself and you will discover that what He said one time, to one person, in one place, was meant for all times, and directed to all persons everywhere. From that day in the garden in the east of Eden, **Doubt** and **Denial**, **Fear** and **Insecurity** have lived in the hearts and the minds of man, beginning with Adam and Eve; and continuing with their offspring, starting with Cain and Abel.

For example, the first travesty of spiritual justice can be found in Cain when "Insecurity" caused him to kill his brother Abel (Genesis 4:6-7). Again, I say, "Include everyone and exclude no one, for we are all guilty." Scripture says, ***All have sinned and come short of the glory of God"** (Romans 3:23).* And to make bad-matters worse, for whatever their individual reasons, instead of **"studying to show themselves approved unto God [as] workmen who need not be ashamed, rightly dividing the word of truth" (2 Timothy 2:15),** members of the organized Church insist on "bathing in the innocence of ignorance" and relying on their pastors who fail to teach the whole truth.

"The pastor said syndrome" is the favorite of most members; thus, allowing the pastor to do their work for them." And at the end of the day, what you have as a result is "ignorance in perpetuity." Translated, people are still fearful and insecure. But that's not how the story ends.

Instead of pastors making their Churches the **path** that leads the people of God from earth's sorrow to Heaven's joy, the Church is set up as the **destination**, leaving the people stumped, stymied, stagnated, and bathing in the innocence of ignorance. The design of God is to take believers from "membership" to "stewardship" and from stewardship to "discipleship." At the risk of sounding extremely critical, what we have today are churches lined up on both sides of the street like canned-goods on a supermarket shelf. And on the inside, we have people who, having itching ears, have heaped to themselves teachers; and these have turned away their ears from the truth, to fables" (2 Timothy 4:3-4).

I don't mean any irrevocable or spiritual harm to my brother or sister preachers, but I have to call a spade a spade and sin by its right name. In each of these Churches, by failing to "preach the word" (2 Timothy 4:1-2), and instead, preaching **from** the word, pastors are preaching a pop-psychology that tells the people what they want to hear, the way they want to hear it. At this point I need to hurry-up and say that it's not what they say that's the travesty of justice. No. No. It's the way they say it. Let me make that clear.

The voice of God told the prophet Jeremiah to tell His people that

> *and He would bring them to Zion: and He would give them pastors according to His heart, which shall feed them with knowledge and understanding'"* (Jeremiah 3:15).

The majority of pastors today have failed to feed the people of God with knowledge and understanding. Instead, they take pivotal scriptures like: ***"Faith cometh by hearing, and hearing by the word of God*** (Romans 10:17), and without giving the people the proper understanding of faith, some pastors strive to build on to their own reputation. Their concentration is on earning a reputation that's built on "entertainment" rather than information. Let me take it to the next level.

Here is the problem in a nutshell. The Church was designed to be voluntary and all-inclusive (whosoever will . . .). That is to say, the Church would be established on faith in our Father-in-heaven, as the foundation. Faith would be the building block, and on it Jesus said He would build His Church and the gates of hell would not prevail against it" (Matthew 16:18). A misinterpretation of that scripture has caused the people of God to be lulled into a false sense of security, looking for "pie-in-the-sky—when they die." Stated another way, the people are looking to "go to heaven when they die." For them, that is their just reward. That is factual, but it is not the whole truth.

CHAPTER TEN

The Impact of Sin

PROLOGUE

IN the words of David in Psalm 51:5, "*all of us* have been shaped in iniquity, and in sin did our mothers conceive us; include everyone and exclude no one. By way of review, the date and time was "before there was a when or a where, OR a then or a there." It was in what Dr. Jeremiah A. Wright (2009) called "The design-phase." The place and setting were in the presence of God, before 'in the beginning' was begun. That's another way of saying God was about to speak everything into existence in real time (Genesis 1:1-25, 27, 31). I perceive that He stretched this old world out on His divine drawing board and evaluated His creation prior to placing his stamp of approval on everything that He was about to make.

PRESENTATION

ADAM was about to be placed in the Garden in the East of Eden. His role and function would be to *"dress and keep it" (2:15).* The Garden was emblematic of a selected place in God's newly-designed world. In Genesis 1:29, God made Adam aware of the provisions that He had put in place for him and his wife. Then, in Genesis 2:16-17, Adam was given some very explicit instructions. Scripture says,

> *"And God commanded the man, saying, 'Of every tree of the garden you ay freely eat; but of the tree of the knowledge of good and evil you shall not eat, for in the day that you eat of it you shall surely die."*

Without wading through a long list of debatable conjecture, let us cut to the chase. Eve had been deceived. In the KJV, Eve said *"She had been beguiled"* (Genesis 3:13). But for Adam things were different. The scriptures doesn't say any different, and I'm not about to put a question mark where the voice of God has placed a period. Scripture says,

> *"So when the woman saw that the tree was good for food, that it was pleasant to the eyes, and a tree desirable to make one wise, she took of its fruit and ate. She also gave to her husband with her, and he ate"* (Genesis 3:6).

Using the spirit of a sound mind that God gave all of us, the best thing I could conclude from that scripture is that Adam "**chose**" to think in opposition to God. There is no record of him thinking about what he was about to do; only that he did it. So, by thinking in opposition to God, he flung open the door to his own mind, allowing Satan's other two of his sons—Fear and Insecurity—to move in and take up residence.

In **Verse 6** we can see when Eve began to **doubt** what God had said in 1:29; and we can see when she actually began to **deny** the relationship that God had with her and her husband, and the connection that she and her husband had with God. Thus, we are able to conclude that Doubt and Denial came into existence with Eve, and Fear and Insecurity came into existence with Adam. We can also say with certainty, that a portion of the nature of God—that is to say, the tendency and inclination to think positive, be productive and progressive on a consistent, continuous and conducive basis—was replaced with Satan's fallen nature.

Paul said, [as a result], *"We now see through a glass, darkly; but then face to face: now I know in part; but then shall I know even as also I am known"* (1 Corinthians 13:12, KJV). It is because of the spiritual myopia caused by the contributions of our fore-parents, that we must now "access and activate" the gifts of God before we can enjoy the promises of God. Looking in retrospect, God created man "In His Own Image," and "after the likeness of the Son and the Holy Spirit" gave Adam and

Eve—dominion over all that He had made. Satan worked his way into the picture, and the image of God in all of us became distorted. Keep in mind that Satan didn't create anything, so he really cannot destroy anything.

The point to be remembered at this juncture is that God, Satan, Adam, Eve, and Satan's two sets of twins: Doubt and Denial, Fear and Insecurity, were all "spirit beings." We know that because in *Genesis* 3: 21, the Bible says *"Also for Adam and his wife the Lord God made coats of skin, and clothed them."* It was then that both of them became fully human. They are still Spirit-beings, but now they are clothed with skin, making them human, and members of the animal kingdom—class Homo sapient.

Why is that important? It's important because it enables us to better understand how Adam and Eve were able to carry on those one-on-one conversations with God—given that He is Spirit—and how Eve could converse with the serpent—given that the serpent is an animal, and Adam and Eve are also members of the animal kingdom. Without that understanding, the reasonableness of it all ceases, and that part of the scriptures will also cease to make sense. No doubt there are other renditions that will make sense to countless others, but this is my perception; I am entitled to it and I have found validation in the scriptures.

What we have is both, the cause and effect, and 'the impact of sin' on the minds of men. Simply stated, disobedience is the cause for the consequence which followed. On the one hand, with Adam and Eve it was more than that; their act of disobedience brought on spiritual death. On the other hand, their act also created the need for salvation—otherwise known as deliverance. Everything started with our first parents and was passed down to all of their children. If we begin with Cain and Abel, include everyone and exclude no one thereafter, the story comes to rest with "you and I." This fact is validated for us in Psalm 14:1-3 and 53:1-4. It is further-validated and spelled out for us in Romans 3:10ff. There, Paul said:

> *"As it is written: 'There is none righteous, no, not one; There is none who understands; There is none who seeks after God. They have all turned aside; They have*

95

> *together become unprofitable; There is none who does good; no not one.'"*

The aims and objectives of *Entering* are to shed light where the people of God are currently walking in darkness. We know that the majority of people love the darkness because the voice of God said, they practice evil (John 3:19-20). But that is not our concern, here. Our responsibility is to turn on the light.

This is new to most people and I am often asked if I am the only one who has seen this vision and given this task. The answer is absolutely not. The Bible has been saying the same thing in English for more than five-hundred years in America. And I suppose there have been others who have done what I am doing. The problem is, only a few will receive and believe this word. Man fell from grace—making him spiritually weak—after which God set Salvation in motion to save him, and he has the prerogative to accept or reject God's gift.

THIS IS MY TIME

EVERY so often we read in scripture where God put opportunities in place for man to take advantage of them and be delivered. My time came in January, 2007. Your time—reader—will come at the will of God. The Spirit of God showed me in a vision that part of my role and function is to carry out the Mandate of the Master. My job—beginning with the great Commitment in Luke 9:23-24, the [two-fold] great Commandment in Matthew 22:37 & 40, and the great Commission in Matthew 28:18-20—is to get the word out. I am to stress that everything must be done decently and in order (1 Corinthians 14:40); that these facets of stewardship are emblematic of love, the most excellent way. And I have striven to do that as the Spirit of God has given me utterance and insight.

Those are the principles of God. They are followed by the promises of God in John 15:7, which says: ***"If you abide in Me, and My words abide in you, you will ask what you desire, and it shall be done for you."*** That is a fact, and I am a living witness. Before you ask, reader, the answer is "No," I have not arrived.

But God, knowing the condition of my heart, has, for the last 6 years, rewarded me unconditionally. However, I think I ought to warn you that there is a direct correlation between what you do, and the blessings that God bestows upon you, as those blessings are designed to keep you fixed and focused. Personally, I have learned not to ask for anything that's not in His will and cannot be validated in scripture.

At the end of the day, I can say with certainty that my prayers are always answered in a positive, productive and progressive manner. That inducement caused me to strive to get the word out to the people of God. I have been at it for just over six years—in pastoral assignments in the 9th District of the African Methodist Episcopal (AME) Church. Inspiration came and writing became a method of outreach to cope with the resistance I received early-on. It is my heart's desire and my daily prayer to God that the people of God will be saved from the power of sin, as the salvation process continues to work in me and in the Bethel Rising Family—especially since it has been proven that I cannot teach what I do not know.

THE SECRET TO SUCCESS

I MENTION these things because according to Jesus in Mark 1:15, it's time for the people of God to know the truth. In *John 8:31-32, NKJV,* Jesus said,

> *"If you abide in My word, you are My disciples indeed. And you shall know the truth, and the truth shall make you free."*

What follows is more of the short version of the longer story that will set forth my personal secret to success in these last six years. However, let me preface by saying that what you read can be used by anyone who desires to rise above mediocrity and access the abundant life; but that person must follow the stated instructions. Because with God there is no respect of person, everything the Spirit of God did for me, He will do for anyone; and the results will enable anyone to begin their journey from earth's sorrow to heaven's joy.

PART THREE

CHAPTER ELEVEN

A Literal Portrait of the Church

THE PROLOGUE

THE prologue is a preview before the presentation. In this prologue of the Church of God which was established in Christ, four questions are raised: (1) "What is the Church?" (2) "What, in this world, is the church supposed to be?" (3) "What did Jesus mean by what He said in Matthew 16:18? And (4) Have we gone wrong in the operation of the Church; and if so, how do we right the wrongs?" It goes without saying that the answers to all four of these questions are subjective for they depend largely on who you ask, and whether or not you are ready to accept the answers you receive. One thing is for certain however: when it comes to the truth about the Church, unless and until the reader is ready to reason with God (Isaiah 1:18) concerning His Church, there will not be an answer to either of these questions that will be both, acceptable and workable.

In 2 Timothy 3:16 the voice of God speaking through the apostle, Paul, has said:

> *"All scripture is given by inspiration of God, and is profitable for doctrine, for reproof, for correction for instruction in righteousness: that the man of God may be perfect, thoroughly furnished unto all good works"* (2 Timothy 3:16). Another translation reads: *"All Scripture is inspired by God and is useful for teaching the truth, rebuking error, correcting faults, and giving instruction for right living, so that the person who serves God may be fully qualified and equipped to do every kind of good deed. (TEV)"*

Having made the decisive-decision to accept what the Bible says, verbatim and without exception, and having received insight and inspiration to write from my experiences and exposure, what follows is my take on truth, backed by Scripture. At the outset let's be clear on at least two points. First of all, according to Scripture God only has one Church: it is "The-Church-of-God" that was established-in-Christ—not to be confused with the local denomination by the same name. God's Church was established on the rock of faith, upon which Jesus stated He would build in Matthew Chapter sixteen, Verse eighteen (16:18).

Secondly, when Jesus said *'upon this rock'* I will build My Church (Matthew 16:18), seemingly, He left the organization of the Church up to the people of God who would subscribe to the same faith to which Peter made reference; and He would do it without any direct intervention from Him.

I suppose it would be safe to say that He—being the embodiment of God—believed that having instilled in each of his creation the Spirit of power, love, and a sound mind, the task of in-gathering for the purpose of organizing His Church would be completed according to His heart. That being said and in an effort to present truth that is void of tradition, I will comment on and criticize, compare and contrast, the apparent successes and failures of the organized Church to meet the criteria contained in the delineation of faith.

Using the sound mind with which all mankind were endowed (2 Timothy 1:7), I coveted the power of God in producing what our Savior had in mind when He declared that *"the gates of hell shall not prevail against it"* (Matthew 16:18).

PRESENTATION

IT goes without saying that the Church means different things to different people, and must be seen that way. However and metaphorically speaking, in a Psalm of praise (Psalm 100:3) David referred to the Church as 'the sheep of God's pasture.' In that frame of reference we can say that even though God has only one flock, He allows them to be housed in many sheepfolds around the world. Add to that the fact that the God we serve must also have a vast sense of humor because He not only allows us to subdivide His flock into many denominations, He permits us to call them by whatever name we choose. Frank S. Mead and Samuel S. Hill, in their *Handbook of Denominations,* have named two-hundred and thirty-nine different bodies as of 1995.

But not to worry, because when it comes to identifying the truth about the Church—in spite of the traditions to which we now subscribe—Jesus, in Matthew 16:18-19, stated very clearly that *"the gates of hell shall not prevail against His Church."* For the record, in that conversation with His disciples He said,

> **"And I say also unto thee, that thou are Peter, and upon this rock I will build my church; and the gates of hell shall not prevail against it. And I will give unto thee the keys of the kingdom of heaven; and whatsoever thou shalt bind on earth shall be bound in heaven; and whatsoever thou shalt loose on earth shall be loosed in heaven."**

That declaration gave Peter—whom I believe to have been the first great leader in the Church at Jerusalem—all the leverage needed to perform the service of organization on the day of Pentecost (Acts 2:38-42) when the first members were gathered together. That said let's get to work.

Definition and Description

The English word 'Church' translates the Greek word 'Ekklesia,' which meant two different things to two different groups of people in those days. To the Jew, Church meant "the called out," for Israel was indeed the called out.'" But to the Greek, Church stood for a political assembly who were, by their qualifications, able to issue out justice in a society. However, when Jesus came on the scene— by virtue of Him being the Ex-officio head of the Church—He understood both meanings. Even though the Bible doesn't say it in words, when He said, *"upon this rock I will build my Church,"*

He was saying, 'My Ekklesia will be a synthesis of what both, the Jews and the Greeks believe.'"

Stated succinctly, "My Ekklesia, said Jesus, will first be called out of the world, rescued and set apart and made spiritually ready." Then they will be sent back into the world to be the moral and ethical custodians of the world—issuing out justice in the world that I made. Translated, this writer is saying that since the body of Christ is one, these two groups must have been designed to be synthesized. Any way you slice it or dice it, the Church, regardless of denominational doctrines, is a synthesized body, built on sanctification and service.

That having been said, for some groups there are creeds and covenants to which all who are involved must adhere. For example, there is the ordinance of baptism. Not only must they be baptized to become a member of the Church; as a member that person—or persons—is expected to be in regular attendance, pay their tithes, and give in the free-will offerings for the support of the various ministries—services—of that local Church. Working in the church to carry out the ministries of that body is also encouraged.

For others "The Church" is a group of called-out individuals who regularly gather in a building secured for public worship, also identified—with a great deal of pride, I might add—as "Our Church." The provident purpose of being a member of that body is to praise and worship God—although like its name, praise and worship also have different meanings and applications. Each of the members will identify him or herself as a Christian—even though their attitudes and actions fluctuate when it comes to living up to their covenant and creed. That may be because we all have "free-will" and it carries with it, the gift of choice.

For still others, the "Church" is a congregation with specific denominational polities, organized to meet the perceived needs of their members. For this group there is a covenant or a code of ethics which defines, regulates and supports its members. For instance, the Baptists have "The Baptist Covenant;" the Methodists have the Doctrine and Discipline; Presbyterians subscribe to the Nicene Creed; and Catholics have the Universal Prayer book called the Missal—to name just a few. And although their sacred texts and code of ethics may read differently, their "core-beliefs" are pretty much the same. That is to say, all of them strive to live by the so-called Golden Rule: "Do unto others as you, in a like situation, would have them do unto you."

Moving right along, I would be remiss if I failed to mention another group which denounces any denominational affiliation. They are classically known as "Non-denominational." Close observation will reveal that each of these groups have selected a portion of scripture to validate themselves, usually one or more of the 5-fold ministries set forth in Ephesians 4:11, to which all of them '**should be**' subscribers. Many have dropped the label 'Church' and affixed the word "Ministry" (ies); but at the end of the day, they all sound alike with one major difference: each of them declares, "Ain't nobody right, but us." The question that remains to be answered is, "how does what they say compare to what Jesus meant by what He said?'"

There is an old saying which reads: "A rose by any other name is still a rose." Borrowing from that phrase, I suppose one could say that when it comes to God's Ekklesia, "a Church by any name is still a Church." However after nearly seventy years of experiences and exposure, I must say that I have become convicted—but not yet persuaded—that in everyone there is value.

Taking all of these differences into consideration, there is one more group about which not much is said, but whose views are prominent and worthy of mention. This group is generally perceived as being cynical because their views are more practical than they are spiritual. The leaders of this group—if you can engage some of them in an interview—will tell you that their views are widely known and could easily be cataloged under the heading, "What If?" The belief-system of each member is unique. The reason is because once the question is raised, each man (or woman) must answer for himself. Their core beliefs are predicated on the question, "What if we are right?" My source, speaking under the veil of anonymity, began talking only after I agreed with one condition: his name would not be mentioned in any of my writings. The leaders of our group agree to one core-belief: they are sworn to secrecy. Their secrecy is bound with the agreement that those who know won't talk, and those who talk really don't know.

To begin with, they are present in every church, regardless of denomination, said he. He went on to say that he was making himself and this interview an exception to the rule, because of the work in which I am engaged, and the boost in public relations that he believed this interview would deliver. It all has to do with what happens in the "hereafter," said he. "Simply stated, this group stops short of saying that they do not believe there is a heaven or a hell, because that would be like saying, there is no God or a Devil." Instead, they are convinced that whatever happens will happen in the span of a person's lifetime—whether it is described as eternal or everlasting—it will happen while he yet lives. Their convictions are founded on the premise that 'when you are dead, you are done.'

I asked him as we continued to dialogue, "What part does the Bible play in his life, and in the lives of his colleagues?" For this group, said he, the Bible is a book of self-contained facts; and it becomes truth when placed in the proper context. In any case, it is through the eyes of the beholder. Simply stated, he was in agreement with me when I said that the Old Testament contains Principles, Promises, and Prophecy in real time; that it forecasts the coming of the Messiah—providing you subscribe to that premise—who will come to seek and to save that which is lost. In addition, I said, the New Testament is a replication of the Old Testament, containing the same Principles, Promises, and Prophecy, along with divinely disseminated procedural-promises added for assistance. These attributes contain clarity and conciseness when it comes to dealing with sin. In his mind the Bible says what it means and means what it says. However, all of us have the prerogative to accept or reject at will, but our choices do not make it good or evil.

When I added that the New Testament chronicles the arrival of the Messiah and His work of redemption—that is to say His death, burial, resurrection, and ascension—and asked if there was agreement? That is where this group—said he—begs to drop anchor. On the whole this group believes the promises of God; but when it comes to Jesus saving His people from their sins, the length of time allowed to "Repent and believe the gospel" (Mark 1:15), is limited to the time each of them has been given to live on earth.

106

WHAT YOU SEE IS WHAT YOU GET

ONE of their prophets who joined in the conversation with this brother in response to one of my questions concerning the context and the content of Revelation twenty-one (21, stated that he believed that the jury was still out on how their believers view the content of this chapter. In other words, they aren't through thinking about the impact this chapter will have on their lives; and no one is willing to firmly put a question-mark where the voice of God has already put a period. For them, God gives each person life and time to live it, and it's up to him what he does with it. Simply stated, for this group heaven is right here on earth, and you catch enough hell every day of your life based on the choices you make. But when you are dead, you are done.

They were in agreement with me when I said that simultaneously, opportunities that are common to all mankind are put before us, and it's up each person to take advantage of any or all of them while they yet live. However, here is where we differ in opinion. For me, God entrusts each person with the same set of gifts to be used in carrying out the tasks that come regularly before them (Genesis 1:27; 2 timothy 1:7). In essence, the Bible is there to enable him or them; and the Holy Spirit—whom they admit lives within each person (Genesis 2:7)—will empower each of them upon request, so that they can rise above mediocrity and access the abundant life that Jesus alluded to in John 10:10b. The issues with which each of us must contend, said he, is deciding whether or not to accept what God has given us.

The belief of this group is in agreement that "God is" and that "He rewards those who diligently seek Him" (Hebrews 11:6). But, those rewards come while you are alive, and not after you are dead. Their philosophy is really rather simple. In the interview both of them asked the question, "What if God had the Bible printed so that man—at his own leisure—could study it; and after studying it, he could not only determine if he wanted to believe what the Bible says, but he can use it to determine the best way to live his life while he is still alive? In other words, "What if we are right?"

After much dialogue, I concluded that they were saying, in effect, that God was literally saying to all mankind: "I have perused all of life from the alpha to the omega, and from the first to the last. Not only that, I have given you "the spirit of power, and of love, and of a sound mind." That Spirit lives within each of you and it's a matter of choice as to how and if you acknowledge Him. But rest assured that I will not transgress your free-will. You have the prerogative to accept or reject at will, any part of the scriptures with one contingency: *"whatsoever you sow, the same will you also reap"* (Galatians 6:7, NKJV).

With all things considered, I had to admit that after meeting with them, "I, too, am not through thinking about some of the things that were said; for there is merit on both sides." Since my Bible says God gave all mankind the Spirit of power and of love and of a sound mind, and since no two people think exactly alike, at the very least, all of us can find what we choose to believe solidly within the framework of scripture.

By the way, God's Omniscience covers His written word, but His written word does not exhaust God's Omniscience. God is bigger than what's written in the Bible. In other words, my Bible has a Judeo-Christian under-pinning; but Jesus had something to say about those who are not Jewish or Christian. And what Jesus had to say may not correlate with what some of us believe the Bible means by what it has to say. Nevertheless, what Jesus said is worth remembering:

> *"And other sheep I have which are not of this fold; them also I must bring, and they will hear My voice; and there will be one flock an one shepherd"* (John 10:16, NKJV).

When it comes to the knowledge of God and how the Church should be operated, we can believe what the Bible says, but there is much more that has not been written (John 21:25). Nevertheless, as for me and my house we have chosen to believe the Bible without exception. I have taught those under my leadership to take what it says verbatim and without exception. Anything else should be filed under the heading of "Ideas" whose time has not come." I call it faith.

Having seen some of what they shared play out in my life in the last sixty years, I urge and I challenge anyone who has developed the mental-state-of-readiness to join me on this journey from earth's sorrow to heaven's joy, to make their choice today, deciding what they are willing to believe; whether it will be the traditional beliefs that blanket the organized Church, or whether it will be the afore-mentioned group, with all of its trappings. As for me, I am driven to wait until my change comes, leaning and depending on the power of the God of creation. Until then, all that my Bible does not cover is categorized under the heading of faith: *'the substance of things hoped for, and the evidence of things not seen.'* When all is said and done, whether the group identifies itself as a Ministry or some other variation of a House of Faith, Jesus put in place a truth that validates. In Matthew 12:33 He said, *"Either make the tree good, and his fruit good; or else make the tree corrupt, and his fruit corrupt; for the tree is known by his fruit."*

CHAPTER TWELVE

The Role and Function of the Church

PROLOGUE

NOW that we have identified, defined, and delineated the contemporary Church, nothing else remains but to delineate the role and function of the Church. The second question to be answered is, "What, in this world, is the Church supposed to be?" I don't claim to have an answer that is both acceptable and workable for all who will read this. However, I was successful in getting some older-aware ones to dialogue with me in a discovery mode. A well-known philosopher once said, "If you want to know how to recognize an apple, remove everything that is not an apple, and that which remains is an apple." In that discovery mode we decided to begin with 'what, in this world, the Church is not supposed to be' in an effort to identify what, in this world, the Church is supposed to be.

What we have today—as it relates to the role and function of the Church—are toys and television instead of thoughts and ideas. The electronic media has all but replaced the assembling of ourselves together (Hebrews 10:25). As a matter of fact, there is a new thing on the horizon called "virtual worship;" it's where believers need only to fire up their computers, turn on their televisions, or download the appropriate 'App' on their "smart phones" and the services will be 'streamed, live,' for them.

Instead of using the spirit of a sound mind to flush out truth concerning the role and function of the Church, the majority of God's people are already content to bathe in the innocence of ignorance, engaged in an exercise in futility while riding a merry-go-round of madness. That's another suitcase that should be unpacked.

Today, almost all of society—including the organized Church—is making an appeal to the younger generation for leadership. The most salient reason is because of technological advancement. Without a doubt it is the younger generation that will position America in the global market. And with all of the advancement in technology, Governments the world over are looking to their youth—21-50—for leadership. Similarly, Churches are looking for pastors among the younger generation—25-50. This, I was told by the leadership of several mainline so-called mega-churches. Why the younger generation? I asked. The answer I received cited two issues and covered two main points.

The first issue is the law of diminishing returns. Translated, we can keep doing what we have always done, but there is an exodus out of the older, mainline denominational churches into the contemporary nondenominational Ministries. Yes, Ministries. Even the use of the word 'Church' has been substituted-out.' The leadership of these congregations state—unequivocally—that the best way to regain, re-train, and retain those who have left the Church is to find a way to attract the younger generation and re-order the worship experience to coincide with their desires. What I hear them saying is that 'we need a new gospel.' With Church growth as the primary target, those Church leaders believe younger pastors would be more successful when it comes to attracting the younger generation.

The second issue is, younger pastors are more attuned to the technologically advanced social media; and just as 'iron sharpens iron,' (Proverbs 27:17) they believe youth will attract youth. While I have to admit that their concerns are valid, more than thirty-one years in the pastorate have convinced me that the real problem with which they are faced is greater than their perception; and if they are not careful, this will turn out to be one of those times when the perceived 'cure will be worse than the disease.' In point of fact, we have reached the turning point in organizational structure, and change is the only absolute. Stated another way, the church is going to have to change; but how will that change look?

I am only one, and this is my perception. More than sixty-five years and four generations have passed since the end of the Great Depression and W.W. II. And since then America has lived through "Old School," "Baby Boomers" and "Generation X." Now, with the retirement of most "Baby Boomers," "Generation X" and "The

Next Generation" in America are now preparing to take the reins of leadership. The "Next Generation" is generation number four, and from where I sit, there is where the problem will begin. There is an old axiom which came up and out of "old school" which reads: "If it's not broken, don't fix it." In *"Entering,"* I have seized the opportunity to segue and to put my spin on that saying.

Having been permitted to see and to reveal the hidden hope, I am convinced that a better reading of that old axiom would be: **"If it's not broken, 'you had better fix it' before it gets broken.'"** That's another way of saying "make sure that the foundation on which you are attempting to build is a solid foundation." In this case revisiting an old Japanese proverb which says, "Plan for the worst, hope for the best, and let nothing catch you by surprise;" is in order. If that sounds curious or perhaps even cynical, count it to my head and not my heart. For this writer, it means that there are some emerging problems on the horizon with which we need to deal, before they get totally out of control. And it's about those problems that somebody needs to say something.

I don't know how others feel about it, but from where I sit there is a need for somebody who has the unmitigated gall and the holy boldness, to stand up against 'what is,' and declare what should be." Stated another way, because I find it very difficult to believe that I am the only one to whom this vision of God has been made manifest, as I prepare to write this manuscript I am apprehensive and in a state of awe. But that's the way I see it. Let me spell it out.

PRESENTATION: 'The way it is'

FROM where I am sitting, Dr. Jeremiah A. Wright (1995) was on point when he said "there is a cruel conspiracy between the high incidence of un-necessary suffering and the dispassionate silence that encompasses the people of God everywhere;" more especially the poor and the indigent people of God who are members of the organized Church. (1) It's a cruel conspiracy. I am well aware of the meaning and the danger in generalizing; but I believe I am on safe ground when I say that somebody needs to say something intelligent, enlightening, enhancive and encouraging, about wide-spread suffering in this mean old world. Stated succinctly, it is time for the true identity and the role and function of God's Church to be made manifest.

For many years I have wished and I have waited for somebody to say something and do something, about these debilitating disturbances. Six years ago, after undergoing what I call "a real conversion experience," the Spirit of God (SOG) spoke into my spirit a portion of the solution to the problem. In answer to my prayer for divine intervention, the SOG said, "If not you, then who? If not here, then where? And if not now, when? Shortly thereafter I heard a song in which the songwriter said, "If the Lord brings you to it, He will certainly bring you through it." It was then that I began to tremble in my spirit. Since then, my perception has had far-reaching implications.

While I am aware of the fact that the solution to the problem involves all of God's people, and not just the organized Church (John 10:16), it is because during the major part of my up-bringing—which encompassed the Civil Rights Era—emphasis were being placed on the Church in the black community. However, since with God there is no respect of person, what I am about to say is applicable to everyone. And make no mistake about it I had to pray long and hard in addition to digging deep into the word, looking for answers to the myriad of questions that came to mind.

So that my convictions did not unfairly challenge the word of God in Romans 2:11, or come across as a negative indictment of the Church, I had to become convinced that there was no other way to record the solution to the problem except to start again at the beginning, and move progressively towards the end.

It did not take long after that to begin to discover the solution to the problem and the answers to my questions. They were found in a lesson taught by Jesus concerning "the way to heaven"—also known as the "narrow gate"—recorded In Matthew 7:13, NKJV. In both, the KJV and the NKJV, Jesus made it clear that the way to life would only be found by a few. After drawing a contrast between 'it' and "the way of destruction; He said the way to destruction is open wide; it is broad and it will be travelled by many. In the KJV, He told His Disciples:

> *"Enter ye in at the strait gate: for wide is the gate, and broad is the way that leadeth to destruction, and many there be which go in there-at: because strait is the gate, and narrow is the way which leadeth unto life, and few there be that find it."*

Again, that's the way it should be. But the message was both, a warning and an assurance. The people of God are being warned that the road to life—while they were being assured that it could be found—they are being made aware that it won't be easy to find. And for people of color who are inclined to believe that they are being singled out by the rigors of racism and the sediment of sin that surrounds it, what Jesus said made it clear that His message was directed to all people everywhere.

While I am using the Christian Bible as my principal resource, reference is not being made to any specific religious group. God's message would be the same if it is read in the organized Church, in a Muslim Temple or a Mosque, in a Jewish Synagogue or Temple, or anywhere else people may gather to worship. That being said, for Christians the onus is on the organized Church and her leaders (Hosea 4:6). Whereas I previously felt guilty about the way I was thinking as it relates to the Church, I no longer feel that way. I have discovered and I have concluded that guilt is not of God. Grace is of God. Guilt is Satan's modus operandi and what Paul told Timothy in his second letter, Chapter 4 Verses 3-4, has already been manifested many times, in many places, and in many ways. Now, I feel that the truth must be told. After reading this, it will be either truth or consequences.

Additionally, I have lived long enough to see that there are some who will catch the vision, while the majority of the members of the organized Church will continue to do the same thing, the same way, hoping to somehow get some different results. Those, who under the leadership of the Holy Spirit, catch the vision; will define, describe and delineate; enlighten, enhance and encourage, those who have an ear to hear what the Spirit is saying to the

Church. That brings us to the central issue facing the people of God. People will say what pleases them—good, bad, or indifferent. The people of God are obliged to "do the right thing, the right way."

That issue is "choice." As a matter of fact, everything centers on our free-will and our ability to make the right decisions and correct choices. With that in mind I began to pray a different kind of prayer. Currently, 99% of my prayers are prayers of thanksgiving (1 Thessalonians 5:18), believing that the perfect plan of God is already in force, and will not change. So it is that each day when I pray, I say,

> *"Lord I thank you for all that you have already done. I thank you for what you are doing right now, and I thank you for what you will yet do throughout this day and the rest of my tomorrows."* When I pray, I also remind the Lord that it was Him who said, *"The steps of a good man are ordered by the Lord and He delights in His way" (Psalm 37:23).*

Not that I am good—absent Christ in my life—so I add to my prayers daily, *"Lord I thank you for ordering my steps."*

Even though the Church of today has many faces, and the congregants are more in tuned to entertainment than for gathering information; on a daily basis I revisit the road over which I have come, remind myself, and continue to thank the SOG for searching me, making me usable, and then using me to get the word out to those who are yet walking in darkness. The answers to my prayers are quite clear. There are many areas of concern, but all of them stem from one source.

The following question was raised by a local group of pastors-in-training. 'Given that all of us believed we were on the right track all the time, "How do we turn the corner? In other words, how do we right the wrongs that have been done?" My answer was both, simple and complex. It involves 'a road less travelled.' The answer is simple when you have made the decisive-decision to hear, receive, and believe. It only becomes complex when you are halt between two opinions. The Scripture says,

> *"For whosoever shall call upon the name of the Lord shall be saved. How then shall they call on Him in whom they have not believed? And how shall they believe in Him of whom they have not heard? And how shall they hear without a preacher? And how shall they preach, except they be sent? Faith comes by hearing, and hearing by the word of God* (Romans 10:16-17).

For clarity and conciseness, I offered three steps to solidarity. As previously stated, I reminded them that:

> *"All Scripture is given by inspiration of God and is profitable for doctrine, for reproof, for* correction, for instruction in righteousness; that the man of God may be perfect, thoroughly furnished unto all good works."

Step # 1 is to hear the word. Jesus said it this way to His twelve:

> "Go not into the way of the Gentiles, and into any city of the Samaritans enter ye not: but go rather to the lost sheep of the house of Israel. And as ye go, preach, saying, 'the kingdom of heaven is at hand.'"

In retrospect I believe it was Dr Jeremiah A. Wright Jr., Pastor Emeritus of the Trinity United Church of Christ of Chicago, Illinois who said in my hearing: "Make Peace with Your Past." (2) Making peace with your past includes, but is not limited to engaging is some close-order introspection, rooting up and digging out anything that is out of sync with the Word and the will of God. When that is done, the believer must then obtain forgiveness from God (Psalm 51:4), and within himself institute forgetfulness to eradicate the wrong—which comes under the heading of making peace with your past.

There is as story of the demoniac in the Gospel of Mark Chapter 5. There we read about a young man who lived in the graveyard and made his home among the tombs. Metaphorically speaking, most of us live in the cemetery of our past, among the tombs of disturbing memories. Examples of making peace with your past, refers to the torment caused by a myriad of bad memories. We hold on to our bad memories, just as tight as we hold on to our good memories. And those **bad** memories are a MOB for they are many. When Jesus asked the man his name, he said,

- "My name is MOB there are so many of us." Translated, he was saying:
- Memories of wrong choices; memories of things that were said to us by those who didn't understand our situation;
- Memories of being Black in a White-man's world—being the last one hired and the first one fired;
- Memories of being called anything by any white person that chooses to call us anything but a Child of God;
- Memories of missed birthdays and shallow alibis that you will not understand in a million years;
- Memories of the moment when your whole world crashed because of death, desertion or divorce;
- Memories of wasted years foolishly spent in the perennial pursuit of perishable products;
- Memories of what it felt like never to have had a daddy in your life; memories of un-confessed sin and therefore unforgivable sin;
- Sins that are haunting and hurting and will not go away. My name is MOB there are So many of us.

Make no mistake about it; making peace with your past is a must. And when that feat has been accomplished, it is followed up by the encouragement to keep the child in you alive. The teachable nature of a child is what God is calling for: God wants us to be childlike without becoming childish. "Don't let the child in you die. Keep the child alive. Somewhere I read or I heard somebody say that:

- To be Child-like is to be teachable, but to be childish is to be immature.
- To be child-like is to be flexible, but to be childish is to be undisciplined.
- To be child-like is to keep a sense of humor, but to be childish is to be just plain silly.
- To be childlike is to play sometimes, but to be childish to play all of the time.
- To be Childlike is to learn something new . . . . . . everyday . . . . . . but to be childish is to know nothing, have nothing, be nothing, and do nothing.
- To be Childlike is to be confident, but to be childish is to be self-diluted.
- To be Childlike is to grow in grace, but to be childish, is to be stumped, stymied, and stagnated, in your development.
- To be Childlike is to be courageous, but to be childish is to be down-right foolish.
- To be Childlike is to use your imagination, but to be childish is to be totally unrealistic.
- To be Childlike is to have respect for others, but to be childish is to have no mind of your own.
- To be Childlike is to be led by the Lord, but to be childish is to be blown about by every wind of doctrine.
- To be Childlike is to Trust in God and Do your Part; but to be childish is to sit back and expect God to Do for you what He gave you sense enough to do for yourself. Don't be childish, be Child-like. Keep the Child in you alive.

Whether or not you are in agreement with me and this unknown preacher out of my past, you can rest assured that it will be truth or consequences. On the other side of the coin are four distinct aberrations from the image of God, in each of us. For the sake of clarification and because all four are spiritual, I have given each of them a name and a personality. Their names are "Doubt, Denial, Fear, and Insecurity." Throughout this work I refer to them as "two sets of twin boys" belonging to Satan, the arch-enemy of God. The bottom line is they are spirits who have taken up residence in all of God's people, and must be dispelled as part of our deliverance.

Doubt and Denial gained entry and took up residence first in the mind and then in the heart of Eve. The conversation between Eve and Satan in which this took place is recorded in Genesis 3:1-6. Subsequently, and in an ensuing conversation between God and Adam in the Garden in the East of Eden, we are informed that "Fear and Insecurity" made their presence known, and had taken up residence in the mind and heart of Adam (Genesis 3:10). Beginning with Cain and Abel, all four spirits were passed on to the offspring of our fore parents: include everyone and exclude no one.

Because of sin, all of God's children after Adam and Eve are plagued with the collective spirits of fear and insecurity, doubt and denial. Each of us, from birth to our spiritual awakening, must be delivered from those diseases which eat away at the fibers of our spiritual fabric (Psalm 51:5). By request, I have been given the task and the authority to shout loud and spare not in my efforts to identify and delineate the cause and effect of these four diseases. And that I will do as long as God gives me grace.

That said, and as a result of limited-learning and mental-laziness, Satan's children—having been created as adults—are permitted to live in the minds of those of us who continue to feel the pain, but who, for whatever reason (s), would rather resort to 'Doubt' and slip into 'Denial', when offered an opportunity to acknowledge their presence and be delivered from them. But that's not how the story ends. The most troubling of all possible outcomes is often overlooked. It takes a close observation to see that Fear and Insecurity are our constant traveling companions; with Insecurity functioning as the linchpin.

Jealousy and envy are fruit off the poisonous tree and the out-growth of fear and Insecurity. Stated succinctly, first comes insecurity followed closely by doubt and denial (Genesis 3:6-10). And with the two of them living large and in charge of our spiritual domain, doubt and denial continue to act as the driving wheel, depositing deception and derision in the minds of all of God's children.

Let me illustrate. "There is a war going on." Contrary to the popular opinion which might suggest otherwise, this world is a "battleground," not a "playground." My research has revealed that whenever covert insecurity is identified—which keeps us fighting among ourselves; covert-fear—which drives that insecurity—gives rise to doubt and denial which also resides within, and keeps up the fight. Using that as the prognosis, the only thing that remains is to record the symptoms and write the prescription.

I believe there is a general agreement among doctors that at best, they can only treat symptoms. So the solution to any illness is for doctors to get the patient to identify the symptom and have it treated, until the real problem cease and desist, and the symptom disappears.

The Prescription

Consider for an example, a person who has a simple headache. A Tylenol or an Aspirin will temporarily relieve the pain. But the underlying truth is, unless and until that person discovers the source of the "tension" which causes the "headache," the pain of the headache will continue to resurface when the tension reaches a pre-set level. Here is the problem. If you suggest that strategy to the patient, he (or she) will quickly resort to doubt and slip into denial, minimizing the cause of the problem and reducing it to nothing more than the intermittent pain that comes with the headache.

He (or she) will dismiss the subject by saying something like: "It's not that serious: everybody gets a headache once in a while. Or, I get them all the time when I get too hot, or if I allow myself to go too long without eating." If that is true, and if there is more to it, I was asked: why doesn't somebody say something or why doesn't somebody do something about the cause?

My response was—and still is—we all have issues with which we need to deal, and there is always "one" issue which generates tension and which causes the symptoms about which we complain and subsequently seek help. And unless and until that issue is identified and dealt with, the patient will be forever treating intermittent headaches. What is the real issue? That issue is highlighted for us by the apostle, Paul, in Ephesians 6:12. In his declaration Paul is seeking to diffuse the in-fighting that goes on between God's children, and acquaint us with Spiritual Warfare. Paul wrote:

> ". . . *For we do not wrestle against flesh and blood but against principalities, against powers, against the rulers of the darkness of this age, against spiritual hosts of wickedness in the places.*"

That Scripture frames a bit of truth in a startling way. It breaks through barriers that have been standing much too long and places blame where it belongs. It leaves us with an awful alternative. From this point onward it's truth or consequences.

CHAPTER THIRTEEN

Truth or Consequences

PROLOGUE

LIFE is about making choices. By creating man in His own Image, God gave him 'Free will', and his free-will carries with it the power and the authority to choose. God has Free-will and He uses it to love us unconditionally. As for me, I believe I am on safe ground when I say that God would be pleased if we loved Him unconditionally, as well. Nevertheless, when all is said and done I have become convinced that there are really only two ways to think; and subsequently, only two ways to live our lives—whether or not we are declared members of the Church. For our purposes here, those two ways are best identified as "God's way" and "Man's way."

PRESENTATION

ON the one hand, without transgressing our Free-will, the content of God's way is spelled out for us in the Bible. On that note we need to be extremely clear. Contrary to the popular interpretation-and-practice of injecting the way we live our lives into the Bible, the Bible was meant to be used as a guide. We are not to paint ourselves into portions of it just because certain fact supports what we believe. That would be suggesting that God is telling us how to live. Instead, the reverse is true. The Bible is to be used as a rule and guide to our faith and practice. Translated, we are to extract selected passages that will help us straighten out the crooked places, raise the low places in our thinking, and level off the high places in our attitudes and actions.

Stated another way, the Bible is a book of facts that, when placed in the proper context, becomes a myriad of truth. The

Bible is fool-proof and fail-safe. It doesn't make our decisions for us; instead, it offers a set of facts that—again, when placed in the proper context—becomes truth on its face.

Man's way on the other hand, is the way of the world. And as we approach the description and delineation of man's way, we must keep in mind that when it comes to living, everything can be found in scripture: the good, the bad, and the indifferent. And since the Bible means everything it says, but does not say everything that it means; what I am calling 'man's way' is really the result of man engaging in the opportunity to do some critical thinking. The ability to engage in critical thinking was accorded to everyone, and can be used to arrive at his (our) choice of direction.

Should the desire to apprehend and adhere to the rules governing the ways of God be our choice, mankind must keep in mind that what he reads in the Bible must be categorized as "content in search for the proper context" before it can be called truth; and then it must be spoken into existence in real time, by each person (Proverbs 18:21).

Ironically and on the other hand, the foundation of man's way is really God's way—given the fact that man was created "In God's Own Image." However, man's way is the manifestation of a combination of more than two-thousand years of long-held traditions being superimposed on top of that foundation of good. Stated another way, the substance of God's way of thinking and living, is spelled out for us in scripture; but it takes the Lordship and the leadership of the Holy Spirit to *"teach us all things, and bring all things to our remembrance that God has already said to us"* (John 14:26). And whether we realize it or not, that is where the problem begins. I call it "mixing and matching," and I perceive that man has mixed evil and good for so long, evil actually looks like good. So it is that when and if change comes in anyone's life, it will be at his (or her) own discretion.

The major problem with which the organized Church is faced—regardless of her self-imposed differences—is making the decision to pay the "high cost of the free gift" that God gave the world, which is recorded for us in John 3:16. Simply stated, the high cost of that free gift is 'submission and surrender.' There are those who will disagree with me, saying, "accepting Jesus as your savior is the primary facet, and the only important aspect." While that statement has a grain of truth, I would argue that many if not most people have made that profession. But because they stopped short of being able to differentiate between good and evil, they are confined to riding a merry-go-round of madness on an exercise in futility.

Given the fact that in most cases, tradition has eclipsed the truth; the only solution to the problem is submission to the Sovereignty of God over our lives, and surrendering to the Lordship and the leadership of the Holy Spirit in our lives. Generally speaking, failing to make those differentiations will cause decision-making to become extremely difficult. Again, they tell me that "I could be wrong, but I don't think so." Sin entered the world and man allowed all of his good to be overshadowed by evil. Previously I called it 'mixing and matching—but for most people, the trade-name is tradition. At best, all of us can say like the late Frank Sinatra: "I did it my way.'" That is the way of the world, with individual specificity.

To make bad-matters worse and using myself as a model, my perception is that people would rather do anything than "think," "face the truth," and "change." Why is that so? I was asked. Remembering the old adage which says, "A man cannot teach what he doesn't know, and he cannot lead where he cannot go," my response was, 'although I am not through thinking about all of the tenets, I have learned one thing for sure: and that is, on my own I only knew one way to live, and that is the way of the world in which we live.' And before I could bridge the gap between man's way and God's way, I had to submit and surrender. And even though that's easier said than done, I found that with a lot of effort and a little help from the friend that I have in Jesus—who is the mirror-image of God—it can be done.

So it is that in *Entering,* using the New King James Version of the Bible (NKJV), Webster's II New Riverside University Dictionary (1984), and more than fifty-years of experiences and exposure as my resources, it is my intent to ***"rightfully divide the word of truth"*** *(2 Timothy 2:15b),* and in so doing, exchange tradition for truth. By saying that, I am not suggesting that all tradition is inherently evil. Let's be clear about that. What I am saying is that, in *Entering*, I am following-up on a self-proclaimed theory that (Carter 2000) penned in a previous publication: *"Truth taken out of context, allows a lie to reign* (3)

Therefore, in the context and content of *Entering*, I will endeavor to set forth clarity where there is confusion. In addition, I will strive to turn on the light where [I believe] the people of God are currently walking in darkness; and as it relates to the word of God, provide a deeper understanding of what the Bible means by what it says, in some of the more familiar, pivotal scriptures.

As it relates to the Church of God, the Spirit of God instructed and inspired the apostle Paul and thirty-five to forty others to make things clear without any confusion. Although spoken to specific Churches by name in the Revelation, Paul's messages were to the Church of God in various locations; more especially, over one-half of the New Testament Churches that he organized.

THE TRUTH WITHOUT EXCEPTION

WHEN "*Entering in the Strait Gate"(Matthew 7:13)* was first introduced in my current pastoral assignment, I shared with them that hundreds of inspirational books are written each year by [almost] an equal number of authors, and most of those authors are pastors and preachers. Additionally, retail sales records will reveal that many of those men (and women) are now very wealthy. The question was quickly asked, "Pastor, do you think the books you are writing are going to make you wealthy?" My answer was quick and candid: "No, I said, I probably won't become wealthy— although it wouldn't be bad if financial assistance to market these books would come my way."

Anticipating the next question, I quickly offered the following insert. There is a reason I said that; let me share it with you. I probably won't become wealthy; and it's because I have discovered that the majority of the men and women who wrote those books and have become wealthy, earned their wealth from writing, not from practicing what they preach or from what they have written. The question that followed was not anticipated either. I was asked, "What are you doing that will show the world that

you are practicing what **you** preach?" I admit that while I didn't anticipate that question, my answer was almost fluid: it came up and out without any hesitation.

I called to their attention the words of Jesus in Mark Chapter 1, Verse 15. There, our Lord issued a very thought-provoking challenge. He said, *"The time is fulfilled, the Kingdom of God is at hand. Repent and believe in the gospel."* In other words, Jesus was, and is currently saying to me and others to whom the Holy Spirit is speaking, "it's your time now." I told them that I received that challenge from Jesus, verbatim and without exception in a vision in January, 2007. And I believe that the Spirit of God speaks directly to me every day. In addition, I took what was said to me in that vision to be my marching-orders, and that they were placed in God's perfect plan before there was a when or a where. And, of course, it was a part of God's perfect plan for me to be with my current congregation, because He knew where I would be in the development of my faith, at this point in my life.

It was at that juncture that I made a commitment to make certain that "I practice what I preached." Those who have known me for any length of time will say that my attitude and actions have dramatically changed since I have been in Alabama. They will also say that a turnabout of one-hundred and eighty degrees from where I was, during the first thirty years of my ministry in California is evident. To put it bluntly, my heart has undergone a modicum of transformation with which I am very grateful. My mind is constantly being renewed, as I make my slow but steady *"turn away from my wicked ways" (2 Chronicles 7:14b),* and I owe it all to the Lordship and leadership of God's Holy Spirit. So it is that I can say with certainty that if I should become wealthy, so be it. And if I do, it will be because I am doing the will of God, and the Spirit of God already had it in His perfect plan for my life. If not, that's okay because I am convinced that the perfect plan of God has something even greater in store for me. In any event I will use this time to allow the inspiration of the SOG to take control.

ON THE ROAD TO REPENTANCE

KEEPING in mind that *"everything must be done decently and in order"* (1 Corinthians 14:40), the first order of business for the Church is repentance. The second part is believing and part of my role and function is to get the word out so that collectively we can right the wrongs that have been done through the sediments of sin. Much has happened to me in these last six years, all of which inspired me to write from my experiences and exposure. Specifically, I was subjected to what I like to call "a real conversion experience."

Prompted by the Spirit of God I made an instant but decisive-decision to submit to the Sovereignty of God over my life; and then I began to slowly surrender to the Lordship and the leadership of the Holy Spirit in my life. These things were done according to scripture, as recorded in 2 Chronicles 7:14. Like everyone else, I am human; and once I learned who God is, in and of Himself, I had to learn how to trust Him.

The first truth that I had to come to grips with was to learn that there is a direct correlation between thinking God's way and being successful. Similarly, continuing to think the way the world thinks will continue to produce perpetual failure. Suffice it to say, learning to trust God is easy once you decide that you have had enough failures in your life. It's hard, but it's fair. I had to **learn** that God is trustworthy before I could **believe God** without exception. I believe I need to pull over and help somebody right here.

There is sufficient evidence to substantiate the fact that the people of God who call themselves a Church, the world over, operate as if a gift of entitlement comes with being Christian. And I suppose it does if things are done the way God had things recorded in His word. But, having stopped short of the requirements of the full complement of salvation, His people are continually being destroyed for lack of knowledge (Hosea 4:6). I have been told that I am wrong, but again, I don't think so. It is my opinion that they believe all they have to do is pray and God is going to stop what He is doing and magically make a miracle out of their mess. My learning came with my burning. That is to say,

I was baptized with fire (Matthew 3:11), born-again of the water and of the spirit, and **made able to enter** into the kingdom of God" **(John 3:5)**. Suffice it say that a believer will know that he is able when decisive-decision-making comes easy.

Let me say that another way. When you no longer follow the leadership of those in your circle of family and friends, but instead set your goal, plan your work and work your plan according to the word of God, you are ready. Once I travelled the road to repentance and spiritually entered into the kingdom of God, my whole life instantly flashed in front of me, and everything that has happened in my life, for the first time, made sense.

The short of a very long story—seventy years (70) long to be exact—is this: I discovered that the Spirit of God has been busy in my life, all of my life, even though I didn't know Him in the pre-pardon of my sins. And no, I didn't understand any of it while it was happening, but today it all makes sense. Stated another way, in these last three years, through revelation, illumination and inspiration, the Spirit of God has set me on-course and has kept me fixed and focused.

I now know for myself that life begins and ends with Jesus—who is called Christ—because He is the way, the truth, and the life" (1 John 5:11-12; and St. John 14:6). And not only that, His way and His truth are the keys to having life and having it more abundantly. Those keys are available to all of the people of God—more especially those who are called by His name—by His power and on His authority—(2 Chronicles 7:14).

We all know we need help, but most of us are unaware that our help comes from the Lordship and the leadership of the Holy Spirit when we allow Him to take the lead in our lives; and that we need to submit and surrender to make it happen. Thus, tradition must be replaced by truth. In other words, we must submit to the Sovereignty of God over our lives, and surrender to the leadership of the Holy Spirit in our lives. Stated succinctly, first comes obedience to the principles, then comes the enjoyment of the promises.

By the way, the reader should be made aware—or reminded if he already knows—that because *"In God there is no respect of person" (Romans 2:11),* what God does for one person, He does for all people. Suffice it to say, those who come after me will have to do the same thing I did, for all the same reasons.

After much prayer and supplication—to make an humble and earnest request—the Spirit of God spoke into my spirit that the perfect plan of God—in concert with His permissive and purposeful-will—is being carried out by His Holy Spirit on a 24/7 basis, 365 days a year. So it is that at the end of the day, what we experience in our lives is the result of God's purposeful will being carried out, after factoring in the rewards and/or consequences of the choices that we have made.

WILFULL SPIRITUAL BLINDNESS

IN all of our lives we are given every opportunity to make the appropriate adjustments in our attitudes and actions, but nothing we say or do will profane or frustrate God's purposeful will. When the time is fulfilled, everyone will see that God has had His way, in spite of and regardless. Translated, everything that happens in our lives is the result of us acting out our free-will, and it happens by omission or commission on each of our parts. We either willfully commit a sin or we omit doing what we should do to prevent sin.

"I still don't understand," a sister said. If what you say is true, 'why does God allow bad things to happen to good people?' And if He is so powerful and so full of Love, 'why doesn't He intervene and prevent babies and little children from suffering?' After all, what happens to them is not their fault. What about that, preacher? My response was that the answers to her questions are simple: but our effort to avoid accountability makes them both, simple and complex; it depends on who is telling the story. Nevertheless I gave her the simple version. On the one hand, man has dominion (Genesis 1:26) over everything God made. So, whatever happens is because man either caused it to happen, or he failed to do what was necessary to prevent it from happening. Keeping in mind, however, that time is relative, what happens today may be somebody's reaction to what was done a year ago; or it may be in accordance with the purpose of God from the beginning. Dominion, which is what God instilled in each of us, is another word for 'supreme authority or control.' And whether we like it or not, God did not give man the power and the authority over everything He made, for him to behave like a baby, cry helpless, and intermittently try to give that dominion back to Him. When a man does that, it's a sure sign that Satan and one or more of his hand-picked demons are at work in the mind of that man, striving to control his heart.

On the other hand, the more complex side is inseparably bound to the full complement of salvation; and that level of understanding requires both, submission and surrender. It works on this wise. There is a general agreement among scholars that the surface meaning of a given passage of scripture can be interpreted from the literal reading. But, when man elects to activate the spirit of a sound-mind that God has given him, there is a deeper meaning which comes only through the leadership of the Holy Spirit. And that meaning comes only when He is at work in our lives; which brings us to the "how" and the "why" of it all.

CHAPTER FOURTEEN

The Battleground

PROLOGUE

THE voice of God spoke to and through the Prophet Zechariah, saying:

> *"This is the word of the Lord to Zerubbabel: 'Not by might nor by power, but by My Spirit,' says the Lord of hosts'"* **(Zechariah 4:6).**

That is the key. We must keep in mind that God said what He had to say to one person, one time, in one place; but what He said was directed to all persons everywhere, and for all eternity. Therefore, the message from Zechariah goes out to all who have an ear to hear, what the Spirit of God is saying to the Church. Again I say, check it out for yourself and you too will discover that God does not repeat Himself. By the way, that's another reason why I am writing to the Church. In the organized Church pastors preach and teach what they know; and many if not most of them, will not get this message unless and until someone helps them by bringing them this message.

So, for the benefit of those who do not know Him in the pre-pardon of their sin, let me hasten to add that God is not some kind of a brow-beating ogre, who sits back and watch you strive to do the impossible, knowing full well that you will not succeed. On that subject, the Bible has this to say:

> *"No temptation has over-taken you except such as is common to man; but God is faithful, who will not allow you to be tempted beyond what you are able, but with the temptation will also make the way of escape, that you may be able to bear it"* **(1 Corinthians 10:13).**

Translated and contrary to the more popular opinion which might say otherwise, "If God has brought you to it, it's because God has already provided a way for you to get through it." The operative word there, is "IF." God does not make your decisions for you, nor will He do your work for you. Those things are left up to each of us, and it's for that reason that we should perpetually celebrate the events that occurred on the day of Pentecost.

PRESENTATION

REVIVAL and Renewal is always in order. Hear the word of God concerning the promise that's available to each of us. By way of reminder, in Acts 1:4ff, Luke wrote,

> *"And being assembled together with them, [Jesus] commanded them that they should not depart from Jerusalem, but to wait for the Promise of the Father, "which," He said, you have heard from me. For John truly baptized with water, but you shall be baptized with the Holy Spirit not many days from now."*

We hear you teacher, the young woman said. It all makes sense, now; but tell us, "How can we know when we have been baptized with the Spirit?" Are we expected to come to Church and demonstrate our baptism by holy dancing in the aisles? Or better yet, are we supposed to start talking in tongues like those people in the Holiness Churches? I don't think I want to do that she said. For me that would be too much distraction and I wouldn't be able to hear the word.

My response directed her to St. John 14:26, which reads:

> *"But the Helper, the Holy Spirit, whom the Father will send in My name, He will teach you all things, and bring to your remembrance all things that I have said to you."*

I left her with this conclusion. Under the tutelage of the Holy Spirit, you will be taught all things by Him as needed. In addition, those things which the Spirit of God has already said to you—those things which you have set aside and / or have decided to forget—will also be brought to your mind. By sending the Holy Spirit on the authority and in the power of Jesus to carry out these tasks, God the Father was actually fulfilling a portion of the Prophecy that He made in Genesis 3:15. By way of reminder, in that verse the voice of God said,

> *"And I will put enmity between you and the woman, and between your seed and her Seed; He shall bruise your head, and you shall bruise His heel."*

Translated, the meaning of that message is plain and simple, and a cursory reading of that scripture will confirm it. However, there is a deeper meaning between the lines that the power of the Holy Spirit will make clear. But for the benefit of those who are totally unaware of the context and the content, I will summarize.

In that passage Moses is making reference to the Messiah mentioned throughout the Old Testament—that would be Jesus who is called Christ in the New Testament (Matthew 27:17). It is He who will pay the penalty for the "Sin" of Adam and Eve, and it is the power of the Holy Spirit that will bruise the head of Satan and his seed. Specifically, the "He" and the "His" in that verse is making reference to the Messiah who will come in the fullness of time. "Your seed and her Seed" refers to the offspring of the Messiah and the children of the darkness: those who failed to meet the requirements for becoming sons of God (John 1:12). The "enmity" is the hostility and the hatred that will perpetually exist between the Savior and Satan.

The KJV says it is the power wielded by the Messiah that will bruise the head of Satan, while the NKJV tells us that it will be the Messiah, Himself, who will bruise the head of Satan. The former refers to Jesus who has all power in heaven and in earth in His hand; and the latter refers to the power of the Holy Spirit, Himself. Any way you slice it or dice it, Satan was defeated, and his defeat is perpetual. Now, we must be careful because his defeat is not to be confused with destruction. Make no mistake about it; Satan was defeated not destroyed by the power of God.

The coming of the Holy Spirit on the day of Pentecost was in accordance with the promise that had been prophesied by God the Father (Genesis 3:15); and with it came the tools needed to put man back in right, relational-standing with God. By sending the Holy Spirit, God was keeping His promise; and the Holy Spirit is the much-needed help and empowerment that man is missing. Simply stated, the Holy Spirit is alive and well, carrying out the will of God the Father on a 24/7 basis, 365 days a year.

In a spiritual nutshell, I believe mankind would do better if he knew better, and it's for that reason that I petitioned the Lord God for revelation, illumination, inspiration, and the permission to write from my experiences and exposure. Am I the first or the only one to have been blessed in this manner? The answer is absolutely not. My new birth 'of the water and the Spirit' came six years ago. Stated succinctly, in January, 2007 it occurred to me that the Spirit of God has been busy in my life, all of my life. But it was when I asked Him to let His Spirit fall fresh on the Church that I was leading, that it was made clear to me that I needed to lead by example. And the Holy Spirit—who was already at work in me—along with revelation, illumination, and inspiration would be the three facets being used to encourage me to write as I would be given utterance and insight.

I wish I could be clearer, but the Holy Spirit is our teacher and I am merely a conduit. In other words, I am limited to identifying the source; I cannot speak for Him. The Spirit of God has inspired me to have previously published two of a trilogy of books. This is book number three. The first was *"In His Own Image, Understanding and Enjoying the Full Complement of Salvation."* It can be purchased by placing the following address in the address bar of your computer: CreateSpace.com/3560208. The second book is *"Rising above Mediocrity, Accessing the Abundant Life: Taking traditional Christian practices to the next level"* (WestBow Press.com) (Search by Title or Author). It can be purchased on my web site: *"Revealing the Hidden Hope.com."*

"Entering in at the Strait Gate, Through the Doorway to an Already Decided Destiny" is book number three—the one you

are now reading. It is designed to shed light where the people of God are currently walking in darkness. More specifically, *Entering* will add clarity where there just might be confusion. *Entering* also points out the fact that the Organized Church has set herself up as the destination, rather than the path which leads to God's already-decided destiny. Jesus, in the "Great Commitment," challenged anyone who desires to follow Him to deny himself, take up his cross daily, and follow Him" (Luke 9:23).

The Great Commandments in Matthew 22:37-40, follow the Great Commitment, and is self-evident. And finally, the "Great Commission" (Matthew 28:18-20) in which Jesus commanded His disciples to go and make disciples in all nations, is the only thing Jesus asked His Church to do. The Scripture says:

> *"Go and teach all nations, baptizing them in the name of the Father, and of the Son, and of the Holy Spirit: teaching them to obey all things whatsoever I commanded you":* **and, lo, I am with you always, even unto the end of the world." Amen.**

I cannot say for certain, but it seems to me that the very things about which I have been questioned the most, have been given to me by God, to be rectified by me. At the risk of sounding like a braggart, it was after *Rising* was published that the Spirit of God gave me to know that I have been groomed to be a lasting part of a superficial-diversity-quota. That is to say, I am to be a perpetual change-agent in the infrastructure of this Zion.

Stated succinctly, I have been given the opportunity to ring loud the bell for everyone to hear. I have the privilege and the pleasure of telling men and women in a dying world— regardless of age, race, creed, color, religion, denominational or sexual preferences—that our God is real, and that there are blessings-unlimited and all-good-things-without-end (1 Corinthians 2:7) awaiting those who will choose to serve a true and a living God. And it is that task to which I am committed, as long as God gives me grace.

What you will read in this book is a combination of realized-truth and a bit of conjecture. However, rest assured that where conjecture has been inserted, great pains were taken to attach supporting scripture that will validate my conclusions. And as it was with the two previous books, the context and the content of *Entering* is not designed to validate what the reader already knows—although it probably will. *Entering* is designed to help a person discover what he doesn't know. That said we can move on to first things first, because there is much to be covered on our journey.

CHAPTER FIFTEEN

First Things First

PROLOGUE

WE begin with first things first: "What is the issue?" And "What is the cause and the effect?" From the foundation of the world, the issue has been what the person of God saw as a need when He said, *"I will put enmity between thee and the woman, and between thy seed and her seed"* (Genesis 3:15). That enmity keeps us aware of the fact that there is a war going on, and that it's a war between good and evil. Scripture calls it spiritual warfare (Ephesians 6:12), and again, I have no reason to put a question mark where God has put a period.

The fact of the matter is that it may be necessary to institute an awareness program that will insure that the people of God take spiritual warfare seriously. I have said it before and I am saying it again: there is a war going on. It is a war that's being fought between the children of the light and the children of darkness.

On the one hand, the children of the light—albeit unknowingly—would be protected by the Holy Spirit under the direction of the Christ—whose human name is Jesus—if they so choose. On the other hand, the children of darkness are under the direction of Satan, the arch-enemy of God. From the beginning, Satan came specifically to steal the joy of God's people, to kill their spirits, and to influence each of them to the point of self-destruction. Relationship is established by blood; and Satan's plan is for them to reject the shedding of the blood of Jesus as payment for their sin. The penalty paid by Jesus enables each of us to re-establish our relationship with God through Christ Jesus. Jesus came specifically to ensure that the children of the light have access to life and that they have it more abundantly (John 10:10b).

PRESENTATION

AS of this writing there is sufficient proof that the people of God are not aware of the war that's being waged between Satan and God. As a matter of fact, God's people are not aware of the person of Satan, his presence and his acquired power. To put it bluntly, their knowledge of him is seriously flawed or altogether lacking. Some say I am wrong, but I don't think so. From that day in the Garden when Adam chose to rebel against God, man's knowledge-bank has been overdrawn. Unknowingly, he has been writing checks on an account that will always come back stamped NSF. And, unless and until "He repents and is baptized 'in the name of Jesus Christ' (Acts 2:38) for the remission of his sins, and "receives the gift of the Holy Spirit", nothing will change.'"

THE Id's of SPIRITUAL WARFARE

LET'S look closely, for example, at a person who is addicted to a controlled substance—and it really doesn't matter which one— the addiction itself is a problem; but that which propelled him to experiment with that drug is a bigger problem. That addiction is evidence of the war that's being fought.

The addict can enter a rehab program to kick the habit, and he might be successful. However, unless and until he becomes engaged in some close-order introspection which allows him to discover the weakness in his spiritual fabric which created the desire for that drug, he is still left with the primary causality.

Let's try another example. Look with me at a person, who inwardly feels that another person is better in some way than he is, or can perform a task better than he can because God made him better; that's a sure sign that he feels inferior to the other person. It is that skill—and the **fear** and **insecurity** which accompanies it—which grips his heart. As a result, he (or she) is left to not only feel insecure, but to live with the idea that the other person is better than he is.

Paul's proclamation to the Church at Philippi—although presented in a different context—sought to reassure them—and us—that we can *do all things through Christ which strengthens us' (*4:13). Nevertheless, rather than think, face the truth and make the necessary adjustments to bring him or herself up to par, spiritually; he covertly slips into denial with insecurity functioning as the driving the wheel.

From that point onward in his life, his **self-perception**—what he thinks of himself—becomes controlled by his **self-esteem**— what he thinks others think of him. He no longer sees himself as "the image of God." Fear and insecurity have set in and because of his newly-adopted attitudes and actions, his circle of family and friends—while looking at him through a glass darkly (1 Corinthians 13:12, KJV)—will actually join in and "help him" to see himself as someone with a handicap.

On a personal note and for many years I fought that same battle: and I spent "a ton of money" endeavoring to buy my acceptance into a desired social network. It wasn't until the Spirit of God (SOG) caused me to discover that my mother had inadvertently and more than adequately, prepared the soil in me for the "planting of the seed" in my life. And when I discovered the meaning of Paul's declaration in 1 Corinthians 3:6, that "One would plant, another would water; but God would grant the increase, in His own time" I was simply amazed.

My mother made the decision to prepare the soil in me by keeping me isolated during my adolescent years, and propping open the door of my heart by restricting my reading to the KJV of the Bible and the Sears and Roebuck Catalog for more than 5 years. And even though I wasn't aware of what the outcome of her actions would be, the end result was the Lordship and the leadership of the Holy Spirit was the only option that I had as a young child.

Unknowingly, Solomon's Proverb in 22:6 had kicked in and kept her fixed and focused. Stated another way, the "SOG" directed the course of human events in my life until I returned to the state of California at the age of thirty-two. That was when I consciously met the Lord Jesus for myself, and verbally accepted Him as Lord of this life and Savior in the life to come (Proverbs 18:21). That was the end of the first beginning, and the beginning of the second end.

THE NEW BEGINNING

IT was in California on the day after my thirty-fifth 35th birthday that I said yes to the Lord and was cognitively re-connected with the purpose of God for my life. I joined a local church as a candidate for baptism, and under the leadership of the pastor "I began to work out my salvation with fear and trembling" (Ephesians 6:5). It was then that I also began a systematic study of the scriptures for myself, which enabled me to begin exchanging tradition for truth. It was then that I realized that the SOG was fighting my battle. It was also then that I realized that my thoughts were higher than those of my circle of family and friends. That realization caused me to enter into the counsel of God (Isaiah 1:18) and reason with Him.

For instance, looking back through my mind's eye I calculated that even as I now write, I have not had a tension-producing headache in nearly forty-five years. Why is that? You might ask. Am I exempt from the myriad of tensions which cause headaches? The answer is a "Resounding No." Although I was not always conscious of it, the truth is, the SOG has had the leadership role in my life for nearly than forty years.

Frankly speaking, early on I didn't have much of a choice. My mother saw to that. I was rooted and grounded in the "Old School" motif from the beginning. Both, she and my maternal grandfather had a rule: "You do as I say do, or else." None of the children— either in her generation or mine—were brave enough to challenge him (or her), or investigate the "or else." I passed that rule on to my six children, and as I look back today, my oldest son was the first to say that "I am certifiably insane" because my attitudes and actions didn't fluctuate, even with the generational changes.

1975

Let me share an example of a story that comes under the heading of spiritual warfare. It was a case of what to do when you don't know what to do. I don't believe I am abusive, but I had occasion to resort to physical punishment with my oldest son when he was fourteen. I had the opportunity to extract the words of Scripture in **'Proverbs 22:15'** which said,

> *"Foolishness is bound in the heart of a child; but the rod of correction shall drive it far from him."*

I *used that rod on that day to straighten out some crooked places in his life."* His mother had come home early from work one day and found him in bed with an older woman (age 34) smoking a marijuana cigarette. As the story goes, the woman was supplying him with weed to sell to his friends at school, and sex was her incentive to play the game. His mother sent for me to have a talk with him the next morning.

After sharing with me the context leading up to the content of the story, my conclusion was I needed to "get to the seat of the problem." He awakened when I entered his bedroom. And when I removed my belt, he made the mistake of getting up and raising his hands to me with one of his martial arts weapons in them. Without a word of warning I endeavored to purposely knock him out; but succeeded only in swelling his eye. When he had sufficiently recovered, he threatened to call the police; to which I replied, "Son, now I know you have lost your mind," as I reached for the telephone.

In the spur of the moment he had forgotten that I carried a badge and a gun as a member of the Reserve Police Force. While his mother applied an ice pack to the swelling, I dialed the telephone for him. The police came and I explained what and why I did what I had done. To those officers I made it clear that I believed that if I didn't straighten him out at home, with his attitude like it was, they—the police—would kill him in the streets.

After questioning his mother and verifying what I had told them, they concluded that not only were both his mother and I in total agreement, but that I was the head of my house and definitely in charge. The lead officer responded, "Man, handle your business" and exited our home. It wasn't a hard sell. It was a matter of resistance to Satan on my part, and as the word says, 'he took flight' (James 4:7).

DOING THE RIGHT THING, THE RIGHT WAY

I BELIEVE in doing the three things that my grandfather and my mother said was a man's responsibility. Papa said, "Son, it is your responsibility to 'provide, protect and pray' for your family; and when it comes to your children, if the Bible says it, you not only have the right, you have an obligation to apprehend and activate it" (Proverbs 22:6; 23:12-13). And although my son's mother and I were separated, I had set those standards for the inhabitants of my house when we were together. Without any fear of civil law I made it their responsibility to live up to them. I was heralded as the head of my house; and that did not include being a friend to any of my children. I was friendly but not their friend.

I believe God has a purpose for every child that He allows to be born into this world. That includes every child being endowed with the attributes that come with the nature of God before the fall. Those attributes are inherently instilled in every child, and they equate to "the image of God." Paul validated this in Romans 2:11, making it clear that every opportunity is given to every person, equally. He (or she) makes the choice to accept or reject those opportunities.

Because God does not change (Malachi 3:6), each person makes all of his own choices; after which the rewards or consequences for his choices are factored in. At the end of the day the outcome of those choices are re-connected and inserted in the purposeful-will of God. That's the short version of a much-longer story; but I believe the point has been made. It's all a matter of choice. And for the benefit of those who still might be confused, Paul makes it plain in Ephesians 6:12ff.

CHAPTER SIXTEEN

The Superiority of Christ

PROLOGUE

FAST—forwarding to the New Testament and combining the next two questions, we are going to put down anchor in an epistle entitled *"To the Hebrews."* The author is unknown so for our purpose we will simply say, "To the writer of the Hebrews." Beginning with Chapter 6 Verse 1, the NKJV reads:

> *THEREFORE leaving the discussion of the elementary principles of Christ, let us go on to perfection, not laying again the foundation of repentance from dead works and of faith toward God, of the doctrine of baptisms, of laying on of hands, of resurrection of the dead, and of eternal judgment"*

There is an old adage which reads, "All you can do with the past is rehearse it or release it." The pre-supposition there is that as a serious Bible student, the reader no longer desires to bathe in the innocence of ignorance, while continuing to rehearse what has already happened. Therefore, as we begin to ascend the spiritual ladder of success, we will release the past, because rehearsing it has become passé.

By saying that, we are not minimizing the importance of Bible history; we are simply moving on up a little higher in our attitudes and actions, growth and development. That said only if you are ready to move forward and access the abundant life of which Jesus spoke in John 10:10b, will you get the most out of this journey. While taking our traditional Christian practices to the next level, we are agreeing to accept the word of God verbatim and without exception. And for the record, the next level—contrary to the more popular opinion which encourages us to do otherwise—encourages critical thinking and requires all participants-in-the-process to be prepared to study the Bible, as opposed to being satisfied with merely reading it every now and then, and memorizing some of the pivotal Scriptures.

Admittedly, this has not been the focus of the organized Church until now, but I have been given to believe that *"the time is fulfilled, the Kingdom of God is at hand, [and it's time for the people of God to] repent and believe the Gospel" (Mark 1:15).* I have become convinced and convicted that "I am being groomed to be a lasting part of a superficial-diversity-quota that, together with the others who will catch the vision, and who will work to re-establish their Relationship with God—which comes by blood—and who will be inspired to speak and write and take this message around the world.

The start-up for me will be part of the infrastructure of a designated campus—Bethel AME Church, Rising, here in Birmingham, AL. *Entering* is but one medium and I am only one person who will rise to the level of need, and plant a seed or water one that has already been planted. In either case, God will grant the increase" (1 Corinthians 3:6) in His own time.

PRESENTATION

RELATIONSHIPS come by blood and Fellowships by consent. The price Jesus paid gave mankind access: now he can re-establish a binding relationship with God. To accept that gift (John 3:16) is a matter of choice. I have said it before and I'll say it again: this book was not written for the purpose of validating anything that any man (or woman) already knows—although it can and no doubt will—but rather it was written to help him to discover and connect what he does not know. The answers to "What, in this world, the Church is supposed to be? "Where did we go wrong? And "How do we get back on track?" are the unknown and the focus of this section. We begin with a comparison between the old and the new.

The Old Testament informs us of God's Law. Obedience to those laws was a sign of living right—doing the right thing, the right way. The New Testament is the New Covenant between God and man. It introduces Jesus, who is the Christ, and it demonstrates His superiority. For example, in John 10:10 Jesus removed all of the guess work out of 'what, in this world the Church is supposed to be' when He said,

> *"The thief cometh not but for to steal, kill, and destroy.*
> *I am come that they might have life, and that they*
> *might have it more abundantly."*

That verse of Scripture, by comparing and contrasting his declaration and using the process of elimination, tells us that "In this world, the Church is to be the bridge over troubled waters between a broken Relationship with God, caused by rebellion; and the re-establishment of a positive, productive, progressive Relationship with God in Christ, based on apprehension and adherence to the DOA in this world. Handling 'first things first' is the key to success.

I keep saying it because I believe it. The first thing is to teach the people. Personally, I believe "People would do better if they knew better." I also believe that it is my task as a divinely-designated 21st Century Prophetic Voice to the Nations, to shout loud and spare not. And since I have concluded that my role and function is to get the word out, I believe God has given me a special role to play. My role includes, but is not limited to alerting the people of God of the existence of a commonly over-looked "basket full of blessings" (1 Corinthians 2:9)—as it were—that are hidden in plain sight, and have been there all the time. We know what's wrong, how do we fix it? That is the question. The answer lies in knowing Christ and making Him known.

CREATION AND CORRUPTION

IN the interest of spiritual justice, we—the Holy Spirit speaking to me and through me—will delineate the most salient of all issues. Because God does not change (Malachi 3:6), and with God there is no respect of person (Romans 2:11), what He said one time to one person in one place was meant for all time and for all people, everywhere. The literal portrait of the creation epic which follows covers three time-frames: **yesterday,** which is the past; **today,** which is the present; and **tomorrow,** which is the future.

How is that possible? Someone asked. Are you going to tell the future? That same person asked. The answers to both questions are a resounding no; but there are reasonable explanations which will satisfy both inquiries. The person of God said *"He would supply all our need according to His riches in glory through Christ Jesus" (Philippians 4:19).* The context is different, but the confirmation still holds. Because of His Omniscience, His Omnipotence, and His Omnipresence, the voice of God was enabling us to say with certainty that "He would take care of all of our tomorrows, today; and He would do it in His yesterday."

YESTERDAY WHILE this story has been told many times, by many different people, and it has been written and re-written by a number of revisionists in several different translations of the Bible, I believe I would be remiss if I did not include a summary herein out of my personal prayer book, for the benefit of those who have not heard or read it for themselves. As noted at the outset, unless stated otherwise, all Scripture references are from the King James Version (KJV). For clarity and conciseness in language usage, however, there are times when I will defer to the NKJV or the New International Version.

In all cases the Bible sets the standard which highlights the mark of excellence in the mind of God, and we either hit the bulls-eye or we miss the mark, it's a matter of choice. There is "no in-between," and "almost" doesn't count. That would be like the man who said, "I didn't lie, I just didn't tell you the whole story." Whether or not one agrees, "a half truth" is still "a whole lie."

INSPIRATION > MOTIVATION

ALL of us from time to time, can use a massive injection of cognitive inspiration as we wrestle with the throes of daily living. And because inspiration comes from the outside which leads to motivation—which comes from the inside—there are times when we seek out those who seem to be successful, and use them to offer a word of inspiration or to jump-start our motivation. Beginning with a word of assurance on the answer to the question, "Who is God in and of Himself?" It is the intent of this writer to enable the reader to dot all the "i's", cross all of the "t's" and fill in the blanks that will make certainty out of doubt, and add faith where there is currently fear in his life.

It is this writer's opinion that not enough is known about who God is, what He is in each of us, and who we are in Him. Therefore, not nearly enough has been said on the subject or taught in the organized church. To that end, *Entering* will seek to enlighten, enhance, and encourage the reader to apprehend and adhere to every word that proceeds out of the mouth of God" (Matthew 4:1), and use it to grow and go from good (Genesis 1:31) to great (1 Corinthians 2:9).

Simply stated, Satan deceived Eve by telling her part of what God said (Genesis 3:1ff). His half-truth—which amounted to a whole lie—started her to thinking. Her decision to use her free-will and think for herself, instead of adhering to what God had already said, opened the door for Satan's two oldest boys—"the twin-spirits of Doubt and Denial"—who were waiting in the wings; and who used that opportunity to take up residence in her mind and subsequently in her heart.

As Eve listened to Satan—even though it is not stated in Scripture—her actions depicted doubt about what God had said. And as she dialogued with Satan, he managed to convince her that God had held something back in the creation epic. Genesis 3:6 reads:

> *"So when the woman saw that the tree was good for food, that it was pleasant to the eyes, and a tree desirable to make one wise, she took of its fruit and ate."*

All of what she saw added up to Eve second-guessing God, and denying the validity of God's word, concerning the provisions that God had made for both of them in Chapter 1 Verse 29. Suffice it to say, when she began to use her free-will and think for herself in opposition to God, everything went down-hill.

Adam—the other half of the parent-equation—said in Genesis 3:10,

> *"I heard Your voice in the garden, and I was afraid, because I was naked; and I hid myself."*

Adam was besieged with fear because he knew he had been disobedient. Take note of the consequences which followed and the order in which they were distributed, starting in Chapter 3, verse 14.

First, God punished the serpent for his part in Satan's plan; that is to say, as a member of the animal kingdom, for allowing Satan to take up residence in him. Then God turned His attention to Satan who had embodied the serpent to carry out his diabolical plan. Next He punished Eve for her part in Satan's plan (v.16) even though she too was a member of the animal kingdom. And last but not least, He punished Adam: "not for eating of the fruit" (Genesis 3:6), but for listening to the voice of his wife (v. 17), and ultimately thinking and acting in opposition to the first Command of God. "Adam's decision to be disobedient came on the heels of choosing not to hear the word of God, but to listen to someone else."

Because the spiritual Relationship had been broken, God did the only thing He could do. Scripture says,

> *"God made coats of skin, and clothed them"* (Genesis 3:21ff.). Then God said, *"Behold the man is become as one of us, to know good and evil; and now, lest he put forth his hand and take also of the tree of life, and eat, and live forever: therefore the Lord God sent him forth from the garden of Eden, to till the ground from whence he was taken. So he drove out the man and placed at the east of the garden of Eden Cherubim and a flaming sword which turned every way, to keep the way of the tree of life"* (Genesis 3:22-23).

For failing to hear, to apprehend and adhere to the word of God, Sin is now alive and well in the world making Salvation a requirement in order to have life, and have it more abundantly.

TODAY

SCRIPTURE says Salvation comes by Faith through Grace (Ephesians 2:8), and that there is a natural progression which follows. The apostle Paul informs us that Faith comes by hearing, and hearing by the word of God. But that's not how the story ends. Several questions are raised: "How shall they hear without a preacher?" "And how shall they preach except they are sent?" The conclusion of the matter is, the people cannot hear without a preacher, and a preacher is not preaching without the Bible. Why is that? I was asked. Simply stated, when defined, "Preaching is the manifestation of the Incarnate Word, by the spoken word, from the written word." Therefore, both, the preacher and the Bible are a must. The Bible informs us that:

> *God gave some apostles; some prophets; some evangelists; and some pastors and teachers; for the perfecting of the saints for the work of the ministry, for the edifying of the body of Christ.*

That said it is necessary to hear one of these gifted persons in order to grow in grace. The problem we have is, when it comes to perfecting the saints, many, if not most of these individuals today, are stumped, stymied, and stagnated. Stated another way, our Christian leaders have missed the mark. The majority of them are satisfied with perpetuating the status quo.

Close observation will reveal that the majority of the membership—in all of our churches—are satisfied with bathing in the innocence of ignorance rather than studying to show themselves approved by God. As a result, they are forced to join the 'pastor-said-syndrome.' When the need arises, they can be heard saying, "I don't know, but the pastor said." It was on that premise that the voice of God sent the word through the prophecy of Hosea in 4:6 saying:

> *"My people are destroyed for lack of knowledge:*
> *because the priests have rejected knowledge, the voice*
> *of God said He will reject them.*

When that prophecy was dispatched, it covered problems that were prevailing between 753 B.C. and 715 B.C.—approximately 2800 years ago. Close observation will also reveal that it is just as prevalent today in 2013, and the causality is still the same. As a result of listening **at** the word of God, rather than listening **to** the word of God, the people of God have made little or no progress. What is the real problem? I was asked. The real problem is ignorance and apathy.

Having failed to utilize the spirit of a sound mind with which they were endowed, they would rather play the 'blame-game,' which is an integral part of 'the pastor said syndrome.'

TOMORROW

THAT portion of the question could easily be answered by saying that "Today is that tomorrow you talked about yesterday." But someone would say, "If that is the case, tomorrow will never come. Besides, that would be too simplistic and the Bible might not support it." So I went in search for an answer that would be both, acceptable and workable. What follows is a statement of the problem.

A STATEMENT OF THE PROBLEM

TO avoid the appearance of conflict before embarking on this journey, I paused long enough to define, delineate and publish an abridged 'Statement of the problem,' followed by a 'Definition of the problem' and a preview of the 'Solution to the problem.' The problem—as I perceive it—is rampant in the Christian community, as well as in numerous other faith-entities, regardless of their names or their denominational polities. That makes it a problem of un-paralleled proportions.

Even though I believe there is general agreement that people would do better if they knew better, this problem transcends ignorance, embraces 'actuality' over 'reality,' pre-supposes and postulates that in order to resolve the conflict and be redeemed, "There is a need for everyone to begin by calling a spade a spade and sin by its right name." That first step will allow an exchange between tradition and truth to take place. If the solemn truth is told, this problem emanated out of rejection: Adam first rejected the word of God. With Adam, fear replaced faith (Genesis 3:6); and with Eve, the "disease-of-deception" gave rise and residence to the twin-spirits of Doubt and Denial; distorting the image of God in which she had been created. And subsequently, mistrust and disbelief—in that order—took precedence over the ability to do justly, love mercy, and walk humbly with our God (Micah 6:8). Collectively, those diseases of the mind, over an extended period of time, have led to un-restrained unbelief. In the simplest of terms, the preponderance of this problem was perpetrated by Satan, the arch-enemy of God. The enemy successfully used the disease of deception to neutralize the Spirits of power and of love, and of a sound mind in the first family. And to this day Satan is still at work; and he continues to steal, kill, and destroy (John 10:10a).

Whatever else we might think, stealing, killing, and destroying are the sum-total of what Satan is all about. Those three facets embody the plan he has for all of us—both Christian and non-Christian. Unlike God, Satan is not a triune being. He exists by using thoughts, ideas, and suggestions (TIS's). Stated succinctly, Satan is not a person, he is a spirit. He has no power in and of himself; and his presence lives only in the minds of men in whom he manages to deposit his TIS's. He uses each of us as his source of power. Jesus made it clear that Satan had but the one reason for coming to the earth (John 10:10a).

And if I may personalize this part of the presentation, clarity will replace confusion and it will make it easier for you, the reader, to see how he operates. Satan came to steal my joy, kill my spirit, and use TIS's to influence me. His intent is to catch me off guard

151

and persuade me to reject the word of God, eat from the tree of good and evil; and subsequently from the tree of life, thereby destroying my relationship with God.

How do I know that is true? James 4:7 states that God has given us more in the way of grace to sustain us. That's why James said, submit yourselves therefore to God. Resist the devil, and he will flee from you. (Note) The reader should substitute his or her name for my name in this statement.

My pronouncement of this predicament and the pain that emanates there-from comprises a very general statement which leads to a very serious indictment. I am acutely aware of that. And not only am I aware of it, I'm also very much aware of the danger that's present in generalizing. However, I also believe that I am on safe ground when I say that this indictment is not meant to be a negative criticism or put-down, but rather the sum-total of a series of facts.

Suffice it to say, when used in the proper context, these facts become un-adulterated truth. My aim is to simply call a spade a spade, sin by its right name and let the chips fall where they may. Again I say, traditional Christianity has a problem; and it's one of un-paralleled proportions. The voice of God said ***"My people are destroyed because of a lack of knowledge"*** **(Hosea 4:6);** but that is the beginning, not the end.

The entire meaning of the message of the prophet goes much, much deeper, for there is also a meaning **behind** the message. In the "b" portion of that verse, Hosea—whose name in Hebrew means "Salvation"—was attacking the problem at the root. When looked at in the proper context, the truth of Hosea's message was that in the eyes of God, the priests and the religious leaders— whom God held accountable—were the source of the people's dilemma. In the simplest of terms, the religious leaders had strayed from the Laws of God. And regardless of the reason why, they had done evil for so long, to them evil looked like good. And subsequently, because of the ignorance of the leaders, the people were being led in the wrong direction.

That prophecy was recorded in the 8th century, B.C. The perfect plan of God sent me as a 21st Century Prophetic Voice to the Nations with a message to His people fourteen hundred years later.

The message is still the same: the leaders rejected knowledge then, and seemingly, they are rejecting it today. My question is, "Do they really know better?" Is this simply a case of fear over-shadowing faith, or is it as Hosea has proclaimed? One of the aims of this work is to insert a measure of certainty sufficient to remove any doubt.

Social Sciences teach that "It's never a good policy to blame the victim for his (or her) own victimization, because there is always an under-lying cause which generates the effect, and with which the victim has little or no control." After giving it some thought I came to the conclusion that the problem in the Christian community today exists primarily because of ignorance and apathy. But why is that so in a country so deeply rooted in the Christian ethos? In my effort to speak truth and hold everybody accountable, I conducted several surveys in several churches, with the intent of obtaining a consensus of what might be the answer to the problem, as perceived by the people.

All of the surveys concluded that, "Deeply rooted in religious tradition that has eclipsed the truth, the Church-of-God has largely become stumped, stymied, and stagnated." We know that people learn differently, but in the Church-of-God on their Sabbath, information takes second chair to entertainment as it comes across the pulpit. That method of delivery allows Satan to have a field-day each week. And much to my chagrin, there seems to be a deep and abiding reluctance among church leaders to speak ill of the enemy. It's almost as if fear has taken precedence over faith, promoting a general reservation about speaking up and speaking out against the powers and the rulers of the darkness of this world, that have taken up residence in the hearts of pastors, preachers and priests. As a result, Satan and all of his henchmen are wreaking havoc in the hearts and minds of the people of God. That is the problem.

A DEFINITION OF THE PROBLEM

IT has been said that "If you tell one lie, you have to tell another one to cover that one up, and another one to cover that one up, and another one to cover that-one up . . ." and the list goes on. Assuming that adage—a short proverb—to also be an axiom, which is a self-evident or universally recognized truth; the crux of the problem with which we are dealing is that those original lies gave rise to unbelief; and over time that unbelief evolved into long-held religious traditions. And those religious traditions have eclipsed truth and permeated the organized Church today.

One of the saddest refrains that can be heard coming from on the inside of the organized Church, is "I didn't know." The people of God claim to love God, but demonstrate an inherent powerlessness when it comes to keeping His Commandments (John 14:24). There is something wrong with that picture, and I have lived long enough to learn that in everything, there is a cause and effect, a cost and a benefit.

THE CAUSE AND THE EFFECT

I LOOKED at the situation and I prayed, asking God the Father for divine intervention. The Spirit of God (SOG) brought to my remembrance God's principles and His promises, His purpose and His plan, (John 14:26). But the SOG didn't stop there. He also opened my eyes so that I could see what was happening with the people of God, as it relates to His purposeful will.

What I saw was a tri-fold problem. First of all I saw the failure to truly repent, which gave rise to the second: the existence of perpetual sin. Thirdly, I saw a religious system where tradition is perpetuated and allowed to eclipse divine truth. All three of these were brought on by what I perceive to be a serious lack of biblical knowledge on the part of religious leaders, compounded by fear and insecurity, doubt and denial.

With their pastor's permission, I talked to the sisters in the Women's Missionary Society (WMS) of the African Methodist Episcopal Church (AMEC), and the brothers on the Deacon's Board of two mainline Baptist Churches in the city. To both groups I asked some very pointed questions, and what follows is a summary of what I learned. Taking it from the top, I first asked if they were sure of their Salvation, and if so, how did they know? After dividing them into groups to collaborate on their answers, a group-appointed spokes-person answered for each group.

I recorded what I heard, and had it transcribed, verbatim. The spokespersons said, "It was a long time ago, but we all remember wanting to be saved; so we came to Church, sat through the service and pretty much followed directions. At invitation time—when the doors of the church were opened—all of us went down front, joined the Church of our choice as candidates for baptism. We were taken in as members and told that after we were baptized we would be given 'The right hand of fellowship' which would give us all the rights and privileges of any other member. There was a slight variation between the Methodist sisters and the Baptist brethren, which included having to have their request presented to the church for the Baptist and to the Quarterly Conference for the Methodist. After that, all of them were baptized.

They continued, saying, "When we had been baptized, we attended several weeks of new member orientation classes." The time varied in both denominations. However, at the conclusion of the classes, we were told that we could now respond positively to the first of the four spiritual laws: *"If you die tonight, are you certain that you will go to heaven?"* The brother who was teaching the classes in the Baptist Church told them, "Now you are saved." I was worried for a while, said one brother, because I had done some pretty mean things. But I was assured that I will go to heaven when I die no matter what, and I wasn't to worry about what I had done, because "my sins had been forgiven." Another brother added that "later his pastor told all of them that even if they should sin, God is going to forgive them because once saved always saved."

I asked this deacon—who was the chairman of the board in his Church—if he thought everybody felt the same, and he stated that "All of the members of our church are saved. Our Pastor taught us the meaning of Romans 10:9: *'If you will confess with your mouth the Lord Jesus, and believe in your heart that God has raised Him from the dead, you shall be saved;'* and as a man of God, we know that he knows.'" The Deacon concluded by saying that all of us on the Board have been trained, and we believe that will get us into heaven. And like the sisters said, "that's really all that matters." One question remains unanswered: "Is that all that matters?"

CHAPTER SEVENTEEN

Salvation: The Procedural Process

PROLOGUE

WITHOUT any malice or forethought, I knew that my next move—in dealing with "first things first"—would call for a written response to the pastors of these people, with a request to let me schedule a workshop on the procedural process that's embedded in God's plan of Salvation—with him (or her) in mandatory attendance. What I had just witnessed was what I call 'an example of ignorance in perpetuity.' I mean no spiritual harm to anybody, but that denominational polity has been present in almost all organized churches for one-hundred and forty-seven years (from 1865 – 2012). And what I believe is sorely needed is what I will call "Systematic Christian Education." Those members needed to be taught so that they can progress in their spiritual growth and development. But my first hurdle would be the pulpit.

PRESENTATION

BECAUSE I subscribe to the theory which says "You don't blame the victim for their own victimization," I thanked both groups for their participation and contribution, and asked them to be on the lookout for my "follow-up" conferences. I then went to work drafting a written response to be shared with the pastors of all three groups. In the draft I stated that we have a problem in the Church, and it's one of unparalleled proportions. That's where I ran into trouble. The problem is with what hasn't been taught, and the unwillingness of the pastors to have their resource banks enhanced. My only recourse was to place all of that information in this book, and let God grant the increase in His own time.

What's missing is the full disclosure of the full complement of Salvation—that is to say, "Salvation in all three stages." The first stage is as those deacons had shared: those members **were saved** but it was only from the "**penalty** of sin" (Genesis 2:17). The second stage is 'to be saved' from the **power** of sin' (2 Timothy 2:15 and Zechariah 4:6). That stage is very important because it will take each participant the rest of his (or her) natural life to overcome. The third stage is **"being saved** from the **presence** of sin (1 Corinthians 13:12),—which is the act of total reconciliation.

Four times the Bible records Jesus coming into Galilee preaching after John the Baptist was jailed (Matthew 4:12; Mark 1:15; Luke 4:14; and John 4:43); but only one time in Mark 1:15 did He say, *"The time is fulfilled"* before announcing that *"the Kingdom of God is at hand"* and that it was time for his hearers to *"repent"* and believe in the gospel."* He said that one time to one person (John Mark), in one place, but His words were timeless and limitless. Mark wrote his gospel approximately nineteen-hundred and thirty-five years ago. The sin of unbelief was rampant then, and it still ranks highest on the list of self-destructive devices used by Satan today to steal, kill, and destroy.

Recently while studying, the SOG spoke these words into my spirit. He said, "Carter, "Now is the time." I re-read that Scripture and perceived Jesus to have meant that Satan's time had run out. God's permissive will had allowed the truth to be eclipsed because of the decisions made by each person. In other words, the choices made in ignorance had controlled the attitudes and actions of the people of God, long enough. It was time for God's people—more especially those which are called by His name (2 Chronicles 7:14), to repent and believe in the gospel; beginning in the pulpit and ending at the farthest pew.

THE SOLUTION TO THE PROBLEM

HAVING no desire to cast blame unfairly, or to deal with the issue of "why" as it relates to anyone in particular, in *Entering* I propose to simply post the lies that were told which created this problem, and then either plant or water the seeds of "the solution to the problem" in the minds of those who have an ear to hear what the Spirit is saying to the Churches. In so doing I will trust and believe that God will grant the increase in His own time (1 Corinthians 3:6).

Beginning at the point of embarkation and moving forward, the solution to the problem is really rather simple. There are several steps in the process. But because Jesus has already paid the penalty for Sin, once and for all time; the only thing remaining is for mankind to make a decisive-decision to accept God's solution to the problem and exchange tradition or truth, beginning with true repentance.

We are saying that the solution is simple because we believe that Jesus tied up all the loose ends when He uttered the sixth saying from the cross: "It is finished." However, in the minds and hearts of most church leaders, the procedural-process that's embedded in God's plan of Salvation, is still a virtual unknown. That bit of information has seemingly evaded the leaders of the organized church; and as a result the tradition which has eclipsed truth brought with it the fear that has replaced faith. In addition, Doubt and Denial have replaced certainty and commitment to the cause of Christ.

Therefore, for most people repentance is superficial at best. That is the problem. Petitioning the Holy Spirit to fall fresh on individual believers is the first step of the process, and the solution to the problem. What I had not considered was that I would need to lead by example. In other words, the SOG would need to first make me usable, and then make me an example for the people to follow.

Peter declared the solution to the problem on the day of Pentecost, in Acts 2:38. He wrote,

> ***"Repent, and be baptized every one of you in the name of Jesus Christ for the remission of sins; and you shall receive the gift of the Holy Spirit."***

However, the failure of pastors and Church leaders to teach the full meaning of Zechariah's message in 4:6, has left the door open wide enough for Satan to slip into their services, blind the eyes of those in attendance, and fix it so that the first step was distorted, but not destroyed. And without the Lordship and the leadership of the Holy Spirit, the people continue to follow the traditional path.

What the voice of God said to king Zerubbabel through the prophet Zechariah—and to anyone in a position of power—must not be over looked or understated. When a Church or Community leader discovers that God's perpetual Principle in Zechariah 4:6 has been overlooked, it is incumbent upon him (or her) to revisit the Scripture, embrace it, restate it and model it to the people with precision and power. It must be made clear that It is not by any perceived power that we might have, or by the leverage that comes with an acquired position. Instead, it is by the Spirit of God says the Lord of hosts.

An integral part of the problem is caused by the people of God having chosen to live life oblivious to, and void of the superintending Spirit of God. As a result, the presence of the Spirit of God is held hostage, because He cannot transgress their free-will, not even to "keep them from falling" (Jude 24).

That was the solution more than seven hundred years before Jesus was born, and the prophecy was carried out by him in His death, burial and resurrection, nearly two-thousand years ago. That is the same solution being recommended today. A word of caution is included for those who will take what they are reading here too lightly, or speak in opposition to it. First of all, it needs to be said that they have every right to do that. However, my experiences, exposure and the voice of God speaking to me and through me after more than thirty-five years of practicing preaching presents the truth, the whole truth, and nothing but the truth.

It has been revealed that any way you slice it or dice it, the Church still has a serious problem, and the end is still the same: **"God's people are still being destroyed for lack of knowledge" (Hosea 4:6).** That lack of knowledge and perpetual biblical-ignorance is the cause and effect of systematic, spiritual self-destruction. And not only that, it will evolve into physical deprivation and denial of the abundant life to which Jesus alluded in John 10:10b. I believe that missing element comprises both, the spiritual and the practical dimensions of life. The challenge in *Entering* is extended to anyone who has the holy boldness to stand up, *"speak truth, love mercy, and walk humbly with our God"* *(Micah 6:8).*

All that all that is required of the reader is to make a decisive-decision to become a participant in the process, and to make this journey from earth's sorrow to heaven's joy, following the dictates of the DOA in this world. In summary, the only antidote to the poison called sin is repentance and obedience to the Laws of God. The voice of God said it in Deuteronomy 6:5; Solomon explained it in Proverbs 3:5-6, Jesus restated it in Matthew 22:37-40, and it's really rather simple if you don't waste your time arguing with its authenticity.

CHAPTER EIGHTEEN

Heaven: God's Already Decided Destiny

THE PROLOGUE

ASK any professing Christian if he or she is certain about their salvation? And no doubt they will say "unequivocally yes;" and if I die tonight, "I am certain that I will get into heaven." Salvation for that person is getting into heaven when this life is over. *Entering* asks and answers the one central question that takes salvation to the next level. Ask that same person "Is there more to Salvation than just getting into heaven?" No doubt he or she would say, "not that I know of." The truth of the matter is, "there is." Oswald Chambers was on point when he said,

One of the dangers of present day teaching is that it makes us take our eyes off Christ and turn them on to ourselves; off the source of our salvation and on to salvation itself. The effect of that is a morbid, hypersensitive life, totally unlike our Lord's life for it has not the passion of abandon that characterized Him. The New Testament never allows for a moment the idea that continues to crop up in our minds and in modern-day teaching: "I have to remember that I am a specimen of what God can do." That view is inspired by Satan, the sultan of sin, never by the Spirit of God. We are not here to be examples of what God can do, but to have our lives so hidden in God, that our Lord's words will be true of us, that *"Men seeing our good works will glorify our Father who is in heaven.*

In this presentation we have argued that there is a procedural process embedded in God's perfect plan of Salvation; one which places getting into heaven at the beginning, and not at the end of a long list of rewards that come with the full complement of salvation. Stated succinctly, simply getting into heaven is the access; but living eternally in the presence of God is Salvation.

Stated another way, the full complement of Salvation is the culmination of the procedural process, and it's in that process that the hidden hope is revealed. What is that hidden hope?

Oswald's chief concern was my greatest challenge while preparing this manuscript: that of being able to stay fixed and focused on the '**Christ** of salvation,' rather than on the '**fact** of salvation,' itself. The enemy is steadfast and immoveable when it comes to catching a believer off guard and keeping him there; and or deceiving him into believing a "half-truth" and using it to steer him in the wrong direction. While writing this book, in addition to persistent prayer it was necessary for me to use pre-set benchmarks to evaluate my progress at strategic times. The participant will also need to make certain that he (or she) stays in right relationship, fixed and focused. Why the emphasis and the urgency? One lady asked. Emphasis is inserted because it is so easy to get off-track. For the most part we are not taught spiritual-warfare as a primary concern. Therefore, believers need to be absolutely certain that they are clear on *who is doing the work.* Scripture says it is the SOG who is busy: binding up the broken-hearted through us, setting at liberty the captives through us, and doing His mighty works through us, and not we ourselves.

We must not allow the enemy to get us off track and deceive us into believing that it is us who are doing a good work. The overall purpose for writing this book is to inspire my readers to become self-motivated, and subsequently become true believers. The next step is to encourage them as believers to 'use the Bible as the rule and guide to their faith and practice in living their lives.' I am acutely aware of the fact that Satan is always on his job. Therefore I cannot say it enough: be very careful. Scripture says,

> *"Be sober. Be vigilant because your adversary the devil, as a roaring lion, walks about seeking whom he may devour"* (1 Peter 5:8).

And that's both, a spiritual and a physical endeavor. Keeping in mind that God works in the heart to purify the mind, while the enemy works in the mind to gain control of your heart; if ever there is doubt about which is which, be reminded that (1) God is

Omniscient: He knows everything. (2) There is no right way to do wrong, and only God can use evil to achieve good. And (3) there is no reason to be afraid because Satan didn't create anything, so he really cannot destroy anything.

GOD FORGIVES, BUT SIN WILL ALWAYS PUNISH

NO doubt both Adam and Eve were forgiven because one of God's properties is mercy and forgiveness. Scripture says He forgave them when *"He made coats of skins and clothed them"* (Genesis 3:21, KJV), transitioning them from "Spirit beings" to full "human beings." He forgave them but He did not cancel the consequence for their disobedience. Their punishment was judicious, not relational. In other words, their Relationship was broken by the sin they had committed, but their kinship—Fellowship—was left intact. They were banished from the garden and as a result of the sin they committed, but not from the family of God. As a result of their sin all of their children and future generations were conceived in sin and shaped in iniquity (Psalm 51:5) but not without a way to re-establish their relationship. We have all been told that the only antidote for Sin— Satan's poison—is Salvation; and that was the promise of God which is recorded in Genesis 3:15. That brings us full-circle, back to where this conversation started. The standard was set, and the plan of God was written in stone.

Deprivation was caused by the lack of an in-depth understanding of what was meant by what was said in Scripture. Deprivation came with deception and through the evolution of sin-practices over the years. Beyond a doubt the organized Church has been deprived and denied. As a result, members of the Church have been allowed to believe that the Principles in Mark 16:15; Acts 2:38, and Romans 10:9 can be circumvented and satisfied by mouthing platitudes.

Stated another way, members believe they can enjoy the promises that come with being saved, simply by answering questions that are asked of them by the preacher, in the affirmative. As a result, they have been lulled into a false sense of security which tells them there is no need to apprehend and adhere to the principles. That, on its face, is unbridled sin. It's unbridled because it continually robs the-people-of-God of the full complement of Salvation, and it robs God of His glory. The outcome is that it keeps us riding this merry-go-round of madness that we call living, engaged in an exercise of futility because no progress can be made. And instead of living the abundant life that God made available through the shed-blood of Jesus, we are constrained to merely exist.

The fact that we say we love the Lord but cannot keep His commandments (John 14: 23-24), ought to send up a red flag, but it doesn't. Add to that the number of Christians who backslide and move from Church to Church out of embarrassment: simply because they are spiritually anemic and too weak to keep God's word; and the number of red flags should increase. And we dare not forget those who are committed to their home-Church and are in attendance regularly, but who, for whatever reason, feel the need to "re-dedicate their lives to Christ" every so often because they feel convicted—which should send up even more red flags—but it doesn't. However, those situations are seldom addressed in the organized church.

THE COST

AS we transition to the 'cost and benefit' of seeking the full complement of Salvation, versus merely being saved by traditional Christian practices, the question is, "Why do we have this dilemma?" There may be many ways to say the same thing, but the shortest distance between two points is still a straight line, and the answer is the same. The reason for our dilemma is wrapped up in the act of "perpetuating the status-quo," instead of growing in the grace of our Lord, Jesus Christ. Stated another way and in point of fact, it is "sin-in-perpetuity." While the solution to the problem is set forth in Scripture, the inability of the Church to solve the problem is largely due to a misunderstanding and/or a deliberate misinterpretation of the concept of sin.

Paul delineated the essence of sin in Chapter 6 Verses 12-13 of Ephesians; and then shot a hole in the hearts of those who fight each other because fear and insecurity in them have not been eradicated. There we read:

> *"For we wrestle not against flesh and blood, but against principalities, against powers, against the rulers of the darkness of this world, against spiritual wickedness in high places." Wherefore take unto you the whole armor of God, that you may be able to withstand in the evil day, and having done all, to stand.*

The problem that prevails would be better defined as spiritual-warfare. In that passage of Scripture Paul is preparing us for becoming engaged in battle—an ongoing battle between "God and Satan." Whether we consciously know him or not, we need to be reminded that Satan is real, and that we need to get to know him. In addition we need to mount an all-out campaign to resist him, for that is the only way to make him leave you alone—even for a moment (James 4:7).

In his proclamation to the Church of God at Ephesus, Paul informs us that the arch-enemy of God is not human. Metaphorically speaking, Jesus called him a thief in John 10:10a, referring to his actions not his identity; and we must be careful not to re-make him into a human-being. In other words, we must not forget that he too is a spirit. That devil—principally because he is a spirit—doesn't own anything. Therefore he is relegated to co-opting that which belongs to someone else. In this case, he is in pursuit of something that belongs to God, and that is God's creation. Let me sum it up for you. Satan's motive is to steal our joy, kill our spirits, and then using TIS's, influence us into entering into the realm of self-destruction, thereby putting us in line to destroy our own relationship with our Heavenly Father. The first lessons to be learned is that we need to take heed to the 2nd Commandment stated by Jesus (Matthew 22:39). Our brothers and our sisters are not our enemies. The enemy is the spirit that they have allowed to invade and control their minds. This spiritual enemy can be found operating in high places, sometimes wielding a tremendous amount of power. He uses that power in a silent, unseen manner. And once we get to know him, we need to learn how to face him in battle. In preparation for this battle, there is both a cost and benefit.

In the simplest of terms, the cost is submission and surrender: Submission to the Sovereignty of God over our lives, and the Lordship and leadership of the Holy Spirit in our lives. The benefit of submission and surrender is the revelation of the full complement of Salvation, while we yet live on this earth. I call it "Revealing the Hidden Hope." It is both, prophesied and promised. Surrender reveals the hidden hope and enables the participant to enter in at the Strait Gate, through the doorway to an already decided destiny. With surrender comes the full complement of Salvation. It is guaranteed but it is not automatic, which is why we must apprehended and adhere to the principle before we can enjoy the promise.

The benefits culminate in accessing the hope that has been there all the time; and they are made possible by the same power that raised Jesus from the dead. In other words, it has already been done. The Son of God hung bled and died on the Cross of Calvary, paying the penalty for the sins of everyone, once and for all time everywhere (Luke 23:44ff); and He was then resurrected for the remission of those sins. His death paid the penalty, His resurrection wiped the slate clean.

Exactly who is this benefactor? What is His name? Looking at Him through Spiritual lenses, Scripture says our benefactor is named *Emmanuel—which being interpreted is, "God with us"* (Matthew 1:23). However, if we look again at this same man through physical lenses, we see a man named Jesus who was called the Christ. Jesus was the [Incarnate] Word who was with God in the beginning and who John, in his prologue, said "Was God." (John 1:1-3, 14).

What must a person do to get these benefits?" That, too, was a question raised by a sister in our Church. The answer is in Peter's response to a similar question, raised by an on-looker on the day of Pentecost. Scripture says the man raised his voice, and speaking for the many he asked,

> *"Men and brethren, what must we do?"* Peter's answer
> is sane and simple. Peter said, *"Repent, and be baptized
> every one of you in the name of Jesus Christ for the
> remission of sins, and you shall receive the gift of the
> Holy Ghost."*

What if I have already done that? The young woman asked. For ease of understanding from this point forward, the participant will need to personalize the process because the plight of all of us is different. The steps are the same, but the sacrifices may be different. All that is required when you hear the word is to receive it and believe it; and you will have access to life through the name—the authority and power—of Jesus.

We must keep in mind however, that understanding is the key. All we have to do is remember that the progenitor of sin is still Satan, and that Satan is still the Arch-enemy of God. I am repeating that because the overwhelming majority of preachers continue to miss the mark, and I believe this is part of the reason. I submit that some preachers may have forgotten, but there is a greater than 50-50 chance that most of them didn't know it in the first place.

That may sound like an indictment of a very large number of preachers and pastors. However, it is not my intent to indict anyone. My job is to produce fruit, not to inspect it. I have been commissioned to write from my experiences and exposure, and everybody knows that "you can't teach what you don't know, and you cannot lead where you can't go." And because it is not readily taught or preached, I perceive the latter to be true. That's another way of saying that this writer once was lost, but now he has been found; he was blind but now he can see.

In writing this book, I am subscribing to the words of Jesus in Mark 1:15:

> *"The time is fulfilled, and the kingdom of God is at
> hand: repent ye, and believe in the gospel."*

So what are we to do and how are we to get our benefits? She Asked. Let me hasten to say that the words are clear. Jesus did

His part and pronounced with a passion that "it is finished" (John 19:30). That leaves the rest up to us, individually and collectively.

THE BENEFITS

JESUS made it clear that His coming was to usher in "Eternal Life" (1 John 5:11-12). Stated another way, the acceptance of Jesus as Lord of this life and Savior in the world to come guarantees us the right of re-entry back into the Garden of God, the privilege of eating from the tree of life on a daily basis, and to live eternally in the presence of God. Jesus came offering mankind a new life, which when translated, includes "life more abundant." Whether or not we choose to accept that gift is predicated on our beliefs and practices.

The trade-name is 'faith' and the only way to know the benefits of trust and belief is to manifest them in our lives. And the only way to manifest them is to know them; and the only way to be certain that you know them is to have an intimate re-established relationship with God-in-Christ, that's based on trust and belief. Stated succinctly, trust and belief are inseparable, and they are bound to our perception of who God is in and of Himself, and what He is in each of us.

THE SIMPLICITY OF SURRENDER

AT the end of the day, God is Salvation and Christ provides the access. Both begin with "True Repentance" as spelled out in 2 Chronicles 7:14. Repentance is not a difficult process, and the steps are rather simple. The problem with which we are faced is two-fold. As a general rule, we don't trust anything or anybody that we don't know. Traditionally speaking, our trust largely depends on what's in it for us, how much time it's going to take, and whether or not we are willing to try something new. As it now stands, we don't believe because we don't trust; and we don't trust because we don't know Him or them in whom we profess to believe. Stated another way, we don't have a clear concept of what it means to trust. Therefore, believing is out of the question.

Again I say, the first steps are submission and surrender. We must submit to the Sovereignty of God over our lives, and surrender to the Lordship and leadership in our lives. In other words, we've got to let go and let God. Translated, we've got to let go of our own way and let God have His way in our hearts and minds, without exception. Simply stated, we must make a decisive—decision to hear the word, receive it and believe it. Whereas our decisions are generally made with the feelings of others in mind, a "decisive—decision" depends only on you. Translated, you've got to trust and believe that God-the-Father is who God-the-Holy-Spirit said God-the-Father is, and that God-the-Father will do what God-the-Holy-Spirit said God-the-Father would do. The use of excessive words is intentional, to set forth clarity and conciseness in the difference between the two persons.

The path to true repentance contains a set of principles which, when completed, will open the door and permit access to the full complement of Salvation. After repenting, the procedure modulates to relationship-building, which comes only by:

> *"studying to show yourself approved unto God as a workman who has no need to be ashamed; rightly dividing the word of truth"* (2 Timothy 2:15).

And it's while you are studying, that the full ramifications of the "Hidden Hope" are revealed. Once you have the access and begin re-building your relationship with God-in-Christ—one that's up-close and personal—the more you know, the more you grow. Suffice it to say, apprehension and adherence to the Divine Order of Authority (DOA)—that is to say, adherence to the written word of God; and obedience to God in all three persons are required in order to fully enjoy the promises of God. Keep in mind that there is a direct correlation between apprehension and adhering and enjoying the promises. There is no substitution and there are no shortcuts. The Bible says exactly what the voice of God meant, and the voice of God meant exactly what the Bible says.

CHAPTER NINETEEN

Continuing in the word

THE PROLOGUE

HAVING examined the prophecy and the promise of Salvation, one must continually embrace his past while living in the present. In other words, he must constantly acknowledge what he did yesterday—to avoid a repeat if his efforts proved to be a failure—while remaining fixed and focused on what he must do today, to consistently remain on target. How is that possible? Some are sure to ask. My reply is very simple. In John 8:32 Jesus said,

> *"If you continue in my word then are you my disciples indeed; and you shall know the truth and the truth shall make you free.*

Look closely and one can see that today is that tomorrow that all of us talked about yesterday; and all we have to do is make certain that what we do today parallels what we expect to see when tomorrow comes. That way of thinking gave rise to part of the title of this book; and the procedural process assists in making it a manifestation. Translated, doing the right thing, the right way enables a participant in the process to enter in at the Strait Gate, through the doorway to an already decided destiny.

THE PRESENTATION

IN his inquiry concerning eternal life, Nicodemus had some very pointed and poignant questions for our Lord (John 3:3-5). Jesus' responses were categorized and positioned to point out the way in which they are often overlooked and taken for granted. Those same questions should be asked and answered by everyone—even those who think they have already arrived. Jesus said to Nicodemus, *"Except a man be born again, he cannot see the Kingdom of God" (3:3).* That message was directed not only to Nicodemus but to all who have a history of following traditional leadership—as did Nicodemus—which was proven to be void of the Spiritual dimension. When asked how this new birth is made possible, Jesus' response both, revealed and concealed. This is the longer version. At the outset let me make it clear that there is an assumption that through apprehension, acceptance, and adherence to the DOA, the participant has re-established his spiritual relationship with God-in-Christ, and has begun his surrender to the Lordship and the leadership with the Holy Spirit. Individuals in this category will have made that decisive-decision to follow the road to repentance that the voice of God declared in 2 Chronicles 7:14. The true road to true repentance will have given him the gift of the Holy Spirit, through which he will have acquired his new mind-set. Then, having been equipped with a new mind-set, the next step is to continue with the edict of Peter in his proclamation to the people on the day of Pentecost (Acts 2:38).

Peter's message went out to everyone in attendance, more especially those who had witnessed the falling of the Holy Spirit on the day. We can be sure of that because of Peter's choice of words:

> *"Repent, and be baptized every one of you in the name of Jesus Christ for the remission of sins, and "you shall receive the gift of the Holy Ghost."*

Peter's message on the day of Pentecost also directed the establishment of 'the Church-of-God-in-Christ'—not to be confused with the contemporary denominational body by the same name. That God-ordained process has been required for membership since the founding of the First-Church on the day of Pentecost. The only exception was Jesus' twelve—including Matthias who had replaced Judas. Suffice it to say, "Include everyone else and exclude no one." Even though the Bible doesn't specifically say it, the use of a sound mind will reveal it: there are three rungs on the ladder leading to the full complement of salvation. Let me make them clear.

Personalizing the process, I believe, will make it even clearer. Today, I can say with certainty that **"I am saved"** from the **penalty** of sin on the profession of my faith; "**I am being saved** from the **power** of sin as I go and grow in the knowledge of the Son of God." And when my time on earth is fulfilled, **"I will be saved** from the **presence** of sin" (1 Corinthians 13:12) when I cross over, and am reconciled. As is self-evident, the process has both, a spiritual and a physical dimension. Therefore, it's not "either/or, it's both/and."

A CLEAR UNDERSTANDING

IN *Entering* I argue that the implementation of both, the spiritual and the physical (or natural) dimensions are necessary. Stated succinctly, we must think on the spiritual level while simultaneously living on the physical or natural plane. A clear understanding of both planes must be internalized and understood in order to enjoy the full complement of Salvation. If the believer desires and expects to enjoy the full complement as stipulated in 1 Corinthians 2:9, he (or she) must embrace both, the spiritual and natural dimensions. Both are equally important and are driven by the believer's attitude, aptitude, and altitude.

As touching the persons' attitude—what he thinks and how he arrives at what he thinks—will govern his success in life, or that lack thereof. Scripture says, *"So God created man in His own image, in the image of God created He him; male and female created He them."* Translated and on the one hand, what a man thinks of himself is what he thinks of God. Similarly, what a man thinks of himself is his 'self-perception; but what he thinks others think of him, governs his self-esteem; which, if not checked, will cause his self-perception to roll up and down like a window shade.

On the other hand, a man's attitude and actions not only manifest his knowledge of who God is, it speaks volumes about 'what God is' in him. For example, we know that God is the source of our being; but the jury is still out on whether or not we know that there is a direct correlation between what we know about God, and what we think and do because of what we know. Let me unpack that suitcase. Let me unpack that suitcase.

I believe there is general agreement that the world knows about God, but I have become convinced that very few of us actually 'know God;' that is to say: that we know God in the sense of having a relationship with Him that's up-close and personal. Relationship is by blood, and the shedding of His blood out on Calvary gives every man access. Once the relationship is re-established, one needs only to center-in on the Nature of God within him. Only God is Omniscient, Omnipotent, and Omnipresent. However a portion of "In His Own Image" (Genesis 1:27) is: Positive, Productive, and Progressive.

Stated succinctly, each of us is in possession of the propensity to think positive, be productive and progressive on a consistent, continuous, and conducive basis. What we choose to do with our possessions is each person's prerogative. If we use our possessions to our advantage, so be it. But if we choose to ignore their collective power, let it be known that the power is still there; and it can still be summoned at will. Since the voice of God says He does not change (Malachi 3:6), we can be sure that He will not rescind them. However, it must be kept in mind that "whatsoever a man sows the same will he also reap.

HEARING THE WORD

FIRST and foremost, the Spirit of God communicated the word of God from on high down to us (Isaiah 55:9). Then, to the extent that we have an ear to hear what the Spirit of God is saying to the Churches, as we study the Scriptures we hear what God wants us to know and do, complete with examples of how things are to be done. At each juncture we exercise our God-given free-will. The choices we make will enable us to receive the information on the physical plane, internalize it and make conscious decisions to respond to it in a positive manner. It is there that the edict of Solomon in Proverbs 3:5-6 should come into play. Pre-supposing that is the direction the reader has chosen to go, what you now have is the spiritual dimension working in concert with and directing the physical dimension, which is the way living our lives should be.

However, if a relationship with God-in-Christ that's up-close and personal, has not been established; that is to say, if you have not accepted God's gift and verbally asked the Spirit of God to come into your heart and take the leadership role in our life (Proverbs 18:21), you will continue to do what you have always done. In other words you will continue on in life following in the footsteps of traditional leadership: winning some battles and losing others, as you struggle to live life void of the positive power of the Spirit of God.

Somewhere it is written that "the Journey of a thousand miles begins with the first step." We prepare now to take the first step on this journey. It is here that the reader will be exposed to the procedural process, line upon line, precept upon precept. It is here that we begin with a period of preparation in which we define and delineate several well-known terms and key concepts that are contained in three pivotal scriptures. It is those three scriptures which point out the principles and the promises related to salvation.

As we approach the target scriptures, keep in mind that in this section the word "spiritual" makes reference to the cognitive realm—what we think—and the word "natural" makes reference to the physical: that which we can see and touch all around us. The target Scriptures are: Mark 16:15-16; Acts 2:38; and Romans 10:9. The operative words in those key terms and concepts are: "Believe;" "Repent;" "Baptize;" "In the Name of Jesus Christ;" and "In my name." These terms are targeted because there is both a spiritual and a natural, dimension that's often overlooked in the traditional teaching of each of them.

For example, simply reading each of them will manifest a literal meaning of the message. However, there is an underlying message inscribed between the lines that ought-not be overlooked. Armed with some good information, the reader will be in a better position to ferret out an in-depth understanding of the plan of salvation, and what it actually means to be delivered.

BRIDGING THE GAP

THIS procedure is being brought to the fore-front to bridge a gap that has been there for hundreds of years. Teaching-preachers differ in their preaching practices than preaching-teachers. On the one hand, "A Teaching-preacher" will observe what is being said in a given passage of scripture, while looking to the leadership of the Holy Spirit for the central meaning of the message. And without going into shut-down mode, he will solicit comparative possibilities from the members of his hearer group and expand on the number of applications he receives. He will then summarize the central meaning from that which was found.

A Preaching-teacher, on the other hand, will do just the opposite. He will seize the literal meaning of the passage, go immediately into cognitive shut-down mode—i.e. defer to rote learning—and begin to build on what he thinks the writer meant by what he said. In addition, a Preaching-teacher will preach the concept of Salvation contained in the above-mentioned scriptures with blinders in place, blocking out the in-depth truths.

For several hundred years these preachers have promoted Salvation as a one-time event, instead of the orderly process that it is—which begins with that event. That kind of teaching manifests the gap between truth and tradition. As a result, believers are lulled into a false sense of security based on a half-truth; and will not be able to bridge the gap.

Oswald Chambers (1982) also said, "The more facile the expression in words, the less likely is the truth to be carried out in life." **(4)** That's another way of saying, "we must not forget that there is a direct correlation between the way the word is delivered, and the effectiveness and follow-through on that which is delivered." Stated another way, the preacher has a peril that the pew doesn't have. The preacher must preach the word, and he must do it without adding to it or taking from it, to make it easy to grasp. Unfortunately, that has not been the case. The enemy has entered the organized church, blinded the eyes and stopped the ears of believers, beginning with the pulpit and coming to rest in the farthest pew. I apologize for the harshness of my tone, but I must speak truth.

Over the years, preachers have become fixed on perfecting their ability to 'preach,'—as defined by tradition. Instead of:

> *"studying to show themselves approved unto God as workmen who have no need to be ashamed, rightly dividing the word of truth"* (2 Timothy 2:15),

Contemporary preachers seem to be content with perpetuating the status quo. As a result, believers have become more concerned with "how well the preacher can preach," rather than on what God would have them to know, and to do. The end result is a message filled with content—minus the context—which allows 'a lie to reign supreme.' That type of preaching has become an entity of entertainment rather than a source of information. It would be good if the pastor / preacher would do both while he is up; but unfortunately, that has not been the case in the last one hundred-fifty plus years.

REASON AND RATIONALE

PAUL informs us in Romans 1:16 that "The gospel of Christ is the power of God unto salvation." The contemporary preacher, by adding rhythm and rhyme to the word to make it more palatable, has succeeded—albeit unknowingly—in diminishing the power of the word by the time it reaches its destination. Stated succinctly, the majority of preachers today are so engrossed in their delivery—striving to earn for themselves the coveted reputation of being a "good preacher"— they succeed only in exciting the people, while at the same time diluting the word. Unwittingly, they negate the power of God unto salvation that's contained in the Gospel, by watering it down.

A LIVING WITNESS

I WOULD be remiss if I didn't mention that the opposite is equally as true. Having walked that road for **more** than three decades, I succeeded only in earning the reputation of being what one pastor called 'a magnificent pontificator.' I was Seminary-trained and steeped in ostentation. The use of 'big words' and 'catchy phrases' plagued my preaching format. I must admit that the people liked what I did, and it helped me to earn a coveted reputation. But at the end of the day, what I did was no better than my colleagues who were bent on earning themselves a good reputation.

And seeing the failure that issued there-from, it is with great pleasure that I say to the world today that "I have been anointed and appointed a "Change Agent" for Christ with no need for ostentation. Today, under the auspices of being a God given pastor and a Bishop appointed preacher, I practice the art of being a good pastor who strives to feed his congregation with knowledge and understanding; and a Bishop-appointed preacher who practice preaching the word, with precision and power. I believe God has given me a special role to play. My role and function is to alert the people of God of the existence of a commonly overlooked, literal, "basket full of blessings" (1 Corinthians 2:9) that are hidden in plain sight; and have been there all the time.

My love for God-in-Christ, coupled with my experiences and exposure, have enabled and empowered me to call a spade a spade, sin by its right name, and let the chips fall where they may. The outcome of my failures, and the failure of others, is that the relationship between God and man, and between man and God is grossly misrepresented, and it's largely because the preacher has fallen prey to the progenitor of propaganda.

The "misrepresentation" about which I am speaking, has evolved over the years from what I believe to be the mishandling of the word of God. When Jesus said, "Continue in my Word" it is certain that He meant under the Lordship and leadership of the Holy Spirit. And I know I'm correct because Part of the problem stems from "limited-learning" and part of it from "mental-laziness." Hundreds of years of "bathing in the innocence of ignorance" and "being satisfied with perpetuating the status-quo," have contributed to the mass-production of "preachers who want to say something, but have little to say." Being less concerned with the context and more concerned with the eloquence of the content, have caused the preacher of today to be more devoted to the members of the Church than he is to his commitment to the cause of Christ.

Am I suggesting that the contemporary preacher is preaching a false doctrine? The answer is a resounding no. What I am saying is he (or she) is unknowingly depriving and denying the people of God the "full complement" of salvation. The wide-spread mishandling of the key terms contained in those pivotal scriptures over time constitutes malfeasance and serves to perpetuate the problem for the organized Church and for Christian people everywhere.

What is that problem in a nutshell? I was asked. Give us an example. The problem has two parts. The first part is the commonly-held misconception of "the nature of the Gospel," with emphasis on how the word **"shall"** in the King James Version and **"will"** in Modern Language Translations—are treated. Those two words should be treated as future tense. However, translated today, shall and will are defined as 'right now.' The second part is "The false sense of security" into which the people of God have been lulled. They are left to believe that they can enjoy the promises of God without apprehending and adhering to the principles that precede them.

The outcome which Paul describes vividly in Romans Chapter 10, verses 1-4, is the perception of this writer: the people are stumped and stymied. And unless and until those believers to which Paul is referring, are quickened and saved by the washing of regeneration and the renewing of the Holy Spirit (Titus 3:3-5); there is a greater than 50-50 chance that because they are traveling on the road to destruction (Matthew 7:13) they will fall asleep with un-confessed sins, which will deny them access to the already-decided destiny that's reserved for the faithful.

Let me hasten to say that whether or not there is general agreement with my perception, the problem still exists. In *Entering,* because I have lived it and am now an advocate for change, I have demonstrated that Salvation actually begins with a lesson on 'True Repentance' that must be learned by everyone. Learning that lesson propels the participant on to the second step: that of beginning to re-establish a relationship with God-in-Christ that's up-close and personal. That relationship is inseparably bound to being both, a hearer and a doer of the word of God. The continued failure to learn that lesson on the part of the preacher will cause the people to remain stumped, stymied, and stagnated. Translated, that means the failure to understand the rudiments of repentance and teach them to his people—will allow the traditional problems of today to continue to exist, and future generations will go on perpetuating the status-quo—although unknowingly— because truth has been eclipsed by tradition.

PART FOUR

CHAPTER TWENTY

The Incarnate Word

PROLOGUE

IN his prologue John wrote:

> *"In the beginning was the Word, and the Word was with God, and the Word was God. The same was in the beginning with God. All things were made by Him; and without Him was not anything made that was made. In Him was life; and the life was the light of men. And the light shineth in darkness; and the darkness comprehended it not."*

I could think of no better way to introduce the person of the Gate Keeper than by the words John wrote. What he wrote has remained a mystery since the beginning of time. As a result mankind knows about Him, but refuse to become acquainted with Him on an up-close, personal basis. But I thank God Almighty for His demonstration of 'Love, the most excellent way.' The voice of God also had John to write,

> *"For God so loved the world that He gave His only begotten Son, that whosoever believeth in Him should not perish, but have everlasting life."*

There is a play on words in that verse that should not go unknown. Jesus said,

> *"I am the true-vine my Father is the husband-man (John 15:1). Every branch in me that beareth not fruit He taketh away: and every branch that beareth*

> *fruit, He purgeth it, that it may bring forth more fruit"*
> *(John 15:2)*

That having been said the reader should understand the concept of perishing not to mean dying, as some might think. Instead, to perish is to wither—while yet remaining connected—until all of the life has been drained. Stated succinctly, the will of God is 'not that man should perish, but to have life; and to have it more abundantly' (John 10:10b).

Contrary to the popular opinion which might say otherwise, the sum-total of all of God's efforts are fixed and focused on reconciling mankind. To say that God loves us is an understatement; because all throughout Scripture the voice of God comes across as a bridge over troubled water. The problem we have is accepting and believing.

PRESENTATION

JOHN continues by saying:

> *"And the Word was made flesh, and dwelt among us, (and we beheld His glory, the glory as of the only begotten of the Father,) full of grace and truth"*
> *(John 1:14).*

From that moment until now, mankind has been privileged to deal with a person who was 'fully God' and 'fully man' at the same time. The apostle Paul called Him "the fullness of the Godhead, bodily" (Colossians 2:9). Still, we have trouble accepting Him. Perhaps it's because Satan has succeeded in neutralizing the sound mind that God gave the man He created in His Own Image. I cannot be sure because I was not there. However, what I do know is unless and until mankind makes the decisive-decision to apprehend and activate this gift that God has given us, nothing is going to change.

Scripture says He lived among us. That raises two questions: What did Jesus say (WDJS)?

And, "What did Jesus do (WDJD) while He was here?" Those two questions cover both, the spiritual and the natural dimensions. If both questions sound the same because they both involve Jesus—and we know that is because He is the embodiment of the eternal God—rest assured they are not the same. It's because Jesus was the Incarnate Word—that is to say He was fully man and fully God. That put Him in the unique position of being the best example of both, our spiritual and practical role model.

The former question: "WDJS" is asking, "What did the voice of God—speaking through His Son, Jesus, have to say on the subject of Salvation?" Or, stated another way, "What would the word of God have us to know and do?" To answer those questions, the participant must have a working knowledge of what the Bible says, and what it means by what it says. He must also have a mental-state-of-readiness that propels him, and inspires him to replicate the attitudes and actions of Jesus. That conclusion is validated by the words of Solomon in Proverbs 23:7: "As a man thinks in his heart, so is he."

The latter question: "What did Jesus do? (WDJD)" is asking us to keep in mind what Jesus did while he lived on earth. Scripture says, ***"He came to save His people from their sins"*** (Matthew 1:21). That verse testifies to Jesus being Incarnate. As a result, everything He did placed Him under the mini-microscope of the Anti-Christ. The Pharisees, who headed up that group, majored in trying to tempt Him. With no trouble at all, we can see that from the day He was baptized and subsequently led into the wilderness to be tempted of the devil—Matthew 4:1—Satan was on his case, but to no avail.

For three years Jesus walked from Dan to Beersheba—a distance of one-hundred and twenty miles from the North to the South—preaching and teaching the Gospel of God. When the time for His public Ministry was fulfilled, He was subjected to several trials at the hands of the Roman government and the Jewish religious leaders. Satan was still on his job. The text which talks about the two thieves on the cross in Luke 23:32-43 validates that conclusion. All in all: stealing, killing, and destroying, is what Satan came to do; and we should not be surprised, when he does just that, non-stop.

The fact that Jesus was the fullness of the Godhead bodily (Colossians 2:9) did not make Him an exception to the rule. Spiritually and physically our Lord and Savior met Satan's challenge, providing us with a perfect role model. Scripture says ***"He came down and lived among us."*** He told us in the summary of the Decalogue what he expected of us; and then He showed us that expectation, 'manifested as love the most excellent way.' Translated, He allowed himself to be crucified on the Cross of Calvary for the sins of the world. Therefore I believe it's safe to say that what Satan did to Jesus, he is yet doing to all of us, even as you read. And because we were created "In God's Own Image," the way Jesus behaved is the way we are expected to behave.

The image of God in us has been distorted, but it cannot be destroyed. Because of the sins of our fore-parents, Satan has us bound. But the power of Jesus' resurrection placed freedom at our disposal. All we have to do is submit and surrender: submit to the Sovereignty of God over our lives; and surrender to the Lordship and leadership of the Holy Spirit in our lives. To surrender means to apprehend and activate the gift of God (John 3:16) and subsequently be set free. Jesus was fully human just like you and I; and was tempted in every way that we are (Hebrews 4:15). The question being asked is, "What did Jesus do? How did He behave?"

In Chapter fifty-three (53) Verse 7, Isaiah prophesied what He would do, more than seven hundred years before He was born; and He lived it out in the three years that He preached and taught before He submitted to death on the Cross.

Scripture says, ***"He was oppressed, and He was afflicted, yet he opened not His mouth."*** We must never forget that although Jesus was emblematic of God in the flesh, He was still our human role model. Therefore, when He said, ***"I am the way the truth and the life, no man comes to the Father but by me"*** in John 14:6, He not only removed all doubts about who He was and what He came to do, He also gave us the best reason for trusting Him. It has been more than two—thousand years since Jesus ascended into heaven and took His place at the right hand of power—according to the KJV of the Bible.

Nevertheless, nothing has changed. As a matter of fact, for some of us the desire to see Jesus is more acute than ever. Such is the case in the sermon that follows. Jesus said, "Freely you received, freely give." If I knew who preached this sermon first, I would give him the proper recognition. The only thing I know for sure is that like the Greek gentleman in the story, "Jesus is the man that I want to see."

CHAPTER TWENTY-ONE

Sermon Title: The Man We Want to See

John 12:20-23

If we had been in Jerusalem on a certain day, we would have seen a great crowd making its way down toward the temple.

If we had NOT known the particular significance of that day,

If we had NOT known WHY all the people were there, we might have asked a passer-by, "WHY are all these people GATHERED here, WHAT'S going ON up at the temple?" The passer-by would have answered, "Why, didn't you KNOW . . . ."

THIS is the day of the Passover Feast and ALL GOOD, LOYAL JEWS have gathered from FAR and NEAR to OBSERVE this solemn but important occasion.

Then . . . . we would have remembered. Our minds would go BACK into Jewish history and we would REMEMBER this occasion. It was a day that REAL Jews would NEVER forget. You see, these people of God had been in BONDAGE in Egypt.

Y'all know WHO those REAL Jews were, don't you? Let me help you out . . . Is it all right if I teach a little right here?

There are many different versions of recorded history. Many books have been written ABOUT and BY different historians. So there are many versions.

You have to take them all with a grain of salt. And, no matter which version you choose to accept and believe, Please, Please, Please leave room for the other versions to be equally as true as the version that you have chosen. Is that all right? Good.

This is MY version. HERE'S the rule that WE must remember . . . IF you are going to accept THIS version.

The concept of the brotherhood of man must be understood within the limitations imposed by Scripture—limitations imposed only by the Word of God. In other words, we ought NOT put our TWO cents in it.

You see, there is a sense in which all men ARE brothers in that they are descendants of ADAM as their common ancestor. That's what we have to keep uppermost in our minds. Here's the lesson.

Genesis chapter 9, beginning at verse 20 tells the story of how Canaan, Ham's son was **cursed; and how SHEM, Ham's brother was blessed. Let me read it for you.**

> *Noah, who was a farmer, was the first man to plant a vineyard. After he drank some of the wine, he became drunk, took off his clothes, and lay naked in his tent. When Ham, the father of Canaan, saw that his father was naked, he went out and told his two brothers. Then Shem and Japheth took a robe and held it behind them on their shoulders. They walked backward into the tent and covered their father, keeping their faces turned away so as NOT to see him naked. When Noah sobered up and learned what his youngest son had done to him, he said, "A curse on Canaan! He will be a slave to his brothers. Give praise to the Lord, the God of Shem! Canaan will be the slave of Shem. May God cause Japheth to increase! May his descendants live with the people of Shem! Canaan will be the slave of Japheth."*

Simply stated, the REAL Jews were slaves to their brothers . . . . who just happened to have been some cruel taskmasters. The Real Jews were the people of God whose lot in life—like mama 'nem used to say—would be a hard row to hoe, because of slavery. Does that make any sense?

Let me give you a little more. The REAL Jews were the descendants of Abraham, literally and figuratively. And this would be the first time that history talks about their enslavement. And not only that, this was the first time that God would use His people to set their OWN kinfolk free. You Bible readers will remember when Cousin Solomon said:

> *"What HAS been is what WILL be; and what HAS BEEN DONE is what WILL BE DONE; and there is nothing new under the sun."*

Solomon was referring to ALL that happened in the Creation story . . . . ALL that happened in the annals of history . . . . ALL that happened in the Pentateuch, ALL that happened and is recorded in the first five books of the Bible. Solomon is saying: anything that anybody says has already been said; and anything that happens to anybody in life has already happened. There nothing new under the sun.

So, Genesis 9:25 sentenced Canaan, the son of Ham to slavery. And if we fast-forward through the pages of history to contemporary times, the record of the second enslavement of the descendants of the REAL Jews IS IN U.S. History, and it starts in this country in 1609.

And that record is the second time that God used His people to set their own brothers free. Let me make that plain. Shem's lineage is the origin of so-called "white folk" THOSE who migrated NORTH into the Nordic Countries: i.e. Norway and Sweden after the flood.

Ham's lineage is the origin of so-called Negroes . . . . those who migrated south of the Sub-Saharan desert after the flood. And Japheth's lineage is the origin of Palestinians— so-called 3rd world people—who populated the so-called Middle East.

All of that is important, but what's MOST important is that the historical record says "in the midst of their enslavement, they cried out to God; and God heard them. You ought to know who they are by now.

They cried out unto God and the Bible says, God sent His servant Moses to go and get them . . . . to lead them out of bondage . . . . to deliver them out of Egypt, into a land that flowed with milk and honey.

And after many strange occurrences—all under the watchful eye of God—that fatal night in Egypt arrived. God said to His people, "You are to kill a lamb without spot or blemish and put his blood on the doorposts OR on the lintels of your doors. And ON THAT NIGHT . . . . I will send the death angel and he will fly over your city. And IF the blood is NOT there, every first born in the land of Egypt will die. But, not even a dog will wag his tail against my people, Israel. THEN God said But WHEN I see the blood, I will instruct the death angel to Passover you and you will be safe.

That night death came and there wasn't a home in Egypt wherein the first son had not been slain. That's when God told His people to KEEP the PASSOVER forever. That was O. T. Now, let's fast-forward to the N. T. and pick up the story for today.

That's why the Jews were in Jerusalem on THAT DAY. They were there to celebrate the feast of the Passover.

But on that particular day, there was, in the city of Jerusalem, ONE who had an altruistic appreciation for the real meaning of the Passover. His name was Jesus. And metaphorically speaking, He knew He was the LAMB without spot or blemish.

He knew He was the LAMB who would be slain; and He knew that IF his blood would be applied to the souls of men they would be safe IN HIM forever. Yes, Jesus knew the real meaning of the feast of the Passover.

But the Bible says there were others present also. There were certain GREEKS among them who had come to worship at the feast. They came NOT so much to worship as TO SEE. They came to SEE the ONE whose fame had spread all over everywhere.

They came to SEE Jesus. The Biblical record says they approached Phillip—one of Jesus' disciples—and said to him, "Sir we want to see Jesus." Now so far as we can determine, the Greeks MUST have had an audience with Jesus because somewhere He said, "those who come to me, I will in no ways cast out."

And I know they were blessed by the visit, but I can only hope that they put their trust in Him for time and eternity. WE WANT TO SEE JESUS . . . . That's the age-long cry of all of humanity!!

Phillip said, "Show us the Father, and that will be sufficient." And the Record says, 'in due time' Jesus came and showed men the Father in His own Person. You Bible readers will remember that in John 14:9 Jesus declared, "The Father and I are one. He that has seen me has seen the Father, and from now on, you know Him and you have seen Him. For when you look in my face, you are looking into the heart of God. The cry of men today is the same as it was in that far-away day.

Just show us the Father, and that will be sufficient. Look with me if you would, at FOUR occasions today when WE want to SEE Jesus.

FIRST, we want to see Jesus when we are burdened with sin—when sin catches up with us. You ought to read Cousin David's confession in Psalm fifty-one (51). It is the cry of a sin-sick soul trying to get back into fellowship with God:

> *Have mercy upon me, O God, [he cries] According to thy loving kindness: according unto the multitude of thy tender mercies, blot out my transgressions. Wash me thoroughly from my iniquity, and cleanse me from my sin."*

Can you imagine the man 'after God's own heart' humbling himself that way before God? Cousin David was a sin-sick soul saying, "I want to SEE Jesus."

There is a story told about a young man who had sunk to the depths of sin. As the story goes, he attended church one Sunday morning and was convicted and converted after giving his heart to God. Afterwards, he would often give his testimony. He would say, "When I walked down that Church aisle to give my heart to God-in-Christ, it seemed that the weight of the world was pressing down upon me.

But when I came to Christ and He saved me, "My load was lifted and became light as a feather." Why? because I had seen Jesus, and my sins had been forgiven.

Now I ask you, today; have YOU seen Jesus? Has YOUR load been lifted?

My brothers and my sisters, we, too, carry the burden of sin. "Oh yes we do." We carry it and there is only one way to get rid of that burden. We must bring that burden of sin to Jesus. We must bring it because HE is our ONLY burden-bearer. What does that mean? It means that we have to let the Word of God cover that burden and the Power of God enter into our minds and hearts in order to wipe it out. Saved people carry sins, and Lost People carry sins. But ALL must bring them to Jesus.

SECONDLY: We want to see Jesus when we are engaged in worship. During the Time of our text there was religious chaos and confusion in Jerusalem much like it is today in Birmingham. Men, women, boys and girls would come to the temple and go through

ALL of their religious ceremonies; but the sin and the guilt would STILL be there. There would be no peace in their hearts.

I don't know how some of you feel about it, but after thirty-six (36) years of preaching, thirty-one (31) of them as a pastor, I still see people coming and going to Church almost every Sunday; going through ALL of the forms of religious worship and YET not truly having seen Jesus, and NOT having had their SIN forgiven.

I don't mean to beat a dead horse, but we've got some problems in the Church. Slavery did a number on some of us. The devil got in some of Shem's lineage . . .

I said, "The devil got into some of Shem's descendants . . ." Oh, y'all don't hear me. I said, the devil got into some White folks and they told some of Ham's lineage . . . . They told some of our ancestors that THEY COULD'T . . . . even when God said they COULD. And those slaves chose to believe what the White folk said. You see, they believed that "the white man's ice was colder than the black man's ice."

They believed the slave owners, rather than believe God. And here we are 204 years later, and the sins of their fathers have been passed on to the second, third, and fourth generation, just like the voice of God said in Exodus 20:5. And some of THEM are members of the family of God. I don't mean any harm, but some of us have got some problems with the burden of Sin.

Some of us right here in THIS Church are still coming and going, trying to carry this burden by ourselves. What IS that burden Pastor? I'm so glad you asked. I've been trying to get that over to you for three long years. That is the burden of "THINKING IN OPPOSITION TO GOD." Some of us have NOT BEGUN to be saved from the Power of Sin. We are members, and we have been saved from the PENALTY of sin; but we have YET to travel the road to repentance. We go through ALL the ceremonies but we have NOT had our Sin washed away. In other words, "we still believe WE CAN'T, even when God says WE CAN. In addition,

WE want to SEE Jesus in the songs we sing and in the SERMONS that are preached. Preachers—me included—fail miserably in their preaching if they DON'T present Jesus to the people.

As a young man in the gospel ministry—it was my FIRST pastorate—I thought people needed to hear intellectual preaching. You understand me.

I thought they needed to hear sermons with BIG words, WITTY epigrams, and HIGH-SOUNDING phrases. I thought they needed that in order to keep them out of the IGNORANT BAG. Besides, that was a so-called Middle-class Church, and back then, the AME Church was touted as the INTELLIGENCIA of the Black community. So, I reached back and pulled up some of the best that Seminary had taught me, and FILLED my sermons with those things. Oh, the Church began to grow in numbers. People were coming and going; Sunday after Sunday they came and together we through all of the rituals and ceremonies. But I found out later that they were NOT coming to worship. They were getting ready for the next round.

They were coming to fight. You see, I was the 12th pastor in 21 years. The Church was called '8th and Towne' in those days because that was the intersection where the Church was located. But later the name was changed, and it became what it is today: The 1st AME CHURCH of Los Angeles. And in those days, that church majored in putting pastors out of the Church.

I tell you, THEY NEDED TO SEE JESUS, but they were COMING to choose sides for the next fight. I was both, young AND dumb about what I was doing. I was a good preacher, but God gives PASTORS according to HIS heart, NOT GOOD preachers. But I thank God for the superintending of His Holy Spirit, for HE let ME see Jesus. That's when I made a commitment to the CAUSE of CHRIST; and "I PROMISED Him that I, would serve Him till I did; I was on the battlefield for the Lord."

I was on the battlefield for the Lord; and the Spirit of God kept me safe and sound from all hurt, harm, and danger. They wanted no part of a Bishop; a Presiding Elder; OR HAVING TO PAY Conference Claims and Assessments. They fought me on those issues for just over four years. Acting on the advice of the late Bishop H. H. Brookins—presiding prelate of the 5th Episcopal District—I did the best I could to take care of God's people. Four years later, we left that facility; and together we planted the Church that I led for an additional twenty (20) years.

And I might as well as tell the whole truth: it's not easy up here. You see, I had earned myself a reputation among preachers. And sometimes it's hard to RESIST the RIGORS that go with an EARNED reputation. I had earned the reputation of being the POETIC PREACHER with a WEALTH of WORDS. My pastor dubbed me the "magnificent pontificator;" AND I could accept that from him because he was mad because I had climbed to the top rung of the academic ladder, and he had barely finished two years of college.

And I have to say it, "every now and then . . . ." Every now and then, shades of De Ja Vous HANG on the HORIZON. In other words, I get caught up in ACADEMIA and SELF—AGGRANDIZEMENT, and I STOP SEEING JESUS. That's the way it was when I arrived in Alabama in August of 2006.

But again, I thank God for the recall of His Word, AND the indwelling of His Holy Spirit: for through His word I have been enabled; and by the indwelling of His Holy Spirit, I am empowered. And between the two I have the assurance—even though it's out of context—I have the assurance that I can do all things through Christ WHICH strengthens me.

THIRDLY, WE want to see Jesus I the details of daily life.

The story is told about a young man who worked in the Los Angeles School District. He had become convicted and converted by the saving-grace of God, through our Lord and Savior, Jesus Christ.

As the story goes, his administrator noticed a change in his demeanor. He approached the young man and inquired about the change. The young man confessed that the DIFFERENCE in him was JESUS. His testimony was that, "His HOURS seemed shorter; his JOB seemed EASIER; and his COLLEAGUES seemed more AGREEABLE. The CIRCUMSTANCES were the SAME, the young man said; but NOW he had the Spirit of God for a daily companion. By the way, THIS is a true story. That young man is me. And I want to SHARE with you that THE SPIRIT of GOD WILL BE YOUR companion if YOU make a quality COMMITMENT.

LASTLY, WE want to SEE Jesus in our Sorrows and shadows.

You see, it's in the midnight hours of our lives . . . .

it's in the midst of DEATH and DARKNESS that WE want to SEE the LIGHT of the WORLD. When those two sisters over in Bethany lost their brother, LAZARRUS, they immediately sent for Jesus. He was the ONLY ONE who could turn their shadows into sunlight.

We want to SEE HIM when sorrows come. He is the ONLY ONE who understands AND can COMFORT us. Some people are beaten into the dust when sorrow comes; because they don't know WHICH WAY to turn. They NEED to see Jesus.

My brothers and my sisters, Jesus died and was resurrected for this very purpose . . . . so that we CAN see HIM when we NEED to. The resurrection has come and gone, but the story lingers on. Jesus did what He came to do. His work is finished.

The DIE has been cast . . . . ALL we have to do is step over the line. All we have to do is MAKE the commitment . . . . Make a decisive-decision to become a faithful follower of Christ. Remember, we said make a decisive-decision. It's about YOU, NOT them. It doesn't matter what the members of your circle of family and friends have to say or do. YOU make YOUR commitment . . . . Annnnnd don't look back, slow down, back away OR be still.

With Jesus, your PAST will be been REDEEMED, your FUTURE will make sense, and your PRESENT will be secure. Simply voice your choice and cross over TODAY. Do that NOW and YOU, like the many who have gone on before you can be THROUGH with LOW living; SIGHT walking . . . SMALL planning . . . . SMOOTH needs . . . COLORLESS dreams . . . . TAME visions . . . . MUNDANE talking . . . . CHINTZY giving . . . . TIMID prayers AND Dwarfed goals.

Stand up and BE the Christian man or woman that God made you to be. IF you stand up AND if you make the COMMITMENT . . . . YOU will no longer NEED Pre-eminence, Prosperity, Position, Promotions, Plaudits, Plaudits OR Popularity.

YOU won't have to strive to BE RIGHT, BE FIRST, BE TOPS, BE NUMBER ONE, BE RECOGNIZED, BE REWARDED . . . OR to BE PRAISED, anymore. IF you make the commitment, YOU can LIVE by His presence, WALK BY FAITH, Lead with Patience, LIFT by PRAYER and Labor with Power.

It won't matter anymore whether anyone agrees with you or not for the RULES of the RACE are set. The GAIT is fast, The GOAL is heaven, the ROAD is narrow, the WAY is ROUGH . . . . companions WILL BE few . . . . but your VISION will be CLEAR and your GUIDE will be RELIABLE.

Don't let anyone or anything STOP YOU . . . . Love Jesus MORE than these. DON'T be DETERRED, LURED back, TURNED aside, DELUDED, DERIDED or DELAYED.

Don't hesitate in the presence of your adversary . . . . Don't negotiate at the table with your enemies . . . . Don't ponder at the pool of popularity OR meander at the maze of mediocrity . . . .

Don't GIVE UP, SHUT UP, BACK UP, or LET UP until you have STAYED UP, STORED UP, and PRAYED UP for the CAUSE of Christ.

He has been too good for YOU to forget WHO you are and WHOSE you are . . . . I cannot speak for you, but I am a follower of Christ, and I've got to GO until HE comes back for me . . . . AND

I've got to GIVE until I drop; I've got to PREACH until ALL have had the chance to HEAR . . . . I'VE got to WORK until HE stops me . . . . an when HE comes back for His own, HE WILL recognize me because MY COLORS WILL BE CLEAR.

What about YOU, TODAY? Will YOU make that commitment?

Will you let Jesus WIPE away ALL of your tears? Will YOU let HIM erase ALL of those memories that keep YOU from moving forward?

Will you let HIM help YOU to make PEACE WITH YOUR PAST?

He said, WHOSOEVER WILL, let him come, and THOSE who come to me, I will in no wise cast out . . . . He also said,

COME unto ME ALL of you who are laboring and are HEAVY-LADEN and I WILL give you rest . . . .

Won't He do it? I said, Won't He Do it? God bless your hearts.

CHAPTER TWENTY-TWO

The Arrival of the Gatekeeper

PROLOGUE

HAVING discussed and delineated the ids of seeing Jesus, nothing remains but to meet and greet the Gate Keeper. Metaphorically speaking, in person He is our Comforter and our Teacher (John 14:26); His presence is felt in all that we do (Zechariah 4:6), and His power keeps us from falling (Jude 24). The attached sermon was prepared to accent the manifestation of His arrival and to further demonstrate His person, presence, and power.

"The Promise Fulfilled"

Acts 1:4; 2:1-4
Delivered to the Lily Baptist Church
Tarrant City, Alabama, December 2nd 2012
Dr. James Francis Brooks, Pastor

PRESENTATION

I shall not be long at all. Your pastor has demonstrated the ultimate in faith by giving me—a total stranger to most of this congregation—the opportunity to preach in his absence. Let me make that clear. Allowing me to share this preaching place in his absence is something that most pastors would not do. That literally forces me to be as intelligent as I know how. Now, here's what I'm going to do. I'm going to tell you what I'm going to tell you; then I'm going to take my time an tell you. And finally, I'm going to tell you what I've told you and take my seat. So, to be fore-warned is to be fore-armed. And I might add that If you are slow getting

198

started, by the time you get warmed up, I will probably be through. Let us pray.

For our lesson text, I want to marry two verses of Scripture. If you have your Bibles, turn with me to Acts chapter 2, put your finger there, flip back to Chapter 1 and stand on your feet in honor of the reading of God's word. Please follow along while I read verse 4 of that first chapter, and then the first four verses of chapter 2. I shall be reading from the NKJV.

> *4. "And being assembled together with them, He commanded them not to depart from Jerusalem, "but to wait for the promise:" "wait for the promise" of the Father, which, He said, you have heard from me."*

> *1. When the day of Pentecost had fully come, they were all with one accord in one place. 2. And suddenly there came a sound from heaven .... as of a rushing mighty wind, and it filled the whole house where they were sitting. 3. And there appeared to them divided tongues, as of fire, and one sat upon each of them. 4. And they were all .... filled with the Holy Spirit and began to speak with other tongues, as the Spirit gave them utterance.*

As you take your seats in the presence of God, I want to think out loud with you about "A PROMISE FULLFILLED." we approach the text, let us keep in mind two things: The arrival of the Holy Spirit on the day of Pentecost celebrated two events: the fulfilling of the Promise of God, and the founding of The Church-of-God-in-Christ. By the way, that Church is not to be confused with the local denomination by the same name. God has only one Church which He calls His sheep. Translated, he has one flock; but He has them housed in sheepfolds all over the world.

In this text, Luke tells us that on the day of Pentecost, when the "promise" of the coming of the Holy Spirit was fulfilled, they were all with one accord in one place. Some of you may not have known it, but pastors and preachers across the country have been praying in recent weeks, months and years-gone-by, for God to let His

Spirit fall fresh on their Churches. With the Spirit of God speaking to them and through them, they were endeavoring to assemble all of their individual families in one place, on one accord.

The task has been troublesome, to say the least. I believe there is general agreement that most people want to live life the way God would have them to live it, but they don't have a mental-state-of-readiness that's proportionate to their desire; hence, they are not ready to do the things that are necessary to bring about God's will. Desire is a wonderful thing, but without a mental state of readiness that's equal to their desire, all of their efforts are an exercise in futility. Developing that level of cognition is a God-sized problem, which demands a God-sized solution, an only the Spirit of God can provide it.

The text says that "At Jerusalem, there were gathered Jesus' twelve—we know that Judas had betrayed Him just before His Crucifixion, but Luke tells us in Chapter 1, verse 26 that Judas had been replaced by Matthias. So gathered there in Jerusalem were Jesus' twelve, Jews and devout men of every nation under heaven. Scripture says: "Suddenly . . ." The use of the word "suddenly," sends a message that is both, timeless and limitless. It tells us that this event can happen, at any time, any place, and anywhere. Our task, as "twice-born" children of the King, is to be ready. And the same thing Jesus told his disciples of old to do, is what He is telling his disciples of today, to do: *"be ye also ready for in such an hour as you think not, the Son of man will come (Matthew 24: 36-44).*

Luke said "suddenly." "Suddenly there came a sound from heaven . . . . as of a rushing mighty wind. That shouldn't be hard for us to visualize, for when the weather is in-climate and there is the threat of a tornado, we get "severe weather warnings on our televisions." And when a tornado hits, the winds are contrary. In Alabama where I live, entire towns have been picked up and blown away. Jesus talked about contrary winds as well. You Bible readers check out Mark, Chapter 4 verses 35 and following, when you get home. Luke said, *"Suddenly, there came a sound from heaven . . . as of a rushing, mighty wind and it filled all the house where they were sitting. And there appeared unto them divided tongues—the*

KJV called them "Cloven" tongues as of fire, and one sat upon each of them."

Stick a pin right there, and permit me to share a word about "the imagery" contained in what Luke said, and I promise I'll come right back. I need to teach right here. Brothers and sisters, will it be all right if I teach for a minute right here? Thank you so much. All of us know that "sensationalism sells." Turn on the television or pick up a newspaper and what you will see are stories about sex, drugs, gangs, death, deception and destruction. All of it is sensational, and designed to hold your interest.

This story is also sensational, but this scripture text is not a "sales-pitch." The "divided tongues as of fire" which sat upon each of them typifies a time of fulfillment. This was a fulfillment of the word of God about the outpouring of the Holy Spirit in Joel 2: 28 and 29; and of John the Baptist about the baptism of the Holy Spirit with fire, that we read about in Luke 3:16.

Why tongues of fire? You might ask. Well, tongues symbolize speech and the communication of the Gospel. "Divided tongues" means that the fire separated and rested on each of them. Fire symbolizes God's purifying presence which burns away the undesirable elements of our lives, and sets our hearts aflame so that we can ignite a fire in the lives of others. You Bible readers will recall that on Mount Sinai in the Old Testament, God confirmed the validity of Old Testament Law by sending fire from heaven in Exodus Chapter 19, verses 16-18. And here at the celebration of Pentecost, God again confirmed the validity of the ministry of the Holy Spirit by sending fire.

On Mount Sinai, fire came down on one place; but on Pentecost, fire came down on many believers, symbolizing that God's presence is now available to all who will believe Him. God made His presence known to this group of believers in a spectacular way—a rushing mighty wind, fire and His Holy Spirit. Let me ask you something. Would you like God to reveal himself to you in a sensational way? He may just do that you know, but we need to beware of trying to force our expectations on God. My Bible tells me that in First Kings Chapter 19, verses 10-13, Elijah also needed a message from God. Scripture tells us that there was a "mighty wind, then an earthquake, and finally a fire;" but God's message came in a "still small voice." My Father's children, God may use dramatic methods to work in your life, or He may speak in a gentle whisper. Your task is to wait patiently, always listening. You can take that pin out, now, I'm back. Luke said, *"Suddenly there came a sound from heaven . . . as of a rushing, mighty wind, and it filled all the house where they were sitting. And there appeared unto them divided tongues as of fire, and ONE sat upon each of them. And they were all . . . . filled with the Holy Ghost, and began to speak with other tongues, as the Spirit gave them utterance."*

Contrary to all that you have heard about those Apostles speaking with other tongues—which some preachers with "closed minds and limited learning" have fashioned into a symbol of sensationalism, and conjured-up doctrinal denominationalism which sent tens of thousands off on a faith-trip, declaring that *"You've got to "speak in tongues in order to be saved."* I stopped by today on my way to heaven to tell you that not a word of that is so. The reference to those apostles speaking with other tongues is another way of saying that they literally spoke in other languages.

Here is the real deal. And I don't want any of you to take my word for it. You ought to read it for yourself when you get home and have some time. It's all there in Genesis Chapter 11, verses 1-9. In the interest of time and pulpit decorum, let me read it for you. But if you read it, read these verses as a participant, so you can hear Moses telling his hearers and you, that the families of Noah, and all of their generations were divided in the earth after the flood. *"And, the whole earth was of one language, and of one speech. And it came to pass that they gathered themselves together, and decided to build [a city and] a tower to the heavens, as a monument to their [own] greatness."*

In verse 5, Scripture says:

> *The LORD came down [from heaven] to see the city and the tower, which the children of men had begun to build. And the LORD said: [in verse 6], "behold, the people are one, and they all have one language; and this they begin to do: and now nothing will be*

> *restrained from them which they have imagined to do.*
> *So God said [to His Heavenly Court], "let us go down*
> *and there confound their language, that they may*
> *not understand one another's speech. So the LORD*
> *scattered them abroad from there, over the face of all*
> *the earth, and they ceased building the city.*

That is the word of God for the people of God. On the day of Pentecost, Luke lists 18 countries from which there were representatives who heard the apostles speak. Scripture says:

> *When the news spread abroad the multitude came*
> *together; and they were confounded because every man*
> *heard them speak in his own language. The people*
> *were amazed and they marveled, saying to one-another,*
> *"behold, are not all these which speak Galileans? And*
> *how hear we in our own tongue, wherein we were*
> *born? Some of them that were gathered there began*
> *to mock, saying, "These men are full of new wine. But*
> *Peter stood up (that's verse 14 if you are keeping up),*
> *lifted his voice (as it were), and said to the crowd: Men*
> *of Judea and all who dwell in Jerusalem let this be*
> *known to you, and heed my words.*

> *(V. 17) And it shall come to pass in the last days, says*
> *God, the I will pour out of My Spirit on all flesh;*
> *your sons and your daughters shall prophesy, Your*
> *young men shall see visions, your old men shall*
> *dream dreams. And on My menservants and on My*
> *maidservants I will pour out My Spirit in those days;*
> *and they shall prophesy. I will show wonders in heaven*
> *above and signs in the earth beneath: Blood and fire*
> *and vapor of smoke. The sun shall be turned into*
> *darkness, and the moon into blood, before the coming*
> *of the great and awesome day of the Lord.*

THE HIDDEN HOPE

YOU can take that pin out, I'm back now. On the day of Pentecost, the Power of Holy Spirit was released throughout the entire world, to comfort and to teach men, women, sons, daughters, Jews and Gentiles, Catholics and Protestants. The word "Now," said Luke, tells us that everyone can receive the Spirit. We have to admit that this was a revolutionary thought for those Christians who lived in the 1st Century. And after Peter's powerful, spirit-filled message, the people were deeply moved when they asked "What shall we do?"

That is the question which must be asked and answered by each one of us who hear or read the words Peter said to the crowd back then. Peter said, *"Repent and be baptized, every one of you in the name of Jesus Christ for the remission of sin, and you shall receive the gift of the Holy Ghost."* The operative word there is *"Repent."* I don't mean any harm with what I'm about to say, but the Spirit of God demands that I speak truth. Contrary to the popular opinion which says "Repentance" is being godly-sorry for your sins. The Spirit of God would have you to know that being godly sorry is a good thing, but it's not enough. The word of God defines and delineates—which means in addition to defining, the word paints you a verbal picture—and that verbal portrait is of "True Repentance." It is a 4-step process. It's spelled out for us in 2 Chronicles Chapter 7, verse 14.

Once again, let me put my "teacher hat" back on for a moment. God is speaking to Solomon in answer to his prayer. God had this to say: *"If I shut up heaven that there be no rain, or if I command the locusts to devour the land, or if I send pestilence among my people, "IF my people, which are called by my name, shall (1) Humble themselves and (2) Pray and (3) Seek my face and (4) Turn from their wicked ways—those are the pre-requisites—'THEN will I hear from Heaven and forgive their sin and heal their land.' "*

Now I don't know how you feel about it, but I am under no illusions. I know there are those who will go on believing that all have you to do is confess your sins—audibly—and be godly sorry. They will continue to live under the age-old tradition of "I just

204

do the best I can, and leave the rest up to God." They won't go any further, and they won't do any better. Like you and I, they too have free-will; and we all know that the gift of choice comes with free-will. But on the contrary, you have now been taught, and you now know that is not enough. That we must be godly sorry for our sins is true—and equally as true is that God is the only one who can forgive us. But the word of God set in motion those four (4) pre-requisites to his forgiveness. Look at it this way: the very fact that they have not been adhered to, and life for us continues to be a merry-go-round of madness, ought to be proof enough that more is needed.

Another reason for believing that completing those pre-requisites are necessary, is that once we are forgiven, we know God expects us to live like forgiven people; but we just can't seem to do it. There has to be a reason for that continued failure. Jesus said, ***"If you love me, keep my commandments."*** Instead of keeping them, our lives are like "a yo-yo:" up and down; and up and down, and up and down. We keep on doing the best we can, telling the Lord that we are godly-sorry for our misdeeds, and hoping that He will forgive us for our weaknesses.

But oh my brothers and my sisters, you know and I know that you know, that God wouldn't ask us to do something that He has not made us able us to do. The songwriter said, "If God brings you to it, HE will bring you through it." That's a good place to say Amen. Take that pin out, and let me share something else with you. If we would hear the word, receive it and believe it, by believing, according to John in 20:31, we will have life through the name—the power—of Jesus.

Having the life that John is talking about means, "No more half-stepping." No more falling back on the old adage that "Ain't nobody perfect (sic);" and besides, "The Lord knows my heart." No, we are not perfect, but our attitudes and actions can be perfectly aligned with the mind of God. And yes, the Lord knows our hearts. He knows that most of us are satisfied with bathing in the innocence of ignorance. That may be the reason God had Hosea to remind us that ***"His people are destroyed for lack of knowledge" (Hosea 4:6).***

The very fact that as of today none of us are able to keep his commands is evidence that we don't have the power, in and of ourselves. And He also knows that we would do better if we knew better. That's why I was sent here to say to you that "It's only when we have been baptized by, and in the Spirit, will any of us be able to keep His words." The question for each one of you today is, "has God spoken to you through His word, or through the words of His preacher, such that you are ready to believe?

In our Interactive Bible Study sessions, I teach my students to read any passage that we are studying twice: first as a spectator and then as a participant. As a spectator, they were privileged to observe whether or not the people are obedient and to see what happens to them. I call this "cause and effect." Then, go back and re-read it as a participant. The second time around you know what to expect, which gives you an opportunity to make the correct decision. Reading this text as a participant calls for you to make yourself part of Peter's listening audience. When the question is asked this time around, the subject is changed. It now reads, **"What shall I do?"** And when Peter tells you to **"Repent,"** you now know **what** to do. It's really not difficult to understand. It simply puts the responsibility where it belongs.

CERTAINTY INSTEAD OF DOUBT

HAVING lived all of these years without following these four (4) steps to repentance, you not only know what to expect, you can easily see why life for you is like a yo-yo: "up today and down tomorrow." I believe the point has been made, and with the help of the Holy Spirit, it has been proven. In verse 38 of this text, **Peter gave us both, God's Principle and His Promise.** He said, *"Repent, and be baptized every one of you in the name of Jesus, for the remission of sins . . .* That is the principle. That is what all of us must do. The English word **"Name"** translates the Greek word **"On-o-ma"** meaning **authority** and or **power.** So, using the power of the Holy Spirit—without which not one of us could do anything—we must complete the four steps to repentance, to have "the sin of oppositional thinking" in us forgiven. But that's not how the story ends. The remission of our sins is also a must, and that comes with His resurrection.

Keep in mind that when Jesus said from the Cross, "It is finished," He declared that **with his death** the **penalty is paid.** Thus, we say that our sin has already been forgiven. But for you and I to be the recipients of that forgiveness, and to be made able to live like forgiven people, we must complete the steps. God said, **"IF"** my people . . . **THEN** will I hear from heaven, **forgive** their sin and **heal** their land. Brothers and sisters, the ball is in each of our court. There will be those who don't and won't agree with me. But this is not about me: it's about what the word of God says. When we have successfully adhered to the principle, then we can enjoy the promise:

> *"And you shall receive the gift of the Holy Ghost. For the promise is to you and to your children, and to all that are afar off, even as many as the Lord our God shall call."*

Peter didn't say, "You **might** receive the gift." He said, "You **will** receive it." But look closely, that phrase begins with the holy conjunction **"and,"** which connects the two thoughts. My Father's children, **IF** on this day, you have repented this **Promise** has been fulfilled in your ears. **If** you have **not**, but you intend to be a follower of Christ, there is no way around it: **you must repent** and **be baptized** in the name of Jesus, **before** you can receive the gift of the Holy Ghost.

I think I need to help somebody right here. I apologize for these interruptions, so please forgive me. But preacher and teacher is what I am, and preach and teach is what I do. We have already dealt with that word, "Repent," but there is a play on words in the rest of that verse that we should not overlook. The English word, **"baptize"** translates the Greek word, ***"Bap-tid-zo"*** which means "to **submerge** or to be **"put under."** Now hook that up to the English word, **"name,"** which is the Greek word, ***"on-o-ma,"*** meaning **"authority or power;"** and "Being Baptized in the name of Jesus now reads: "to be put under the authority or the power of God the Father, God the Son and God the Holy Spirit." In the name of Jesus Christ meant all three, because Jesus declared that *"All power in heaven and in earth was in His hands."* So when Peter said, *"Repent and be baptized every one of you in the name of Jesus Christ,"* He was stating an absolute fact that included the dual role that the Son of God performed here on earth.

And I think I need to say this: "That did not give some of these "Bible-toting, scripture quoting, judgment-spewing, hope-to-die Christians" the license to step down on un-learned and un-suspecting people; telling them that "Unless they have been baptized "in the name of Jesus, **only,** they are not saved." The Bible says, "Let God be true, but everyman a liar" (Romans 3: 4). Putting it all together, "to repent" means to change the direction of our lives: **from** a life of selfishness and rebellion against the Laws of God, **to** a life of Christ in which you depend on him first for forgiveness; then for continuous mercy, guidance, and purpose.

My Father's children, it goes without saying that we cannot save ourselves—that only God can save us. Well, His plan is non-negotiable. No doubt all of us have been to the water to be baptized. But water Baptism is only an outward sign of an inward intent. Baptism, as used by Jesus in Matthew 28:19 and by Peter here in Acts 2:38, goes much deeper than the baptism pool. You must be born again. And that's more than mouthing platitudes— just saying you have been born again. To be "born again" literally means that:

(1) You have come to the realization that "your way is not working in your best interest, you admit your short-comings, and petition the Spirit of God to intercede for you"—that's called 'humbling yourself;' (2) When you have talked to God and have asked for His forgiveness—that's called praying; you are to (3) "seek God's face." That means following the edict of the apostle Paul in 2 Timothy 2:15. Under the authority and the direction of the Holy Spirit, you search the scriptures for the 'will and the way' of God—A.K.A His face—and in so doing, when the time is fulfilled you will receive a "new life" complete with a "new mind." And with your new mind, you subscribe to the re-statement of the principle and promise in Romans 10:9, NKJV, which says that:

> *"if you will confess with your mouth the Lord Jesus,* **i.e. the [Lord-ship of Christ],** *and believe in your heart that God raised Him from the dead, you will be saved"*—

That would be emblematic of your desire to live life God's way. Lastly, you begin to (4)—*"turn from your wicked ways."* It is the turning that takes you to the second step in the procedural process: "To be saved from the power of Sin."

When you have completed those four steps, you will be forgiven for the 'Sin' of oppositional thinking. You *can* now claim the "New birth." Stated succinctly, you are ready, willing, and able to do more than just say, "I know I've been born again." Salvation is free; but as you can now see, there is a high cost to the free gift. In addition to the water, you've got to be baptized with the Spirit. And being baptized with the Spirit is being put under the complete authority and power of the Spirit of God the Father; God the Son; and God the Holy Spirit, once and for all time—which is total surrender.

The first thing on your agenda as a new person in Christ is to revisit 2 Timothy 2:15 and begin to:

> *"Study to show thyself approved unto God, a workman that needeth not to be ashamed, rightly dividing the word of truth."*

That directive is one of the most often quoted—but the most often overlooked—when it comes to paying the high cost of that free gift. It was spoken one time to Timothy in one place, with a specific application to him as a young pastor. But I believe I'm on safe ground when I say it will enable everyone to borrow Peter's words—to go and grow in the knowledge of Jesus. That requires the work of "God-in-all-three persons," working in concert **in** you and **on** you, to make all of that happen.

And when you have been born again, in Romans 8:16 Paul says:

"The Spirit itself bears witness with our spirit, that we are the children of God: for the natural man receives not the things of the Spirit of God: for they are foolishness to him: and neither can he know them, because they are spiritually discerned."

In other words, a relationship with God cannot be developed because what he has heard is a traditional application, and not of God; because it has been naturally discerned. Sadly enough although very true, even after reading these words there are those who will not heed them. But that will continue to remain their problem, not yours. That has always been one of the drawbacks to free-will. No doubt Jesus had these folk in mind in Matthew 7:13-14, when He urged those who were striving to be one of His disciples to "stay focused and stay on course. That is not a problem when you have been born-again of the water and of the Spirit. Your walk will match your talk, and you will feel so good about it you will tell somebody.

At the outset, I told you what I was going to tell you. Then I took my time and told you. Now I'm going to tell you what I've told you, hitch this thing up to Calvary and take my seat. Are you still with me? Good. Keep in mind that depending on your gift as a disciple, your task is tell somebody what the Lord has done for you. If you are not a preacher, don't try to preach. If you are not a teacher, don't try to teach. Simply tell those whom you meet what the Lord God has done for you. In other words, by sharing your joy, you are planting the seed; or what you say will water a seed that has already been planted. Do that and leave it to God to grant the increase in His own time.

And for the nay-sayers: with or without you, somebody is going to say something. The Bible says, "Let the Redeemed of the Lord say so." And make no mistake about it . . . There will be a witness to God in this Church. As a matter of fact, there will be a witness to God in this neighborhood and in this community. Justice **will** roll down like **thunder** and **righteousness** like a mighty **stream.** Paul said, **"Be not deceived, God is not mocked . . ."**

Weeping **may** endure for a **night**, but **Joy will come** in the morning:

God **WILL** make a way . . . Prayers **WILL** be answered . . . Hearts **WILL** be changed . . . . Minds **WILL** be made whole . . . Hurts **WILL** be healed . . . . Lives **WILL** be lifted . . . . Songs of praise **WILL** be sung . . . . Testimonies **WILL** be told . . . . Praise **WILL** be positive . . . . Grace **WILL** be given . . . . Salvation **WILL** be sustained . . . . You and I **WILL** do better and God **WILL** get the glory . . . **Why**? Simply because somebody is going to stand up and say something . . . .

But I have to tell you that, **IF you** are **too Sophisticated** to say amen . . . And if **YOU** are **too Educated** to cry hosanna . . . And if **YOU** are **too Opinionated** to say thank you Jesus . . . And you are **too Assimilated** to shout hallelujah . . . And if **you** are **too acculturated** to say praise the Lord . . . and **too acclimated** to cry **holy** . . . **Too DIGNIFIED** to say **Glory** . . . . **Too Smart** to **shout** . . . . Too **Cute** to **cry** . . . . and too **Cool** to **care** . . . . Just you remember that Jesus said, "If these hold their peace, the **rocks WILL** cry out . . ."

The **Heavens WILL** declare the Glory of God . . . and The **Earth WILL** show forth His handy work . . . **Not** when the **preacher** steps up to **preach** . . . . **Not** when the **choir** gets ready to **sing**, but when **GOD** comes into **HIS** house . . . **When God** walks among the seven golden candle sticks . . . . **When HE**, out of **his** love for **us**, pours out **His Spirit** . . . the heavens **will declare** the glory of God and the earth **will show** forth His handy work. And because I am a living witness to the faithfulness of God to His word, I use every opportunity afforded me to tell the world that our God is real; and that 'there are blessings unlimited and all good things without end' (1 Corinthians 2:9) awaiting those who make the decisive-decision to serve a true and living God.

With that outpouring on the day of Pentecost, the promise of Jesus to His Disciples was fulfilled (Acts 1:8). In accordance with the KJV of the Bible, that was nearly two thousand years ago. At His command, some of us have made the remembrance of it perpetual; and rightfully so, for the Spirit of God is still with us today. He is our comforter, our teacher and our keeper. His overall task is that of "Gate-Keeper." Our task, metaphorically speaking, should we decide to get on board this "Old ship of Zion," is to submit and surrender. It is our choice to submit to the Sovereignty of God the Father **over** our lives. And should we decide to submit, we must also surrender to the Lordship and the leadership of His Holy Spirit **in** our lives. I pray that the Spirit of God will shower you with Blessings-unlimited and all good things without end.

CHAPTER TWENTY-THREE

Entering in at the Strait Gate

PROLOGUE

THE voice of God the Son said,

> *"Enter ye in at the strait gate: for wide is the gate, and broad is the way, that leadeth to destruction, and many there be which go in there at: because strait is the gate, and narrow is the way, which leadeth unto life, and few there be that find it."*

Another translation records it this way:

> *"You go in through the narrow gate because the gate to hell is wide and the road that leads to it is easy and there are many who travel it. But the gate to life is narrow and the way that leads to it is hard, and there are few who find it."* (TEV)

Either way you slice it or dice it, the Bible sets the standards which highlight God's mark of excellence. We have the choice to either hit the bulls-eye or we miss the mark. There is no "in-between," and "almost" doesn't count. That would be like the man who said, "I didn't lie, I just didn't tell you the whole story." By the way, whether or not one agrees, "a half truth" is still "a whole lie." Hear the truth, the whole truth, and nothing but the truth.

What is it that's on the other side that makes entering in at the strait gate the preferred route? In other words, "Why the Strait Gate?" Personally, I chose to call it "An already decided destiny." But I must hasten to say to you, reader, that the choice of gates through which any of us enter life is always ours. Like everything else that Jesus said to us while He lived here with us,

His recommendation to 'enter in at the strait or the narrow gate' comes in the form of a suggestion.

PRESENTATION

JESUS said the gate to destruction—hell—is wide; the road that leads to it is easy to find, and there are many who travel it. Metaphorically speaking, the gate to hell is guarded by Satan; and it was him who deceived Eve by telling her half of what God said (Genesis 3:1ff). That half-truth started her to thinking. Her decision to use her free-will and think for herself, instead of trusting the word of God, opened the door for Satan, who dispatched his two oldest boys—the twin-spirits of Doubt and Denial—who were waiting in the wings, and who took up residence in the mind of Eve and subsequently in her heart.

As she listened to Satan, she began to doubt what God had said. Simply stated, she doubted the word of God in Chapter 1 Verse twenty-nine (1:29). And as she dialogued with the devil, he managed to convince her that God had held something back in the creation epic. Genesis 3:6 in the (NKJV) reads:

> *"So when the woman saw that the tree was good for food, that it was pleasant to the eyes, and a tree desirable to make one wise, she took of its fruit and ate."*

All of what she saw added up to her 'second-guessing God', and denying the validity of what He had said concerning the provisions that He had made for both of them. Suffice it to say, when she exercised her free will and began to think for herself, everything went down-hill after that.

WHO IS YOUR SOURCE?

ADAM—the other half of the family-equation—was heard saying in Genesis 3:10,

"I heard thy voice in the garden, and I was afraid because he was naked, and I hid myself." Adam was besieged with fear because he had been disobedient. Take note of the consequences and the order in which they were distributed, starting in Chapter 3, verse 14. **First,** God punished the **serpent** for his part in Satan's diabolical plan; secondly, He turned His attention to **Satan** who had embodied the serpent for his part in the play. Thirdly He dealt with Eve (v.16) for her contribution in Satan's scheme. And last but not least, He let Adam's consequence fall on him: **"not for eating of the fruit"** (Genesis 3:6), but for **"listening to the voice of his wife** (v. 17)." Adam's decision to be disobedient came on the heels of "not listening to the word of God." In natural progression, because the *spiritual connection had been broken, God did the only thing that He could do. The Scripture says:*

> *"God made coats of skin, and clothed them" (Genesis 3:21ff.). Then God said, "Behold the man is become as one of us, to know good and evil; and now, lest he put forth his hand and take also of the tree of life, and eat, and live forever: therefore the Lord God sent him forth from the garden of Eden, to till the ground from whence he was taken. So he drove out the man and placed at the east of the garden of Eden Cherubim and a flaming sword which turned every way, to keep the way of the tree of life" (Genesis 3:22-23).*

For failing to hear and adhere to the word of God, Sin is now alive and well in the world, and Salvation is required, in order for any of us to be restored.

A WORD OF WARNING

THE Bible confirms that *"The people of God are destroyed because of a lack of knowledge"* (Hosea 4:6). But that's not the whole the story. That verse begs to be delineated. Perhaps it would be easier to understand if we add the following. Throughout the Old Testament, to obtain forgiveness the priests offered the sacrifice and a sin offering; and the Chief Priest went behind the curtain into the Holy of Holies to ask forgiveness—for atonement of the sins of the people. And in response, God sent His message to the people by His prophets. At the crucifixion of Jesus, the curtain in the temple was torn in two leaving the way open so that the people could go to God for themselves.

The meaning of the message of the prophet Hosea went much deeper that it appears. In the "b" portion of that verse, Hosea—whose name in Hebrew means "Salvation"—attacked the problem at the root. When looked at in the proper context, the truth of Hosea message was that the priests and the Chief priests were the source of their dilemma. In the simplest of terms, those religious leaders had strayed from the Laws of God. In other words, they had done wrong for so long, to them wrong looked like right; and subsequently, ignorance-in-perpetuity was leading the people in a wrong direction. The prophet's message was recorded in the 8th century, B.C.

Here I am thirteen centuries later, a 21st Century Prophetic Voice to the nations, and the message is still the same. There is one dramatic exception: a few of us have caught the vision and are striving to do it right. The leaders rejected the knowledge of God back then, but a few of us—comparatively—have been designated change-agents for Christ. We have made the decisive decision to accept, rather than to reject the word of God. We search the scriptures daily under the leadership and the direction of the Holy Spirit, looking for truth, justice and the way of God. We are looking for truth. The question was asked, "What happens when you do what is right, the right way?" In other words, what will be the rewards? I really can't speak for the others, but I can tell my part of the story.

The Entering

I was more than sixty-five years old when I made the decisive-decision to submit and surrender. With all that I knew about the Bible, and in spite of all of my experiences and exposure, for the first time I began to take the Bible at its word, verbatim and without exception. In making my decision about how I wanted to live my life, I verbally acknowledged the Sovereignty of God over my life (Proverbs 18:21) and made a respectful request of the Father to let His Spirit fall fresh on me. In response I found the passage where Jesus said:

> *"The Thief does not come except to steal, and to kill, and to destroy. I am come that they might have life and that they might have it more abundantly" (John 10:10b).*

Without assumption, presumption, conjecture or prognostication, whatever Jesus meant I wanted some of it. I soon discovered that translated, I was asking the Spirit of God to take the Lordship and leadership in my life. That's when I also discovered that after being saved from the penalty of sin, instead of following through in accordance with the voice of God in 2 Chronicles 7:14 and Paul's edict to Timothy (2 Timothy 2:15), I had chosen to live the last three decades of my life doing things my way. I had done evil in the sight of God because I had lived life the way those who came before me had lived it.

After a while, time and circumstances dictated and I said to myself and to my God, "enough is enough." Things were not working out in my favor. I really didn't know what to expect, but I was so far down, spiritually, it was an uphill climb to the bottom. On the advice of a friend and brother, I embarked on a diligent and protracted study of the Bible. And following the edict of the voice of God in 2 Chronicles 7:14, I gained forgiveness for my sins. The problem was, I had stopped short and had not been forgiven for the one major sin in my life: "Thinking in opposition to God." For others it may have been different, but for me, a word to the wise was made sufficient.

PERCEPTION, PRESUMPTION AND PURSUIT

WHAT I hoped for was still unseen. But one day while studying the Scriptures, I heard the voice of God—the-Holy-Spirit speaking in Matthew 7:13-14. Because I had grown spiritually to the point of accepting the word of God without exception, after hearing His voice I began praying for God to make me usable, and then use me in kingdom building. In essence, I began endeavoring to enter in at the Strait Gate through the doorway to what I have learned to call an already decided destiny; and I did it without a clear understanding of what lay in store. Stated succinctly, I acted on faith.

My perception was since I had retired from leading a Church in Los Angeles, CA, relocated to Birmingham, AL with the desire to teach at one of the Historically Black Colleges and Universities, I presumed that following up on my dream would not be a problem. I was highly educated and saw no reason why I couldn't pursue my dreams. That's when things took what I'm going to call a drastic turn. I received a telephone call from an old friend stating that he had a problem and my help was needed. In retrospect I see now that the perfect plan of God included me answering the "Macedonian call" from my friend who was the presiding prelate of the African Methodist Episcopal Church in Alabama (AMEC).

STARTING ALL OVER AGAIN

ON the 15th of December, 2006, he appointed and God anointed me to become the pastor of a Church family in Calera, AL. Last week, I began what is now my 6th year of service with the 9th District of the AME Church. One of the aims of this work is to grasp the measure of truth that has been invested in me and use it to replace tradition. Simultaneously, as I performed my duties as a pastor, I strove to replace doubt with certainty. What about those who don't or won't hear? I was asked. The answer to that question has created a problem that will no doubt remain until Jesus returns. I could be wrong, but I don't think so. I sincerely believe that those who can't or won't hear, are part of the group to which Jesus was referring when he said, **"The poor you will have with you forever," for they are deserving of pity and/or mercy** (Mark 14:7). Simply put, they are victims who have fallen in battle. They are down but they don't have to be out. There is still a chance for them to recover.

Somewhere I read that "It is never a good policy to blame the victim for his (or her) own victimization," because there is always an under-lying cause which generates the effect, and with which the victim is powerless to control. Furthermore, I believe there is general agreement that the problem in the Christian community today exists partly because of ignorance; and partly because of apathy. Collectively, those two diseases have caused many of us **'who, having itching ears' have turned away our ears from the truth, and turned them into fables'** (2 Timothy 4:4). But why are things that way in a country so deeply rooted in the Christian ethos? I was asked. My answer is "I'm really not through thinking about that yet; for that question continues to cause me anxiety and concern.

SUMMARY

WHEN it comes to life-application and the writing of this book, I sometimes wonder if I have done my work well. I have to ask myself, "Did I answer the relevant questions?" For example, "Who is God, in and of Himself?" "What is God in each of us, and who are we in God?" Essentially my objective was to demonstrate that God placed in each of us the propensity—the inclination and tendency to think positive, be productive and progressive on a consistent, continuous and conducive basis—thereby making us usable. Those are some of the attributes which describe and delineate the nature of God. All nine of those attributes are foundation gifts.

However, the first six—like every other gift that God has given us—because of sin, must be apprehended and activated. And our ability to move forward in either of them can only be accomplished by the Spirit of God, working through the word of God, in the child of God, who is doing the will of God (Zechariah 4:6). The last three—Able, Accessible, and Accountable—are restricted. Let me personalize. To be "Able" is to put your spirit of a sound mind to good use: maximizing your ability to hear the word, receive it and believe it. Then, as you go and grow in the knowledge of Jesus, the Christ, care must be taken to not let your academic altitude mess up your spiritual attitude. Keeping in mind that regardless of how many letters you have behind your name, your approach to God must be in humility; care must be taken to guard against replicating my mistakes. It took me almost three decades climb down off that ladder, make myself humble, and talk to God about my problem.

The decent to the bottom made me accessible both, to the Spirit of God and to my circle of family and friends. The only thing that remained is the accountability factor. As I strive to enter in at the Strait Gate, through the doorway to an already decided destiny, I am constantly struggling to remain accountable. By now, one should have deduced that "Entering" is ongoing. The "How" factor is clear. All I had to do was "Do the right thing, the right way, on a daily basis."

Since that day the SOG has kept me acutely aware of the fact that I am not travelling alone. The Spirit of God is my guide. His role and function is to ***"keep me from falling and to present me faultless before the presence of His glory with exceeding joy"*** *(Jude 25)*. You have heard the old saying which reads: "Nothing from nothing, leaves nothing;" well, close observation will reveal that in those days, pastors told their parishioners next to nothing; so they knew next to nothing; therefore, they did next to nothing. Subsequently, when the final bell was toll, they had next to nothing. And if those same conditions persist, one-hundred (100) years from today, we will still have next to nothing. It is on that note that I made the decision to hear the voice of God in scripture as if He was speaking directly to me. The voice of God said, ***"My people are destroyed for lack of knowledge" (Hosea 4:6)***.

Scripture says Jesus came into Galilee preaching the gospel of the kingdom of God, and saying,

> ***"The time is fulfilled; the kingdom of God is at hand: repent ye, and believe the gospel"*** **(Mark 1:15).**

I took Him at his word, verbatim and without exception.

CHAPTER TWENTY-FOUR

My Ever-present Past

PROLOGUE

IT has been said that "You cannot teach what you do not know, and you cannot lead where you cannot go." So it is that I end this project with a page out of my ever-present past. Purely for my own edification and enjoyment, I carry with me in my heart these words from an old hymn of the Church.

> *"I sing because I'm happy, I sing because I'm free, for His eye is on the sparrow, and I know He watches me."*

Let me hasten to differentiate between 'happy' and 'joyful,' because it is the 'joy of Jesus' that blankets my spiritual fabric. Being happy is not out of the question—so long as it is within the context of the first Psalm of David. But if the content is taken out of that context, I revert to being joyful. In addition, please allow me to make it clear at the outset that I have not arrived. But like the Apostle Paul, this is what I do:

> *"Forgetting those things which are behind, and reaching forth to those things which are before, I press towards the mark for the prize of the high calling of God in Christ Jesus" (Philippians 3:13-14).*

Stated succinctly, I am in the process of becoming all that I will become; but I have a head-start on those who have not caught the vision. **"I have been saved' from the penalty of sin on the profession of my faith; I am in the process of being saved from the power of sin' as I go and grow in the knowledge of Jesus;** and when my time on earth has been fulfilled, **I will be saved from the presence of sin when I make the transition from**

'now until then' (1 Corinthians 13:12b). Meanwhile back at the beginning.

STONY THE ROAD I HAVE TROD (1946)

I begin my reflection at the age of six when my mother moved me and my siblings to Richmond, California from Birmingham, Alabama. I don't remember much before that time, except that my maternal grandfather was a Primitive Baptist preacher who rode circuit in and around Phenix City, Alabama, and I was allowed to go with him wherever he went. During my pre-pubescent years, my family ranked high on the list of dysfunctional families in our community. We were poor but we didn't know it because all of the families around us were on the same economic strata. My sister and I had the same mother and father, but there were two others who had different fathers, who, like us, didn't know them. We were reared by our maternal grandmother while my mother worked in the shipyards. We lived in government projects which had been provided for workers in the Shipyards in Richmond, CA, during WW II; and my mother—one of the many—was on 'Aid to Families with Dependent Children' (AFDC) to supplement her income.

During those years my mother defined our reality and gave us no room in which to wiggle. She and her father before her had a pivotal rule in their houses: "You do as I say, or else. I brought you in—and and with a snap of the finger—she clearly indicated that she would take us out." Neither of my siblings was brave enough to challenge the 'or else,' so we did as we were told. My mother believed solidly in a literal reading of the KJV of the Bible, and used it to a fault in rearing her children.

For example, Proverbs 22:6 reads:

> *"Train up a child in the way he should go: and when he is old, he will not depart from it;"*

And Chapter 23, Verses13 & 14 housed the rule and guide to her faith and practice. Those verses read:

> *"Withhold not correction from the child: for if thou beatest him with the rod, he shall not die. Thou shalt beat him with the rod, and shalt deliver his soul from hell."*

My maternal grandfather had deposited those verses in my mother's mental file cabinet, and she deposited them into my knowledge bank and an early age. Like mother, like son, I passed them on to my six children as they came into the world, and they were not negotiable. Not only were they the rule and guide to her faith and practice, I believed solidly in them and used them to straighten out the crooked places in the lives of my children.

I grew up isolated and without many friends at all. Between the age of six and fifteen, when school was out I was confined to the room that I shared with my sister—until I turned ten and she turned eleven—or we worked in the fields harvesting fruits and vegetables—literally, anything that grew. It was during those years that our older brother left home and joined the Army-Air Corp, and I inherited his room. Instead of allowing me to go out and play after school, my mother made me sit and read to pass the time. At the risk of making my mother sound like a 'brow-beating ogre' let me explain. I was a 'big kid.' I came into the world weighing twelve (12) pounds, nine and ½ ounces; and at the age of eleven, I was five feet eleven and weighed one-hundred and ninety-eight (198) pounds. By the way, I was the biggest kid in the seventh grade.

Parents of children my age were afraid I would hurt one of them if we played together; and my mother was afraid that I would get hurt if she allowed me to play with children my size, because they were several years older. The alternative was for me to stay inside. That explains my isolation. Staying inside had its advantages. I had a good memory and I used to my advantage. I memorized quite a bit of the KJV of the Bible, which made me sound more mature when I spoke, than I really was. By the time I was fifteen, I was out of high school with nothing to do.

College was a figment of somebody's imagination in our house, but not mine. With no other recourse in sight, I elevated my age, convinced my mother to sign the enlistment papers, and joined the Air Force. A man at the Probation Office in our town echoed my conviction, and convinced my mother that signing the papers would be the lesser of two evils.

To put it bluntly, I went from being an adolescent child of fifteen, to a full grown man of twenty-one in a matter of minutes, with a few strokes of a Remington typewriter. From there on—as I look back—life was like riding a merry-go-round-of-madness on an exercise in futility. I spent several years pretending to be what time and circumstance had not allowed me to become: a mature man. Of course I didn't know any of this until the Spirit of God (SOG) opened my eyes and I was made able to see; and that was at the age sixty-five (65).

A lot happened to me in the fifty years between fifteen and sixty-five. The most important of the lessons that I learned was that 'there is no right way to do wrong.' Another lesson that I learned at age sixty-five—that I didn't know before then—was that what I struggled to figure out on a daily basis—the purposeful and permissive will of God-the-Father had already worked it out in the design-phase—before the beginning was begun. I perceived that He had directed His Spirit to carve out a prominent place for me in His perfect plan. That plan included, but was not limited to me discovering that I was divinely gifted to be a 21st Century Prophetic Voice to the Nations.

I call this part of my story 'a page out of my ever-present past' because everything that happened to me had happened to someone else before me; and I found out, as the Scripture says, "there is nothing new under the sun" (Ecclesiastes 1:9). The literary version of my story actually starts when I was about six years old, and has continued until this very day. In retrospect, my story and yours—if you decided to tell it—would sound like this.

AN INTERESTING PARALLEL

BIBLE readers will recall that in Genesis Chapter 3, Satan deceived Eve by convincing her that God had omitted something in the creation epic. As a result she became easy prey for Doubt and Denial—whom I identify as Satan's two oldest boys—to move in and set up residence in her mind and heart. With nothing to stop her or to protect her, she began to use her free-will to make decisions for herself. Everything went down-hill from that point onward. Simply stated, Eve began to see herself as Satan saw her, rather than as God had made her.

Satan told Eve that *"her eyes would be opened, and she would be as gods, knowing good and evil."* My beginning paralleled Eve's. I did wrong for so long, wrong began to look like right. Scripture says,

> *"When the woman saw that the tree was good for food, and that it was pleasant to the eyes, and a tree to be desired to make one wise, she took of the fruit thereof, and did eat, and gave also unto her husband with her; and he did eat. And the eyes of them both were opened, and they knew that they were naked; and they sewed fig leaves together, and made themselves aprons."*

In Genesis 3:8 the Scriptures say,

> *"And they heard the voice of the LORD God walking in the garden in the cool of the day: and Adam and his wife hid themselves from the presence of the LORD God among the trees of the garden. And the LORD God called out to Adam (Genesis 3:9), and said, 'Where are you?'*

Adam answered, saying:

> *"I heard thy voice in the garden, and I was afraid, because I was naked; and I hid myself"* (Genesis 3:10).

The answer that Adam gave God informs us of his—and our—dilemma. Fear and Insecurity—Satan's other two boys—had taken up residence in the mind and heart of Adam. Collectively, they neutralized his spirit of power, of love, and of a sound mind (2 Timothy 1:7). Doubt, Denial, Fear, and Insecurity became permanent birth defects in all of Adam and Eve's off-spring. And unless and until each of us submit and surrender to the Lordship and leadership of God's Holy Spirit, they will remain within us as our constant traveling companions. That's the long way around of saying that what happened to Adam and Eve also happened to their children; and it explains what happened to me as well.

David made it plain in Psalm 51:5. He informed us that he and all of humanity would be born in sin and shaped in iniquity. Specifically and using the purest principles of piety and virtue, my mother nurtured in me an acute case of fear and insecurity. Giving her the benefit of doubt, as an adult whose eyes have been opened, I can say with certainty that my mother prepared the soil in me for the planting of the seed when the time was fulfilled. The seed in me was actually planted in January, 1938, to come forth on the first day of the year in 1939. But, as time would have it, I wouldn't say yes to the LORD God and accept the LORD Jesus as my savior until the third Sunday in January in 1974. On that day, on the profession of my faith I was saved from the penalty of sin (Genesis 2:17). The next step for me was 'to be saved from the power of sin;' which would start when I began the first phase of true repentance.

ME and MINE

WHAT happened to me in the next three decades is a clear picture of what will happen to anyone if he—or she—endeavors to circumvent the principles that are embedded in the procedural-process which leads to 'the full complement of salvation.' Translated, I followed the traditional path of repentance (Romans 10:9) and began to live my life according to the Golden Rule: "Doing unto others as I, in a like and similar situation, would have them do unto me." After more than three decades of living

226

my life that way, I can now say with certainty that 'good is always good,' and evil can only be mistaken as good. Let me make that clear.

Solomon once said,

> *"Wisdom is the principal thing; therefore get wisdom: and with all thy getting get understanding" (Proverbs 4:7).*

Translated, I can also say with certainty that understanding is the missing factor in most of our lives. "What do you mean preacher?" I was asked. The answer is simply this: I had studied to show myself approved unto God as a workman who had no need to be ashamed, because I could rightly divide the word of truth" (2 timothy 2:15); which is what I thought that verse meant. As a result, I had a firm grasp of the written word, with a lot of it committed to memory. But, paralleling Solomon, I was lacking in wisdom. Getting an understanding—according to Webster— requires an equal amount of wisdom and knowledge in a given subject area. I had the knowledge, which means in most situations I knew what to do. But I was lacking in wisdom—which is HOW to do it.

Dr. Martin Luther King, Jr. once said,

"Knowledge without wisdom makes you an educated fool;" and "Wisdom without knowledge locks you in the strait-jacket of your own mind;" which is tantamount to you going the wrong-way on a one-way street, and everybody knows it but you. "The solution to the problem said he, is synergistic" (5).

In other words, there must be an equal amount of wisdom to accompany your knowledge in a given subject area, in order to arrive at an understanding. Such was the case when I arrived in Alabama in August, 2006. I had gone through a failed marriage, which, for me defied all logic because I had done all that I thought was expected of me. But because I believed solidly in the power of prayer, I petitioned the LORD God for divine intervention. I had a God-sized problem and I needed a God-sized answer.

HIS EYE IS ON THE SPARROW

IT had taken me more than six decades to reach this point I my life, but today I can sing because I'm happy. Better still, I sing because I'm free. His eye is on the sparrow all the time, and that makes me know that He is watching me. The songwriter was on point when he asked the question, and many if not most of us, would do well to engage in introspection, until we can see clearly, ask and answer the same question.

"Why should I feel discouraged, why should the shadows come, why should my heart be lonely and long for heaven and home; when Jesus is my portion? My constant friend is He: His eye is on the sparrow and I know He watches me. His eye is on the sparrow, and I know He watches me. I sing because I'm happy, I sing because I'm free, for His eye is on the sparrow, and I know He watches me."

At the ripe old age of sixty-five years I reached the point of surrender. Let me pull over and park, and help somebody. Only after I had repented—following the edict of the voice of God in 2 Chronicles 7:14—and was born again of the water and of the Spirit (John 3:5), was I able to wrap my head around my part in God's plan. Given the life that I had lived and the choices that I made along the way, it was easy to blame someone else for what I did, or what I failed to do. But I thank God Almighty for His superintending Spirit which kept me and never left me— He kept me safe and sound from all hurt, harm, and danger; and never left me to my own devices, or I would have certainly stumbled and fell; and no doubt, I would have become a victim of self-destruction.

When the time was fulfilled I was able to speak truth to myself and to the Lord; forgive myself and begin to walk humbly with Him (Micah 6:8). Today I am not ashamed of the gospel I preach for I know it is the power of God unto salvation. It is my hope that something will be said in this book that will enlighten, enhance, and encourage others, such that they will hear, receive and believe, and be made able to know the joy of Jesus and forgiveness God's way (2 Chronicles 7:14b). There is an old cliché which reads, "Everybody wants to go to heaven, but nobody wants to die." Dying for me, however, now that I have a spiritual hook on the subject, is not a problem. Seven years ago I made a decisive-decision to "enter in at the strait gate" (Matthew 7:13) and began doing the right thing, the right way. Does that make me any different from anyone else? The answer is emphatically no. Like everyone else I started out with a fallen nature—albeit unknown as it relates to the fullness of its failures—and I needed to be saved before I could have life and have it more abundantly.

For the first sixty-five (65) years of my life, I blamed my mother—and others—for my failures. However, once I made the decisive decision to submit and surrender—submit to the Sovereignty of God over my life; and begin a systematic surrender to the Lordship and leadership of the Holy Spirit in my life—dying, on a daily basis became second nature. Today, my role and function as a twice-born child of God is to tell the world what the Lord has done for me. That is the primary aim and objective of this literary endeavor.

My journey on this road from earth's sorrow to heaven's joy began nearly seventy-five years ago. And like everyone else, until I reached the age of sixty-seven I attributed my inability to get where I wanted to go in life to someone else. However, when the Spirit of God opened my eyes so that I could see, I asked myself what we all ask ourselves at some time in life: "Who am I? And why am I where I am at this time in my life? The Spirit of God (Zechariah 4:6) also opened my ears so that I could hear, and then began a renewal process in my mind so that I could receive and believe.

From that point onward, the answers became crystal clear. To make a longer story short, my journey began on the road to repentance. By the way, what I did is a must for everyone. I say that because with God there is no respect of person and every opportunity is made available to everyone equally; which makes this path to perfection the same for everyone. Translated that means you, my brother (and sister) will have to offer your selves as candidates for baptism by the Holy Spirit as stated by Jesus in Matthew 28:18-20. And let's be clear, I am talking about becoming a "Disciple of Christ," not a member of a local church, which includes but is not limited to engaging in a diligent and protracted study of the Scriptures in search for the face of God—His will and His way. Stated succinctly, you must be in search for His approval of you as a workman who no longer has a need to be ashamed because of his ignorance; and that's because you will have been taught by the Holy Spirit to rightly divide the word of truth (2 Timothy 2:15).

Along with that opportunity also comes the same set of keys to the Kingdom that Jesus gave Peter (Matthew 16:19), and the gift of faith to use them. For clarity and consistence, since the meaning of that verse has been the subject of debate for centuries, I have included an overview of a short commentary found in the Life Application Study Bible (1996, P. 1624) which attracted and held my attention, and which I have added to my resource bank for future reference. It is not the only way, but I believe it to be a good way—one that works. That commentary reads:

> ***Some say the keys represent the authority to carry out church discipline, legislation, and administration (18:15-18); while others say the keys give the authority to announce the forgiveness of sins (John 20:23). Still others say the keys may be the opportunity to bring people to the Kingdom of heaven by presenting them with the message of salvation found in God's Word (Acts 15:7-9). The religious leaders thought they held the keys to the Kingdom, and they tried to shut some out.***

That said I am inclined to believe that we cannot decide to open or close the Kingdom of heaven for others. Instead, God uses us to help others find the way inside. Therefore, for all who believe "God is" (Hebrews 11:6) and are willing to make the decisive-decision in favor of the cause of Christ, and are willing to be obedient to His word, the Kingdom doors will automatically swing open.

It has taken me more than six years to reach the point of this writing in my quest for truth and God's way of living. However, the journey thus far has been well worth the effort. As previously stated, there was never any doubt in my mind about my calling in life, but access to my gifts on occasion, have caused me problems with doubt-and-denial. Sometimes I momentarily forget that the rewards and consequences of and for the choices that I have made in life getting to this point, have already been included in the perfect plan of God. And frankly speaking all any of us have to do is wake up each day to see what is in God's plan. Those acts of rebellion that I committed along the way caused the permissive will of God to push up the time-factor in my life to the point of my surrender.

In the fullness of time, according to the perfect plan of God for my life, the words of Jesus in Mark 1:15, became my reality. When I arrived in Birmingham, AL in August, 2006 it was time. Jesus said, *"The time is fulfilled, and the kingdom of God is at hand: repent ye and believe the Gospel."* It was then that I was made aware that just as it was with the prophet Jeremiah in Chapter 1, Verse 4, the purpose of God for my life had also been ordained before He formed me in my mother's womb. The voice of God said to Jeremiah, *"Before you were formed in your mother's womb, I ordained you a prophet to the nations."*

IN THE BEGINNING

BECAUSE of my insecurity most of my early adult life was spent striving to be accepted. Having been isolated almost all of my childhood I had no friends and my family members numbered few and far-between. As a matter of fact, they consisted of my grandmother, my mother, her brother, my brother and my sister. There might have been others, but I didn't know them. The bottom line is, when I left home at the tender age of fifteen (15), I had to cultivate a circle of family and friends; and that I did at a tremendous cost.

I didn't recognize my weakness or the dilemma it produced until I endured a failed marriage at the age of sixty-five (65). As the story goes, I was forced to hire a Psychologist in 2004 to help me work through the throes of a lop-sided divorce. For more than thirty years I had striven to live by the tenets of the Bible, and for me divorce was not an option in a marriage that I believed was sanctioned by God. One of the lessons I had to learn was that of 'the role and function of a husband in a godly marriage.' To this day I still believe that the role and function of a godly husband is to provide, protect, and pray for his family; as God did for Adam and Eve. My problem was, I had the knowledge but I didn't have the wisdom. I knew what to do, but I didn't know how to do it.

Even with a Seminary degree—one in which I Minored in Marriage and Family and Children's Counseling—it wasn't until I hired the services of a practicing Psychologist that I was made able to develop a mental-state-of-readiness—in the wisdom department—that was equal to my knowledge-bank. Beginning in 2004, Dr. Jackson—not his real name—helped me to turn the hands of time back to when I was a child so that I could see how and when fear and insecurity moved in and took up residence in my life.

It was in early 2006 when my eyes came open, and I was able to see clearly. As a result, between 1954 and 2004 I spent an inordinate amount of time, talent, and treasure striving to be accepted. Since then I have learned to forgive myself, acknowledge my weaknesses and embrace my strengths. None of that would have been possible had it not been for the penalty paid by Jesus out on Calvary. Paul's declaration to the Church at Rome in Chapter 10 Verse 9 identified the solution to my problem, and the phrase used by the writer to the Hebrews in 11:6 validated my needs. After travelling the road to repentance, I searched the scriptures until I discovered what Paul and the writer to the Hebrews meant by what they said.

It was then that I called on the 'name of the Lord'—i.e. summoned His power and authority—for the strength to stand fast in my faith. After that I followed through on what I believed, and since then the recall of the word has been my source of enablement, and the indwelling of the Holy Spirit has been my source of empowerment. Collectively they have caused things to grow and go from good (Genesis 1:31) to great (1 Corinthians 2:9). What follows is a page out of my ever-present past. Look closely and you might find that the events look strangely familiar.

MOVING TOWARDS PERFECTION

ENTERING in at the Strait Gate requires everyone to do things decently and in order, and I am no exception. That having been said let's move to the crossroads where choice and consequence grips most of us. Generally, we stop with 'mouthing platitudes'—merely saying that we believe and that we accept Jesus as our Lord and Savior.

The fact is there are four steps to forgiveness and a new life in Christ. Upon completion "I was given my new life in Christ." With my new life I was enabled to live; and under the Lordship and the leadership of the Holy Spirit, I was empowered to move and have my being with a transformed, renewed mind and a changed heart" (Acts 17:28).

Now that I know the sediments of sin brought on by Satan, the arch-enemy of God, rather than continue to do the same thing the same way, hoping to somehow get some different results, I became a participant in the procedural-process which led to the full complement of salvation. Under the Lordship and the leadership of the Holy Spirit, I thank God for the opportunity, and respectfully request that the reader bear with me while I take time out to replicate the "rules of thumb" for this work.

In the proclamation of Peter in Acts 2:38, we were told **to:**

> *"Repent and be baptized in the name of Jesus Christ, for the remission of your sins, and you shall receive the gift of the Holy Spirit.*

Close observation will reveal that in that verse, there is a principle and a promise. The **principle** is to repent and be baptized; and the **promise** is to become the recipient of the Holy Spirit. Translated, the four steps to repentance are the principles. They are the contingencies. They are the laws of God and they satisfy the requirements of God for repentance. Satisfaction of the principles guarantees enjoyment of His promises.

In this case I am going to individualize and personalize. Having made the four required steps, I was forgiven and the Spirit of God healed my land; that is to say, He again made me prosperous. But that's not all. I began again a diligent and protracted study of scripture as Paul told Timothy in in his second letter, Chapter 2 Verse 15. And having begun that study of the word of God, I was also brought face-to-face with the beginning requirements for baptism, in the name of Jesus Christ.

By way of definition and delineation, when it comes to baptism, there is a play on words which begs to be translated and then transmitted. Using Strong's Exhaustive Concordance of the Bible as my reference, I found that the English word **"baptism"** translates the Greek word **"baptidzo,"** which means "to be put under;" and the English word **"name"** translates the Greek word **"O-no-ma"** which means "authority" or "power." Summarily, when I was baptized in the name of the Father, and of the Son, and of the Holy Spirit, a transliteration of that verse would have heard the voice of God saying, "Put him under the authority and the power of God the Father who created him, God the Son who redeemed him, and God the Holy Spirit who will keep him from falling; and present him faultless before the presence of My glory with exceeding joy—that is to say, "seal him unto the day of redemption" (Jude 24).

Considering the fact that "all power in heaven and on earth" was given to Jesus upon His resurrection, when Peter made his declaration he was saying to me that I was now qualified to receive the gift of the Holy Spirit. And for the record, it is from that vantage point that I am writing. Stated succinctly, the word of God enables me, and the indwelling of His Holy Spirit empowers me, giving me the assurance that *"I can do all things through Christ which strengthens me" (Philippians 4:13).*

Being able to do all things through Christ which strengthens me includes, but is not limited to, having the power to carry out the Great Commandment in Matthew 22:37: *"You shall love the Lord thy God with all your heart, with all your soul, and with all your mind. While* I am empowered to carry out the Great Commandment, in that embrace we must not forget that the Great Commitment in Luke 9:23 precedes the Great Commandment. It was there that Jesus said, *"if anyone desires to come after Me, let him deny himself, and take up his cross daily, and follow Me."*

The Great Commission in Matthew 28:18-20 is the culmination. It reads:

> *And Jesus came and spoke to them, saying, "All authority has been given to Me in heaven and on earth. Go therefore and make disciples of all the nations, baptizing them in the name of the Father and of the son and of the Holy Spirit, teaching them to observe all things that I have commanded you; and lo, I am with you always, even to the end of the age.*

Suffice it to say, to fulfill the **Great Commission,** Disciples of Christ—out of necessity—must have already made the Great Commitment, which gives them the ability and the power to carry out the Great Commandment.

In the Great Commission, the Disciples of Christ were commanded to go and make disciples of all nations, and teach them to obey all things that Jesus commanded. I began my personal journey after wrestling with the tenets of Great Commitment. And because of the difficulty I had elevating my own belief and making it progressive, I have developed a great deal of compassion for my fellowman. In other words, I found that I—along with all of the people of God with whom I have interacted—have been stuck in the "membership mode" for more than five-hundred years in America. Simply stated, we become members of the church, and there remain fixed and focused on getting into heaven when we die, as our just reward.

The failure to respond to the procedural process of repentance supports my belief that to persuade the people of God to exchange their traditional Christian practices for biblical truth, will require a tremendous amount of effort, and a whole lot of time. There is nothing difficult about making Disciples of Christ. The Instructions for making Disciples of all nations are clear. I suppose a lot depends on which version of the Bible you are reading. The following are four versions that I used for comparison and contrast, as I prepared to write this manuscript.

The NKJV reads, *"All authority has been given to Me in heaven and on earth. Go therefore and make disciples of all the nations, baptizing them in the name of the Father and of the Son and of the Holy Spirit, teaching them to observe all things that I have commanded you; and lo, I am with you always, even to the end of the age."*

The KJV reads, "All power is given unto me in heaven and in earth. Go ye therefore, and teach all nations, baptizing them in the name of the Father, and of the Son, and of the Holy Ghost: teaching them to observe all things whatsoever I have commanded you: and, lo, I am with you always, even unto the end of the world."

The Good News Bible—Today's English Version—has it this way. "I have been given all authority in heaven and on earth. Go, then, to all peoples everywhere and make them my disciples: baptize them in the name of the Father, the Son, and the Holy Spirit, and teach them to obey everything I have commanded you. And I will be with you always, to the end of the age." One last example is:

The NIV reads: "Then Jesus came to them and said, "All authority in heaven and on earth has been given to me. Therefore go and make disciples of all nations, baptizing them in the name of the Father and of the Son and of the Holy Spirit, and teaching them to obey everything I have commanded you. And surely I am with you always, to the end of the age."

Although each of these versions read slightly different, in all four renderings, three things stand out and are constant: baptism, teaching and learning. When it comes to baptism, the traditional view involves taking the people to the water—which is an outward expression of an inward change. However, baptizing them "In the name of," or better stated "Putting them under the authority and the power of God the Father, God the Son and God the Holy Spirit," involves baptism by and with the Holy Spirit, which elevates truth over tradition. Collectively, it amounts to taking our traditional Christian practice to the next level. That level has its focus on the authority and the power of God the Father, God the Son, and God the Holy Spirit; and includes the follow-up to Jesus' proclamation in Matthew 28: 19—20. Hear an exposition of that word.

> *"I have all power in heaven and on earth. Heretofore I have sent you only to the Jews; but I am Lord of the entire world. Therefore I command you to go into all the world and make disciples of all nations. Enroll the people as scholars / learners, putting them under the authority and the power of God the Father, God the Son, and God the Holy Spirit; Teaching them to obey everything that I have commanded you, and surely I will be with you always, even to the end of the age" (Acts 16:15; Matthew 28:19-20).*

For the record and so that there is no longer confusion, make note of this. There is a direct correlation between "the apprehension of, and the adherence to, the expanded word of God," which grows out of your study and your ability to handle the Great Commitment. To the extent that you conform to the dictates of scripture, your ability to enjoy the promises of God will be manifested.

That said your positive mental attitude and your productive and progressive actions demonstrate whether or not you have been baptized in the name of Jesus Christ for the remission of sins. And as you submit and surrender to the Lordship and the leadership of the Holy Spirit, He will take His rightful place in your life. By the way, submission is instant. It simply requires a decisive-decision. But surrender is gradual. It is a growth process that will take you the rest of your natural life as you "are being saved from the power of sin," and will move you from "good" (Genesis 1:31) to "great" (1 Corinthians 2:9).

THE TIME IS FULFILLED

AS previously stated, when Jesus began His Galilean Ministry, scripture says He came into Galilee preaching the gospel of the kingdom of God. Bible readers will recall that in His sermon Jesus issued a very thought-provoking challenge. "He said,

> *"The time is fulfilled, and the kingdom of God is at hand. Repent, and believe in the gospel."*

It was with that in mind that I made a commitment to submit to the Sovereignty of God over my life, and began my surrender to the Lordship and leadership of the Spirit of God in my life. It was with that in mind that I extend this challenge to you, the reader. It's time for you to also become a follower of Christ.

Metaphorically speaking, believing that sin has caused all of the gifts of God to be placed in a discretionary account, and placing the onus on the believer; the first order of business for me was to make a decisive-decision to conform to the principles of God, so that I could enjoy the promises of God. Because sin had distorted the image of God in me and in all mankind, it was necessary for me—and it is necessary for all the people of God—to apprehend and activate all of God's gifts. I cannot speak for anyone else. But for me, access and activation was necessary because, between January, 1974 and August, 2006, I didn't have to worry about "getting lost in the shuffle," simply because "for more than a quarter-century, I had been shuffling along with the lost (sic)."

That position in life has **one** central drawback and downfall. Again, albeit unknowingly, those of us who have not been born-again of the water and of the spirit (John 3:5), would rather do anything than think, face the truth, and change. That is the outcome of Satan using thoughts, ideas, and suggestions (TIS's) to neutralize the spirit of a sound mind that God inherently instilled in each of us. In other words, that is the mark of sin. Having "been saved" from the penalty of sin on the profession of my faith, and being steadfastly involved in "being saved" from the power of sin by the indwelling of the Holy Spirit, made me more than willing to think, face the truth, and make the necessary changes that caused me to start growing and going from good (Genesis 1:31) to great (1 Corinthians 2:9).

Make no mistake about it, the task is extremely difficult, but it can be done. All it takes is—under the leadership of the Holy Spirit—making a decisive-decision to think positive, be productive and progressive, and live out your life according to God's way of thinking. That's another way of saying that the Holy Spirit must be on the throne of your heart. When that decisive-decision has been made, you will discover that you are at the turning point.

For clarity and conciseness, I need to rewind back to the beginning. My mother and her father before her subscribed to the Primitive Baptist motif. They both enforced the same rules in their respective homes: "If it's not written in the Bible, it's a sin and you don't do it or you will go to hell." And for my mother's children, hell was not an option. My mother not only believed solidly in a literal reading of the King James Version (KJV) of the Bible, she used it as the rule and guide to her faith and practice. For example, she followed Solomon's proverbs without exception. Chapter twenty-two (22) Verse six (6)—*"Train up a child in the way he should go: and when he is old, he will not depart from it"*—formed the foundation for rearing her children. And Chapter twenty-three (23) Verses twelve through fourteen (12-14)—*"Do not withhold correction from a child, for if you beat him with the rod, he will not die. You shall beat him with a rod, and deliver his soul from hell"*—set the boundaries.

THE TRUTH IS THE LIGHT

With nothing else on which to fall back, after being discharged from the Air Force I set my course for Las Vegas to possibly hook-up with my older brother, with a stop-over in Los Angeles. I went out to one of the prominent night spots in Los Angeles where a very popular R & B orchestra under the direction of Erskine Hawkins was playing. And while sitting and enjoying the music I noticed that no one was playing the piano. In addition, several requests for the orchestra's signature tune—Blues after

Hours—came in. The leader of the group kept putting the people off by telling them that his Piano-man had not arrived. That was my chance. One of the tunes I had learned to play quite well while growing up in isolation, was that particular song which had a 7-minute piano solo.

As of that night I began working as a "sideman" with the Erskine Hawkins—who was enjoying a modicum of fame because of two of his signature tunes: "Blues after Hours" and "Tuxedo Junction." It was my first night in Los Angeles at the infamous 'five-four' Ballroom. Erskine's piano player—the late Averill Paris—had an alcohol habit which rendered him incapacitated almost every night. Erskine had let me sit in and was highly impressed by my ability to not only play "Blues after Hours", but I could also hold my own with the other tunes that the group played. With no further discussion, I was hired to fill in for the piano-man when necessity dictated, pack instruments and drive for Mr. Hawkins in the interim.

I traveled across the country with the group and back to Los Angeles before being offered a job playing the electric piano with the "Ike and Tina Turner Revue," which called for me to play the piano on a regular basis. With Ike I worked six nights a week making $15.00 a night plus hotel-room and board, for about a year. That may not sound like much money, but that was the going rate in those days. We had a two-week layover in East St. Louis, Illinois—Ike's home town—preceding a scheduled recording session in D.C. in February, 1960.

In that two-week period I made telephone contact with and traveled to Chicago to meet my biological father. He was glad to see me and that made me feel good. In one of our many conversations he told me that he didn't see how I could make enough money to support myself playing music, but if I would go to school he would help me. Needless to say I was broke and when he said he would help me that sounded pretty good. I didn't waste any time, I enrolled Crane Junior College—which was later changed to Malcolm X Community College in March of 1961.

My father retired from Sears Roebuck and Company in May of 1960 at the age of sixty-two (62).

At his retirement dinner he introduced me to his supervisor and asked him if I could have his job. My father had been a janitor for a number of years and was well liked by all who knew him. His supervisor asked me about my back ground, about which I didn't dare tell him the whole truth. But, with my fingers crossed, I blocked out my ever-present past, revealing only that I recently arrived in Chicago and was attending Community College with a desire to become a Lawyer. He suggested that I come into personnel and take a battery of tests which would better enable him to see if he could find a place for me. I did that and was hired into Sears Operations Department.

THE SOIL HAD BEEN PREPARED

BECAUSE of the way I had been reared, it was easy for me to be polite, courteous, and well-mannered. In addition, I was a thinker and a hard worker. You might say that the soil had been prepared and the seed had already been planted. Starting in 1958, I began to live large like the man in charge, that I thought I was. Translated, I began to learn the ropes in life. I learned how to smoke, drink, cuss, spit, stay out all night, and get into an occasional bar fight because "my friends" thought it was the thing to do. Like the late Frank Sinatra once said:

> *"I have been a puppet, a pauper, pirate, a poet, a pawn and a king. I've been up and down, and over and under, and I've learned one thing: every time I found myself flat on my face, I picked myself up and got right back in the race, 'cause that's life: that's what people say; you're riding high in April and shot down in May; but that's life."*

In other words, I paid my dues. My circle of friends led, and I followed. I was a smoker and a drinker. Some of those with whom I worked in the clubs experimented with drugs, but I steered clear of all controlled substances because I had read about too many entertainers being out of control and subsequently dying from an over-dose of first one drug and then another and I wanted very much to live. Instead, I drank Covoisiere and Hennessey—the best of Cognac when my money wasn't funny—and Christian Brothers Brandy when it was. For the next twelve (12) years I worked 5-days a week for Sears and Roebuck and played music six nights a week and a matinee on Sunday in one of the local night clubs.

1965

EVERY night I drank at least a half-pint of cognac or brandy while I worked, and I went to bed each night with a drink to help me sleep. In addition, I started each day off with a Coffee Royale—a cup of coffee with a shot of brandy to clear my head. Some said that I was an alcoholic, but I didn't agree because I never got drunk or missed a day of work. I worked my way into Middle Management and did a stellar job as a Senior Buyer for Sears. Besides, "I only drank when I was by myself or with somebody (sic)." The history of my ever-present past states that I was only drunk two times in my life: my first night in San Antoine as an Air Force Recruit, and on my birthday on January 1st 1974, after which I quit smoking, drinking, chasing women, and doing all of those things that my mother called sin.

Since my story is partly instructional, I believe I would be remiss if I didn't include an example of the consequences of failing to think for yourself and letting someone else write your agenda. In January, 1961 my older brother committed a felony using my car, a crime for which I was arrested because the ownership of the car was traced to me. And because I let my mother influence me, I spent seventy-one (71) days in the Los Angeles County Jail. Had I spoke up for myself I would not have gone to jail; but my mother insisted that "God had blessed me more than He did my brother," and that if I loved my brother, I would simply keep my mouth shut. To do otherwise would have caused him to be convicted and spend more than ten years in prison. Again, I did as I was told, and because I refused to speak up for myself I was locked away.

On the night when I was first picked up, I was placed in an interrogation room in the City jail. Because I didn't answer his question the way he thought I should, one of police officers hit me in the side with what I believed to be a piece of rubber hose rolled up in a towel; and I had no better sense than to 'spring up off the stool on which I was sitting and hit him back.' A second officer in the room knocked me unconscious. When I came-to, I had been transferred from the City Jail to the County Jail. In the interim I was never charged or arraigned. Seventy-one (71) days later my brother was summoned to court and I was summoned as well. My brother was convicted on circumstantial evidence because I refused to testify against him. He was sentenced to probation for five years and ordered to make restitution. When asked if there was anyone there whose name had not been called, I raised my hand and responded to the Judge's questions. When it was determined that I had not been charged or arraigned, but had been locked up for eleven days beyond the statute of limitations, I was immediately set free.

I learned a lesson in life from that experience that I have never forgotten: "let no man write your agenda." That included my mother. From then on, I was determined to think for myself, face the truth, and change my attitude and actions when necessity dictated. I strove to file a law suit against the city for keeping me locked up longer than the 60-day statute of limitations. However, the Attorney I hired discovered that not only had I not been charged and arraigned, there was no record of me ever being incarcerated, and I couldn't prove different. In the long run, that was to my advantage, because my record was clear. You might say I earned a degree from the university of hard knocks.

OCTOBER, 1973

FOUR months after my arrival in Los Angeles, the supervisor for whom I worked in Chicago telephoned me and put the following suggestions on my mind. In a thirty-second telephone call, he asked, "Have I ever lied to you?" To which I said, no. "Have I always treated you like a son?" I said yes. He said, "Freeze your stock and get the hell out; they have got you pegged." This time he hung up. I sat there holding the receiver dumb-founded. I didn't

243

know what to make of the conversation, but I knew AL Zavinagus. Almost like a robot, I went to personnel and froze my stock. While I was trying to think of what I would do if I left Sears, I received a telephone from All State Insurance telling me to come to Chicago and close the deal on my house.

Sears had a policy that if a person was involuntarily transferred and couldn't sell his house within ninety (90) days, Sears would buy it. That telephone call alerted me that Sears was buying my house. I took a week off and flew to Chicago. I located AL who had since retired and moved to southern Illinois. He asked me if I had taken his advice and froze my stock. I told him that I had and was trying to figure out what I would do when I left Sears, when I received the telephone call from All State Insurance. He made me aware of the fact that if I could buy for sears, I had the best training in the business and that I could buy for anyone. I thanked him for his advice without asking what prompted him to give it.

Two months later after returning to Los Angeles, I noticed that Sears Stock had started dropping. In the past month I was told that it had fallen from $120 dollars a share to $83 dollars. I was locked in at $103 dollars a share so it didn't bother me. I resigned from Sears and went into business for myself. I cashed in my stock and used the profits to purchase a Shell Oil Company Franchise with an attached Service Station. Gasoline was $.29 a gallon and there was no such thing as "self-serve." When a person drove into a service station, he (or she) received "Full Service." In addition, I had two service bays in which to earn money doing light repairs— something I learned to do by reading Chilton Repair Manuals while passing the time as a buyer.

I worked that unit twelve hours a day for eighteen (18) months saving all of my profits. When the time was right I used my savings to purchase a second unit that was twice as large as the first one. That enabled me to use all the profit from the first unit to pay the taxes on both units, leaving the profit from the second unit virtually free.

December, 1973

The money was rolling in and I had been living "high on the hog." On December 31st 1973 I took the night off, and hired a local musician to work in my place. I invited two of my employees, their wives and my girlfriend out to celebrate my birthday on New Year's Eve. We visited several clubs but ended up at the 'TiKi-Island' where I normally worked 7 nights a week and a matinee on Sunday. I ordered a fifth of Hennessey and a set-up for six. I really don't remember much after 11:00 P.M. because the audience persuaded me to sit in with the band. I played and I sang—or so I was told—until well after midnight. I was very drunk but my employees and my girlfriend saw to it that I got home safely. The next day I woke up with a big head and a hangover. But a Coffee-Royale fixed that. It was called "a hair off the dog that bit you;" and it was guaranteed to cure you.

At the suggestion of my girlfriend later that day, I went to the club to pay my bar tab. When the bartender gave it to me, imagine my surprise to see a total of $47.50 on the tab. Did I get that drunk? What did I buy? I knew that a fifth of Hennessey only cost $12.50; and I knew that because I had bought many of them over the years. The bartender told me all I bought was a fifth and a set-up for six. I paid the tab but made up my mind that I was through with alcohol as of that night. I took to spending my spare time at the service station after that.

THE END OF THE FIRST BEGINNING

THEN it happened. I reached the turning point in my life. The date was January 1st 1974. Recalling some of the words which my mother drilled into our heads from one of Solomon's Proverbs, to wit: ***"Train up a child in the way he should go: and when he is old, he will not depart from it,"*** I called on the Lord. That was the end of the first beginning of my life, and the beginning of the second end.

On the second Sunday in January, 1974, I attended church and the preacher spoke from the subject: "Life's stormy seas."

Half way through his sermon he touched on the 'religious storms' that will confront us. That sermon got my attention, and when the time was right I accepted Jesus as Lord of this life and Savior in the world to come. I united with that church as a candidate for baptism. I had already been baptized at age seven, but that was because my grandmother told me to. This time it was because I had accepted Christ for myself.

I joined the young-adult Usher Board, but because I was a college graduate I was asked to also teach Sunday school. I simultaneously began to read through the Bible a second time, and by force of habit, memorized quite a bit of the New Testament. By the time I completed the second reading, I was convinced that my mother and my grandfather had spent their lives trying scare people into heaven, out of fear of going to hell. I remember entering Graduate School with a desire to become a Lawyer and then a Federal Judge. However, eight months later things changed again. Time and circumstances convicted me, and I became convinced that there was a higher calling on my life. I announced what I believed to be my calling to the gospel ministry to my pastor, and instead of Law School I switched to Seminary to sharpen the tools with which I had been entrusted.

Building on what I believed to be the true foundation for godly living, I travelled the road to repentance in accordance with the dictates of the voice of God in 2 Chronicles Chapter 7 Verse 14. And when the time was fulfilled, the Spirit of God spoke into my spirit that I had been ordained a 21st Century Prophetic Voice to the Nations. The validation was in the fact that I couldn't otherwise explain the advanced revelation and illumination of scripture that had been given to me.

Prior to writing *Entering,* I concluded that the context and the content of the two books that I had already published were clearly "years ahead of their time." In each of them one will find parts of my story. This is an expanded version. It is my hope that by telling my story, my readers will find a portion of their own ever-present past, and that it will serve to enlighten, enhance, and encourage them to get on the right track and to stay fixed and focused. Translated, that's another way of saying that I hope what the Spirit of God has revealed and subsequently inspired me to write, will enable my readers to bridge the gap between traditional teaching that's being taught in the organized Church, and what they will read in my books.

The fact that I wasn't allowed to come forth until the 21st Century, I believe is because of the choices I made along the way. Time had to be allowed according to the permissive will of God, for the Spirit of God to factor-in the rewards and consequences of my choices. In that capacity and since there is nothing new under the sun, unlike the prophet of old who for hundreds of years "foretold the future," my task is to "go forth telling the future." That is my endeavor both inside and outside of the Church, using revelation illumination and inspiration to the very best of my ability.

I have identified "Who God is in and of Himself" and a portion of "Who we are in God." We come now to the answer to "What is God in each of us?" As previously stated, having been created in God's own image, characteristically speaking we have several advantages without which all of us would be powerless. For instance, we have the propensity—the inclination and tendency— to **think** positive, **be** productive and progressive; consistent, continuous and conducive at will. These six attributes delineate a portion of The Nature of God which He inherently instilled in each of us. John said it this way in the prologue to his Gospel: ***In Him was life, and the life was the light of men.*** Thus, with a healthy degree of certainty, regardless of what we have been taught, all of us can say with certainty that God is the life and the light of men. More will be said on this subject as we proceed.

AIMS AND OBJECTIVES

KEEPING in mind that the primary and terminal aims and objectives of *"Entering"* are to enlighten, enhance and encourage believers to cultivate an ear to hear what the Spirit of God is saying to the Church, I have determined that the first order of business for me was to replicate the rules for learning how to trust and believe. According to Webster's II New Riverside University Dictionary (1988), the definition of "trust" is **"having complete confidence**

in the ability, integrity and Character of another," and belief
is activated trust. Stated another way, the definition of belief is
having complete confidence **in a trust that has been activated.**

Since the person in question is the LORD God, I dare say there
is no need to delineate the validity of His character. Therefore, we
will proceed on the basis of Solomon's declaration in Proverbs
3:5-6:

> *"Trust in the LORD with all your heart; and lean*
> *not on your own understanding. In all your ways*
> *acknowledge Him, and He will direct your paths."*

That said—using the same source of reference—the ability to
trust and believe is left up to the discretion of the participant-in-
the-process. That means you me, I we, us and they. Personally, I
have come to grips with the fact that by believing, any of us can
have life through the name of Jesus (John 20:31). It is my hope
that my readers and all of my future hearers will become willing
participants in the procedural-process that will inspire them
to endeavor to enter in at the Strait Gate (Matthew 7:13), by
doing the right thing, the right way. How do we do that? I was
asked recently. The answer is simple provided we don't spend
an inordinate amount of time arguing with the concept or its
authenticity.

ABOUT THIS BUSINESS OF "HOW"

WITHOUT any fear of contradiction or condemnation, I can say
with certainty that this process is both, healthy and wholesome. It
has been tried and proven to be true. I did it and it works. The only
obstacle is one's belief system. Previously we said that there are
only two ways to think, and subsequently only two ways to live
our lives: God's way and man's way. On more than one occasion
Jesus taught the "narrow way" and admonished his disciples to
make the best choice. In Matthew 7:13 (NKJV), Jesus said, ***"Strive***
to enter through the narrow gate, for many, I say to you, will seek
to enter and will not be able;" and again in Luke 13:24 (KJV),

Jesus said, ***"Strive to enter in at the Strait Gate: for many, I say unto you, will seek to enter in, and shall not be able."*** Thanks to Adam, the only way man really knows is how to live life the way Adam left on record. Therefore, without going any further, there must be an agreement that "change—from the inside-out—is a must."

Keeping in mind that Jesus came to save mankind from his sins, I soon learned that the correct choice was self-evident. Needless to say, all of this is easier said than done; nevertheless, the way is simple. There are six sequential steps: (1) Discover where you are, (2) Choose where you want to go, (3) Decide the best way for you to get there; (4) Set your goal, (5) Plan your work, and (6) Work your plan. As you prepare to begin your journey, ask yourself, "Where am I?" And here, I trust I don't have to delineate the importance of adhering to the old adage which says, "To thine own self, be true."

Having discovered where you are—relative to where you desire to go—you need only determine that God's way is the best way to get there. That second step fluctuates with each person because no two people think exactly alike. The best way to get there is determined by one's ability to hear the voice of God, receive it and believe it (Romans 10:17). At this juncture I believe I would again be remiss if I didn't slip in a reminder for good measure. It involves a struggle with which all of us must contend.

Simply stated, we must learn to think positive and to be productive and progressive as we strive to live our lives. That involves taking the word of God verbatim and without exception. By way of reminder, new participants in the process should read each passage of scripture as a **spectator,** observing how the Bible writer's target-population received and reacted to the word; and how the Spirit of God's behavior was affected by the choices they made. Then the participant should take a good look at his own life, re-read the same passage as a **participant**—having been fore-warned and fore-armed—and making the correct decision the second time around should be easy.

All of this should be accomplished before he (or she) attempts to help others to think right and be right. That last step is most important. Each person must remember that when he (or she) is sharing, he is telling his own story; and if his story doesn't sound like the story of the person with whom he is sharing, it will be rejected. But he should not allow that to stop him from going forward.

So far we have used three attributes of the Nature of God that were inherently instilled in each of us. Each person has the propensity to think positive and to be productive and progressive. The question to be asked and answered by each of us at this point is, "Do I have a mental-state-of-readiness that's equal to my desire to choose God's way?" Oswald Chambers (1982) was correct when he said,

Everyone has to begin with this struggle for self-denial; and striving to enter in at the narrow gate is a picture of the struggle. Anything that does not enter in at the narrow gate, for example, will discover that self-interest, self-indulgence, and self-determination will always end in destruction. The struggle to enter in, no matter with what it may be in connection, braces us morally. Self-indulgence is a refusal to struggle, a refusal to make ourselves fit. **(6)**

So it is that we say if you ultimately choose to engage in the struggle and gain the victory, you will be a benefit to all with whom you meet. But if you choose not to struggle—and the choice is always yours to make—your attitudes and actions will manifest themselves as moral pollution. I made my choice and followed all six sequential steps. Once I determined who God is, in and of Himself, I was able to better—determine who I am and what [the power of] God is in me. The problem that remains is for each person to make his (or her) choice.

THE CHOICE IS YOURS

I HAVE said it before and I'll say it again. I believe that if an inquiry was held, there would be a general agreement that by nature, the human heart accepts the existence of God; but still we willfully run from God and rebel against Him. The question is why? That is one of the questions that this book has striven to answer. The Bible—the sacred book of the Christian faith—provides us with the only verified, acceptable word of God: which calls that rebellion "Sin." Romans 3:23 informs us that *"All have sinned and come short of the glory of God. In addition, Romans 3:10 reminds us that "there is none righteous, no, not one."* Yet, the Bible says that God loves us, all of us: you, me, I, we, us, and they: include everyone, and exclude no one.

The Bible says that not only does God love us, He wants to save us. In other words, God wants to deliver us from the self-destructive forces of sin, and offer us a new life filled with hope. In the simplest of terms, God wants to be reconciled with the man whom He created in His own image (Genesis 1:27), but who was overcome by sin. God wants mankind to have a New Life in Christ (John 3:5), which is inseparably attached to a hope that's built on nothing less than the blood of Jesus and righteousness.

That hope is available only through the acceptance of God's free gift: the sacrifice of His Son. Scripture says,

"God loved this world so much that He gave His only begotten Son so that those who believe would not perish, but would have everlasting life."

Translated and in simple terms, His Son paid the penalty for our sin, granting us the right of re-entry into the garden of God (Genesis 3:23), where we can eat from the tree of life on a daily basis, and live eternally in the presence of God. But that is not how the story ends. We cannot speak positively about Christ without mentioning Satan—whose real name is Lucifer (Isaiah 14:12). Satan, the arch-enemy of God, has mounted an ongoing campaign against the cause of Christ, with the terminal aim of stealing your joy, killing your spirit, and causing you to self-destruct—destroy your own relationship with God. Let me make that clear. Satan is alive and well, but he is powerless in and of himself. Instead, he draws his strength from those of us who either refuse to resist him, or who goes to sleep at the switch and allows him to take up residence in our minds.

THE ACCUSER

SATAN in our lives is like the District Attorney in the court room. He is the accuser and his aim is to bring in a verdict of guilty. Even though the voice of God has said:

> *Therefore, if anyone is in Christ, he is a new creation; old things have passed away, behold all things have become new" (2 Corinthians 5:17);*

Satan will use the same thoughts, ideas, and suggestions (TIS's) that he used with Eve and Adam, and then Jesus, to deceive you. Satan's onslaught is never-ending. It took me several years to learn how to resist Satan. I followed Jesus. Jesus did it by using only the word of God. Suffice it to say, the only thing that works is the "word of God" (Matthew 4:4). Rest assured that the Spirit of God works only through the word of God, in the child of God, who is striving to do the will of God. It works on this wise. Salvation requires submission and surrender: submission to the Sovereignty of God over our lives, and surrender to the Lordship and leadership of the Holy Spirit in our lives. That is the formula. Anything else is an abrupt waste of your time.

That is a summary of the procedural process which leads to the full complement of salvation. The outcome is reconciliation. The full complement of salvation differs from traditional salvation in that it requires apprehension and adherence to the principles of God, in full expectation of enjoying the promises of God. Simply stated, the full complement grants every man (and woman) access to salvation that's guaranteed, but not automatic. That access, when activated, will enable and empower the participants in the process, to be reconciled to God in real time.

A POIGNANT QUESTION

IN a testimony to the Glory of God in creation, King David wrote to the Chief Musician on the instrument of Gath, raising the question, ***"What is man that you are mindful of him?"*** The answer appeared first in the twenty-seventh verse of the first Chapter of Genesis: *"So God created man in His own image; in the image of God created He him: male and female created He them . . ."* That verse is followed by the simplicity in verse sixteen of the third Chapter of St. John: *"For God so loved the world that He gave His only begotten Son that whosoever believes shall not perish, but have everlasting life."* Collectively, those two verses speak volumes about the love that God has for His creation; and I have learned not to inadvertently put a question-mark where God has arbitrarily put a period. And by learning from my experiences, my readers do well by adopting this strategy. We call God Our Heavenly Father because it was He who created the heaven and the earth (Genesis 1:1) as well as the progenitors of the human race and calling their names "Adam" (Genesis 5:2). But "Who God is and what He is in each of us" are the questions which drive this inquiry; and will propel us on to higher heights.

OLD SCHOOL THINKING

I AM out of the "old school" and my perceptions are built on the "tried and the true" with limited variability. Therefore, in *Entering* my delineation is based on the cause and the effect; and the cost and benefit of embracing change from the inside-out. For me, everything begins with the cost and benefit of our base-scripture (Genesis 1:27-28) which reads:

> *"So God created man in His own Image; in the image of God He created him; male and female He created them." Then God blessed them, and God said to them, "Be fruitful and multiply; fill the earth and subdue it; have dominion over the fish of the sea, over the birds of the air, and over every living thing that moves on the earth."*

It is my conviction that man, having been created in the image of God, came into the world with portions of the nature of God. Specifically, the attributes used to describe the nature of God gave man the propensity to exercise each of them at will, with the proper preparation. It is also my belief that those two verses of scripture identify what was "REALITY" in the mind of God, prior to the onset of Sin. Reality does not change for it is both, the Character and the Nature of God. However, "REALITY" became "ACTUALITY" in Real-time, once it was spoken into existence."

It works on this wise. When God spoke His Reality into existence, it became Actuality in Real-time—the time in which we live. Stated another way, "God's Reality" is the foundation of our "Actuality." Who we are, was meant to be the super-structure that was been built on that foundation. And although God's Reality will never change, our actuality ebbs and flows and is dictated by the choices we make.

PERCEPTION

THE ability to see the difference between Reality and Actuality is a matter of spiritual perception. For example, I perceive that when God spoke, Reality became Actuality and that which emerged was "Existence," coming up and out of "Essence." By way of definition, **"Essence" is "The indispensable or intrinsic properties that characterize or identify something." That which follows is Existence, and the manifestation in real time is the Evidence.** So it is that we can say with certainty that "Essence precedes Existence, and it's always followed by Evidence."

In *Entering*, I begin by comparing and contrasting "Reality" with "Actuality," and follow up with a comparison of "Cost and Benefit." Those are the lessons that I have learned, and my objective in *Entering* is to pull back the spiritual covers and reveal that which is hidden, but has been there all the time.

For instance, when God created man in the image of Himself, man was—and still is—a Spirit-being. However, when sin was allowed to enter into His world, God made coats of skin and clothed the man and the woman (Genesis 3: 21), transitioning them to human beings. I also perceive that God's intent was for His image to remain intact; that is to say, it, like Him, would never change (Malachi 3:6). In other words, His image in mankind would always be "Reality." It identifies what's on the inside, regardless of any changes which may occur on the outside.

At this point I am going to fast-forward, and intermittently flip back and forth between the Old and the New Testament—between the foundation and the superstructure—using what the SOG has inspired me to write, and at the same time, explain and validate what's going on in my mind, and what I believe goes on in the mind of modern man. That said, a literal reading of 2 Timothy 1:7 will reveal that Paul provided validation of my convictions thus far. There, Paul said, **"For *God has not given us a spirit of fear, but of power, and of love, and of a sound mind."*** And we know Paul was correct because characteristically speaking, God is Omniscient, Omnipotent, and Omnipresent—which is another way of saying that God has all knowledge; He is all powerful, and He is everywhere-present at the same time equally. Therefore, what you read and what you do with what you read is your prerogative.

As previously stated, God's way of thinking and living is spelled out for us in Scripture. Make no mistake about it, God does not make our decisions for us; and He will not transgress our free-will. Stated succinctly, in the creation-epic—among other things—man was given the Spirit of a sound mind. However, Satan—using TIS's—entered the minds of Eve and then Adam and neutralized the soundness of their minds. Thus we can again say with certainty that because of sin, all of God's gifts must now be apprehended and activated.

All of God's gifts are now discretionary; that is to say they are guaranteed but they are not automatic. Each of them is up to the discretion of each person. And, in order to apprehend and activate them, all of the "i's" must be dotted and all of the "t's" must be crossed, in accordance with both, a literal reading and an in-depth understanding, of what the Bible means by what it says.

FILLING IN THE GAP

THAT said, with the advent, the advances, and advantages of computer technology, I believe that the saddest refrain that can be heard coming from a self-declared born-again Christian is,

"I don't know." Why is that so? A member once asked. "No one knows everything," she added. My response, I believe, was self-explanatory. When examined closely the answer is both self-evident and scriptural. For instance, it stands to reason that if you lend yourself to a diligent and protracted study of the Bible, the word of God will be made so clear a fool and a wayfaring stranger need not error. And if the participant-in-the-process has really been *"born-again of the water and of the Spirit" (John 3:5)*, the use of modern technology allows the Spirit of God to be his Comforter, Teacher and his Keeper (John 14:26) without the benefit of knowing history.

Secondly, if you add to that equation the fact that the voice of God, speaking through the apostle, Paul, said: *"Study to show yourself approved unto God, a workman who needs not to be ashamed, rightly dividing the word of truth" (2 Timothy 2:15)*; when you have sufficiently engaged in that study, you will have achieved the ability to read the biblical road-map to successful living. Not only that, if you tack on the words of Jesus in John 8:32, (KJV):

> *"If you continue in my word, then are you my disciples indeed; and you will know the truth, and the truth will make you free."*

You will not only have your road map, you also have the keys to spiritual freedom. The operative word in that verse is **"IF."** Either way, what you have is self-evident truth, backed up by scripture. Let me press the point. Continuing with a literal reading of the scriptures, which inform us that Adam and Eve were the only ones to whom God gave the truth about living life and the subsequent death that would follow if they chose to be disobedient (Genesis 2:16-17), their ensuing disobedience placed the onus squarely on their shoulders and ours. Now that we know who did what, the only thing left to do is examine the cause and the effect, to see how the people of God within and without the Church today, figure into the equation.

In Matthew 16:18, Jesus made a very poignant but piercing proclamation which continues to tickle the emotions of Christians the world-over, in the two-thousand years that have followed. In response to Peter's declaration that: ***"You are the Christ, the Son of the living God;"*** Jesus answered and said to him,

> ***"Blessed are you, Simon Bar-Jonah, for flesh and blood has not revealed this to you, but My Father who is in heaven." "And I also say to you that you are Peter, and on this rock I will build My church, and the gates of Hades shall not prevail against it."***

How that is interpreted depends largely on how one interprets the word of God. For example, I tend to think that since time is relative in the eyes of God—that is to say, "one day is as a thousand years when it is passed" (2 Peter 3:8), all statements of fact should be looked at as already-done. For instance, the "b" portion of the above-scripture should be preceded by "When the time is fulfilled," and would read: "When the time is fulfilled—i.e. when the end has come—the world will know that upon the "rock of faith" Jesus built His church, and that it was impregnable; that is to say the gates of hell could not prevail against it."

On that note, the events which occur in our lives each day should be seen as a natural part of the perfect plan of God, being carried out by the Spirit of God on a 24/7 basis, 365 days a year. However and for the record, the perfect plan of God includes, but is not limited to both, the purposeful and the permissive will of God, and it's all recorded for us—in the proper context—in the Bible. Translated, the Bible was given to the world especially for the Church. And even though Satan is on his job striving to convince us otherwise, the Church was designed to be the path that leads to the final destination—notwithstanding limited learning and mental laziness have established her as the final destination. Let me make that clear.

My perception is that the design of the organized Church would function better if it contained this order. The first step would be membership; the second step would be stewardship; and the third and final step would be discipleship. Specifically, while a candidate is showing him or herself to be a good member—that is to say, being taught and learning how to be a good steward—he is also being taught the rudiments of repentance, leading to the "Great Commitment" in Luke 9:23.

When he has mastered the steps of self-denial, the next rung on the ladder is learning to "Love the LORD his God with all of his heart, and with all of his soul." If it looks like I have overlooked a portion of that verse, not to worry because—just as Jesus summarized the Decalogue (Matthew 22: 37 & 40)—He also summarized the original rendering of this commandment in Deuteronomy 6: 1-6. Hear the voice of God in its entirety:

> *Now this is the commandment, and these are the statutes and judgments which the LORD your God commanded to teach you, that you may observe them in the land which you are crossing over to possess, "that you may fear the LORD your God, to keep all His statutes and His commandments which I command you, you and your son and your grandson, all the days of your life, and that your days may be prolonged. Therefore hear, O Israel, and be careful to observe it, that it may be well with you, and that you may multiply greatly as the LORD God of your fathers has promised you—'a land flowing with milk and honey.' Hear, O Israel: The LORD your God, "The LORD is one!" "You shall love the LORD your God with all your heart, with all your soul, and with all your strength." "And these words which I command you today shall be in your heart." You shall teach them diligently to your children, and shall talk of them when you sit in your house, when you walk by the way, when you lie down and when you rise up. "You shall bind them as a sign on your hand," and they shall be as frontlets between your eyes. "You shall write them on the doorposts of your house and on your gates." [And as a caution against disobedience] when the LORD your God brings you into the land of which He swore to your fathers, to Abraham, Isaac, and Jacob, to give you large and beautiful cities which you did not build, houses full of all good things which you did not fill, hewn-out*

> *wells which you did not dig, vineyards and olive trees*
> *which you did not plant—when you have eaten and*
> *are full—then beware, lest you forget the LORD who*
> *brought you out of the land of Egypt, out of the house*
> *of bondage."*

Speaking as an African in diaspora, I believe I am on safe ground when I say that the above-passage is especially applicable to all people of color residing in the United States. Why? Someone asked. It's because they are the progenitors of the human race, even though Satan has convinced them that they are nothing, nobody, and unnecessary. And we can know the truth of that conclusion because it pleased God to geographically begin creation with people of color among the inhabitants of the African Continent before the Caucasian race came into being. The Bible is replete with the number of times that they seemingly forgot the LORD their God, even while in transition out of Egypt.

The Life Application Study Bible has a commentary on the above passage that's worthy of repeating in this presentation. The editors wrote:

This passage is often said to be the central theme of Deuteronomy. It sets a pattern that helps us relate the Word of God—that would be the words of Jesus, who is called Christ, in the New Testament—to our daily lives. We are to love God, think constantly about His commandments, teach His commandments to our children, and live our daily lives by the guidelines in His Word. (Note the spelling of Word.) God emphasized the schools cannot be used to escape from this responsibility. The Bible provides so many opportunities for object lessons and practical teaching that it would be a shame to study it only one day a week. Eternal truths are most effectively learned in the loving environment of a God-fearing home.

For the record, therein lies one of the first connections between the Old and the New Testaments. Recalling early elementary English language grammar, children are taught to capitalize the name of a "Person, Place, Thing or Idea," calling it is a proper Noun. Close observation of the first verse of John's gospel in every translation of the Bible, reveals that "WORD" is capitalized, which indicates that reference is being made to a person; yet the term is traditionally used as if it is inanimate.

That same reference appears in verse 14, this time linking two living persons: one who is prominent in the Old Testament, and one who makes His presence known in the New Testament. The curious part is that the two persons are one-in-the-same; which brings us to point number one. The first person is the Creator-God; the second person is Christ.

Therein is a mystery which has raised many questions, but for which there seemingly were no ready-answers; at least none that were both acceptable and workable. I once heard the late Dr. C.A.W. Clark, pastor of the *Good Street Baptist Church* in Dallas, Texas, offer in a sermon what I believe to be the most succinct explanation, one that's both reasonable and acceptable, and also biblical. Dr. Clark said,

The Creator-God, being Omniscient, Omnipotent, and Omnipresent, took out of Himself just enough to reproduce Himself, thereby allowing Him to be absent from Himself, while yet remaining with Himself. He spoke, and the Word went out. Scripture says that word was, "for unto us a child is born, unto us a Son is given: and the government shall be upon His shoulder: and his name shall be called Wonderful, Counselor, The Mighty God, The Everlasting Father, The Prince of Peace" (Isaiah 9:6). **(7)**

What we have there is both, prophecy and a promise. God the Father spoke through the mouth of the prophet and declared the end from the beginning (Isaiah 46:10), as only the Creator-God can do. Isaiah records this rendering:

> *"Remember the former things of old, for I am God, and there is none like Me, declaring the end from the beginning, And from ancient times things that are not yet done, saying, "My counsel shall stand, and I will do all my pleasure," Calling a bird of prey from the east, the man that executes My counsel, from a far country. Indeed I have spoken it; I will also bring it to pass. I have purposed it; I will also do it."*

Therein is the connectivity between God and man, and between man and God. This connection between the Old and New Testament is often overlooked, but remains just the same.

Fast-forwarding to the New Testament, in Matthew Chapter 22 Verse 37, we hear Jesus' response to a question by a young Jewish Lawyer. Jesus said to him, ***"You shall love the LORD your God with all your heart, with all your soul, and with all your mind."*** Deuteronomy 6:5 uses the word, "strength" rather than "mind" which seems to suggests "combining all of your faculties." At any rate, following the Great Commitment is step number two: otherwise known as the "Great Commandment" (Matthew 33:37 – 40).

If we Pre-suppose that the tenets of the Great Commitment and the Great Commandments have been met, the third rung on the ladder is the Great Commission (Matthew 28:18-20). Simply stated, using the Great Commitment as the launching pad, the first stop on the path to an already-decided destiny, is the Great Commandment (Matthew 22: 37, 40); with the Great Commission (Matthew 28:18-20) as the starting point to becoming a follower of Christ.

In essence, the goal of the organized Church is to evangelize with the common, collective objective of making disciples of all nations. The role and function of the Church is to perfect the saints for the work of ministry (Ephesians 4:11), for the edifying of the body of Christ. Stated succinctly, members of the Church are to become disciples, go out and make more disciples; at which time the cycle begins again.

Part of the problem with which the organized Church is faced today, is reversing the trend that now exists: that of making the organized Church the path rather than the destination. Currently, Church members strive to get people to join their local church-family and take part in making manifest the vision of their pastor. That makes the Church come across as the final destination instead of the path leading to the destination.

As it now stands, the growth of the church has become stagnated, fails to grow; and the cause of Christ is thwarted. When that trend is reversed the world will see what Jesus said come to fruition. That is to say, Chapter 16 Verse 18 of the Matthean

Gospel would now read: "When the time is fulfilled, all will see that My church was always impregnable, and incapable of being taken by force." That conviction also underlies Hosea's prophecy in Chapter 4 Verse 6, which should be understood as the voice of God saying: "When the time is fulfilled, the world will see that many of "My people were destroyed for lack of knowledge," and there was no need for such destruction. For the sake of clarity, Hosea's prophecy reads:

> *"My people are destroyed for lack of knowledge. Because you have rejected knowledge, I also will reject you from being priest for me; "Because you have forgotten the law of your God, I also will forget your children." "The more they increased, the more they sinned against Me;" I will change their glory into shame." "They eat up the sin of My people; They set their heart on their iniquity. And it shall be: like people, like priest." So I will punish them for their ways, and reward them for their deeds. "For they shall eat, but not have enough; They shall commit harlotry, but not increase; Because they have ceased obeying the Lord." (Hosea 4:6-10).*

When I look back through my mind's eye, using my spirit of a sound mind, this is what I hear and see. My perception is, the voice of God said what He meant, and He meant what He said, with no time-constraints considered.

But currently, when a person expresses a desire to unite with the Church, he is taken in; membership and stewardship are combined, and that person, instead of being taught to be the Christian that God would have him to be, is guided into one of the Church auxiliaries or ministries, and begins fulfilling the vision that the pastor has for His Church; almost completely obliterating "discipleship."

WE REAP WHAT WE SOW

FOR more than fifteen-hundred (1500) years—from 500 A.D.—the organized Church has perpetuated this status-quo and thereby missed the opportunity to correctly define herself. One writer—and if I could remember his name, I would give him his proper credit—said that "the organized Church has also missed the opportunity to rediscover a world that has long been forgotten: a world in which the 'Hidden Hope' was actually common-place.' "

For lack of a better way to say it, the sins of oversight, limited-learning, mental laziness and apathy have caused the Church to become sequestered; and according to the Bible, the perpetuation of the sediments of those sins, makes "The pastor-said syndrome" the principle cause. People will refuse to think for themselves. Instead, they answer questions by saying, "I don't know, but the pastor said . . ."

A local pastor recently said to me, "In summary what you are saying is, unless some radical changes are made, the church is going to hell in a hand basket, and pastors are pushing it." My response was, look at it this way: "Since continuing to do the same thing, the same way, hoping to somehow get some different results, is 'a working definition of insanity,' instead of criticizing pastors—unduly or otherwise—why not let change begin with you, and share with the pastors you know how change—from the inside-out—can affect their attitudes and actions?'" His response was, "Personally, Dr. Carter, I would if I could." Tell me what I should change, and how to change it. Tell me if you know. My response is included in the Epilogue that follows.

EPILOGUE

THE primary aim of this work was to develop a medium for getting the word out by painting a literal portrait of how to do the right thing, the right way. The way is clear; all the participants-in-the-process have to do is enter in at the strait gate (Matthew 7:13-14) to an already decided destiny. Specifically, it was my intent to set forth the two mindsets that are open to all of God's children: 'thinking God's way' and 'thinking man's way.' Having made my choice, in this work I have striven to provide written assistance to those who desire to choose God's way over our current traditional ways.

Paul delivered the will of God when he said to Timothy: *"Preach the word."* And since I have been led to believe that "Preaching the word" (2 Timothy 4:1-4) is exactly what the voice of God meant, for all the same reasons that Paul proclaimed; I made the decisive-decision to call a spade a spade, sin by its right name, and let the chips fall where they may. On the one hand, "Preaching the word" is *"The manifestation of the Incarnate Word, by the spoken word, from the written word."* On the other hand, preaching **from** the word—which is what contemporary preachers do—is when pastors select a pivotal scripture, affix a catchy subject, and use it to interpret the scripture for their hearers, using it to 'tell the story' while at the same time endeavoring to solve their problems.

Simply stated, pastors are content with using this method of interpreting the Scriptures for their parishioners, which does two things. It restricts the hearer to the mindset of the preacher—which becomes their truth—closing the door on any other way of understanding the word of God; and it denies the people their ability and their right to *"go and grow in the knowledge of the Son of God, unto a perfect man, unto the measure of the stature of the fullness of Christ"* (Ephesians 4: 13); by activating their own personal 'spirit of a sound mind. Am I saying that preaching from the word is in error? No, but close observation will reveal that in most cases you will find those sermons to be insufficient.

Why? Because the former is designed to prevent sin; while the latter is designed to deal with sin the only way the preacher understands it.

In John 5:39-40, Jesus said,

> *"Search the scriptures; for in them you think you have eternal life: and they are they which testify of me. And you will not come to me, that you might have life."*

I have searched the scriptures, attempting to find instances where Jesus set out to solve problems as a matter of purpose. I read where He healed all manner of sickness and He even raised the dead; but nowhere did I find Him engaging in solving the problems of the people as a matter of purpose. Even though I did hear Him say *"I am come that they might have life, and that they might have it more abundantly,"* I would be the first to say that there are many ways to interpret that scripture. However, when the solemn truth is told, that verse means much more than what we have traditionally believed it to mean, and problem-solving is not a principle part of it.

And after thinking about it, I suppose it wouldn't be too far out of order to include some "problem-solving" in the phrase "more abundantly." But that would be our doing, not His. It seems to me that we have given everything else a chance, so it might be time to give God a chance. It is clear to me that pastors and preachers are faced with some difficult days ahead. I have had some in these more than seven decades, and I expect to have more in the years to come.

Long-time members are on an exodus out of the mainline denominational churches into the so-called "non-denominational" [mega churches]. While they try as hard as they may, pastors cannot get their traditional churches to grow, quantitatively or qualitatively. To put it bluntly, churches have become entities of entertainment with programs for profit, rather than sources of information which point the way back to Christ. And it's precisely because the days ahead are difficult, that now, more than ever, in the words of Henry H. Mitchell (1979), a former Adjunct professor at my Alma Mater, Fuller Theological Seminary, Pasadena, CA "There must be a recovery of preaching."(8)

Personally, I have been led to believe that "The time is fulfilled; that the Kingdom of God is at hand; and that it is time now for all of God's people to *'repent and believe the gospel"* (Mark 1:15). Translated, **I submitted** to the Sovereignty of God **over** my life and began a systematic **surrender** to the Lordship and the leadership of the Holy Spirit **in** my life, in January, 2007. Since then I have been growing and going from "good," (Genesis 1:31) to "great" (1 Corinthians 2:9); and the best part of it is, God is not through with me yet.

The words of the apostle Paul in Philippians 3:13 ring true in my life:

> *"I count not myself to apprehended: but this one thing
> I do, forgetting those things which are behind, and
> reaching forward to those things that are before me, I
> press toward the mark for the prize of the high calling
> of God in Christ Jesus."*

That which I have experienced and to which I have been exposed, is proof-positive that God is good all the time; and all the time, God is good. I have no "real regrets" because until I was made able to submit and surrender, I did what I was big and old enough to do—that is, until I grew tired of doing it, falling down and struggling to get up. The last time around I was left pondering the question, "What, in this world, is the Church supposed to be? While I'm not through thinking about the specificity of the answer, there is one thing I would do differently if I had the chance to start all over. Without a doubt I would start on this road thirty years sooner. Nevertheless, *"The Lord [has] rewarded me according to my righteousness; according to the cleanness of my hands has He recompensed me"* (Psalm 18:20).

I have been paid according to my work; and I thank God that I am still able to produce. My heart's desire and my prayer to God on a daily basis, is for His people to be saved, and for the salvation process to continue in me. It is my hope that the reader finds what he (or she) needs to help him see that there are 'blessings-unlimited and all good things without end' (1 Corinthians 2:9) awaiting those who have the holy boldness to choose to do what's right, the right way.

Translated, I am challenging all of my readers—and hearers—to do what God would have you to do the way God would have you to do it. Let me close by saying that "to know Jesus and the power of His resurrection" is to be the participant-in-the-process. Believers must be willing to have their minds renewed on a continuous basis (Romans 12:2). In essence, each must be willing to acknowledge the fact that he is not the captain of the ship. Jesus is the Captain and the Spirit of God (SOG) is the Executive Officer (XO). By the way, only the XO can guide steer the ship. Being able to find and enter in at the Straight Gate must be left to the leadership of the Holy Spirit. I believe I am on safe ground when I say that most of this is new for most people; and it's going to take some time to become acclimated.

However and metaphorically speaking, the objective is to get all who will, to get on board this 'old ship of Zion.' Oh, and by the way: this is a war-ship, not a love-boat. To get on board you will have to fight. But once you are on board, you can leave the fighting up to the SOG. He will fight your battles if you will be still and know that He is God; and that He will be exalted (Psalm 46:10). Paul said to the Church at Philippi, "In all things give thanks." He did not say, "For all things," but "In all things." I fashion my prayer on a daily basis on what God has already done, what He was doing at that very moment, and what I believed He will do throughout that day and in the rest of my tomorrows—which, I believe has already been done and included in the perfect plan of God.

My prayer is repetitious, but it is real and not in vain. It captures all of my thoughts on a daily basis. Examine it and you just might see your desires as well. To be able to enter through the narrow way—the Strait Gate—one must be willing and able to trust the word of God implicitly. Age is no factor, and a formal education—or the lack thereof—is not a barrier. One merely needs to believe. When Jesus said, "Lo, I am with you always, even to the end of the age" (Matthew 28:20); He was referring to the consistency in the character of God the Father. **The fact that God** is Consistent tells us that He is always on task. If we apply a literal meaning to the promise of God in Jeremiah 33:3: *"Call to me and I will answer you, and show you great and mighty things, which you do not know,"* what you have in the content of *Entering* is an example of a perpetual principle and promise.

I mention it because this verse is often taken out of context; which, by the way, allows a lie reign supreme. I believe that because we have been told that we can call on God, and that God always answers prayer. The attitudes and actions of many, if not most people, seem to suggest that 'by some stroke of genius' God will stop what He is doing and perform at our will. Nothing is farther from the truth. All that God the Father is doing these days—VIA the other two members of the Supreme Court of Heaven—is superintending what He said He was going to do in Genesis 3:15. What makes me so sure? I was asked. My perception is based on three words in Genesis 1:26: "Let them have dominion . . ." That says to me that God, having made man in his own image, and subsequently having Moses to write "And God saw everything He had made, and behold it was very good;" nothing was omitted from the purpose and the plan of God. Therefore, it's only a matter of picking up where God left off in that twenty-sixth (26th) verse, and getting a good understanding of what God meant by what He said.

Close observation will reveal that God the Father sent Jesus the Christ to fulfill His promise. His divine plan was put in place, and God the Holy Spirit is carrying it out on a 24/7, 365 days a year basis. And as it relates to the work that He came to do, Jesus—who was "The fullness of the God-head, bodily" (Colossians 2:19),—had this to say while He was dying on the Cross of Calvary: "It is finished" (John 19:30). In other words, what He came to do was already done, and all we have to do is believe, to make it so.

Scripture says only a few of us will find the strait gate (Matthew 7:13), to say nothing about entering it, apprehending and adhering to the principles that will take us to the other side; or enjoying the promises that await us. Perhaps it would be easier to accept if we think in terms of the perfect plan of

God already being in motion. It is, you know (Genesis 1:31). The perfect plan of God, complete with the rewards and the consequences of our free-will already factored-in, is being implemented by the Spirit of God; and it covers all of existence from 'the alpha to the omega; from the first to the last' (Revelation 22:13).

The truth of the matter is, the perfect plan of God contains all there is and all that will ever be. As each day opens and enlivens, God has one goal and one objective in mind. I call it 'His Reality.' The outcome of that goal is recorded for us in Genesis 3:15. And there is a direct correlation between it and "doing the right thing, the right way. **"Stated succinctly, His terminal objective is to reconcile mankind to Himself. In spite of the popular opinions which might say otherwise, that is all that God the Father is involved in on a day to day basis.**

In the design-phase, the heavenly die was cast, and the divine mold was poured, giving everybody their purpose and everything its place in the plan of God. There is nothing more that He needs to do. What you and I have been given—by the grace of God—is the power and the authority which came with free-will. And our free-will gives us the opportunity to see— from day to day—what's included in the plan of God. Through His word we're enabled, and by His Spirit we are empowered. And between the two, we have the blessed assurance—even though the reference-scripture is written in a different context—that we 'can indeed, do all things through Christ, which strengthens us" (Philippians 4:13). All we need to do is make the necessary adjustments in our lives.

Finally, I have set forth the ideas and strategies in this book in the spirit of humility. Sometimes it was difficult, but I have striven to not be pedantic—that means, marked by a narrow, often ostentatious concern for book learning—in my presentation. However, I did endeavor to be persuasive because we have only one life to live, and none of us know how much time we have. Ever since I discovered that having been created *"In His Own Image"* actually gave the Spirit and Soul of man pre-eminence, I have been in awe of our Heavenly Father, the Lord Jesus who is our Christ—who is our only way-maker and in whom we live and move and have our being (Acts 17:24-28)—and the Spirit of God (SOG) who makes all things happen.

Today I count it a double honor to know Him in the pre-pardon of my Sin, and to have been given this opportunity to tell somebody what I know about the God of creation. So it is that I beseech you and all of my readers to join me on this journey from earth's sorrow to heaven's joy, which begins with a walk down the road to repentance, and ends behind the doorway to an already decided destiny. By way of description, hear this: *"Entering in at the Strait gate"* is the beginning, and it is ongoing. In other words, it is non-stop. Once you start the journey from earth's sorrow to heaven's joy, you must be ready to go all the way. Those are not my words. Jesus said, ***"No man, having put his hand to the gospel plough, and looking back, is fit for the kingdom of God"*** (Luke 9:62).

I don't believe that Jesus, by saying that, was sounding the death knell for those "who are lacking in knowledge" (Hosea 4:6). I believe He is simply saying that you are not worthy of the kingdom in that posture because you have not been born again. That means that a decisive-decision must be made before you put your hand to the plough. Stated another way, whatever it is that caused you to look back will manifest itself as "a product of the wide gate that leads to destruction." Every pastor / preacher must keep in mind that when you announced that you believe that God had placed a higher calling on your life and that you believe that calling is to preach the gospel; there was no one present but you and God. And when Jesus said, "Lo, I'll be with you always, even to the end of the age;" He was simply looking out for you. Know this: once you have made that decisive-decision, you will never walk alone.

Look closely and you will see that ***"you are approaching the doorway"*** *to 'An already-decided destiny"'*. Another way to see what you are looking at up ahead, is to envision it as a bright light. What you see 'is a light;' but it is more than that. I perceive it to be the face of Jesus, who is the "Light of the world;'" sitting on the right hand of God the Father making intercession for you, me, and all believers who make it that far. On the other side is what we have **traditionally called heaven,** and even I cannot describe what's over there.

What I can say is that from the beginning it has been the dwelling place of our Father-in-heaven, for even the Temple that Solomon built could not hold His presence (2 Chronicles 6:2ff.). Oh, how I would love to be able to see it, describe and delineate it; but I can't. This is where conjecture takes the place of truth with no biblical validation. You and everyone who comes after you will simply have to believe; for it is one of the gifts of God that must be apprehended and activated to enjoy the promises of God.

You have heard me fondly describe 'the already decided destiny' as "one of the blessings-unlimited, and all the good things without end" that await those who have the holy boldness to receive the word, believe it and make the decisive decision to serve a true and a living God.

You cannot assume, presume, conjecture, or procrastinate. You cannot go back or relive the past. At best, you can only go forward. Your task, should you make the decisive-decision to become a participant in the process, is to go forward and "do the right thing, the right way." The SOG will lead, guide, and protect you all the way. He will keep you and never leave you: keep you safe and sound from all hurt, harm, and danger; and never leave you to your own devices lest you stumble and fall. Ultimately, His task is two-fold: to save you and to seal you until the day of redemption (Jude 24).

By the grace of God we will see you on the other side. There are only two ways to travel: your way, and God's way. Translated and in the words of Charles G. Adams (1980), "All things are yours. The past is yours: learn from it. The present is yours: fulfill it. The future is yours: preserve it. The Bible is yours: believe it. The Church is yours: claim it. Jesus is yours: accept Him. The Holy Spirit is yours: receive Him. Death is yours: delay it. Eternal life is yours: seize it. Heaven is yours: meet me there" (9)

NOTES

1. Dr. Jeremiah A. Wright (1995) From a sermon delivered at Ward Chapel AME Church Los Angeles, CA
2. Dr. Jeremiah A Wright (1996) From a sermon delivered at his Home Church: Trinity Church of Christ: in Chicago, IL
3. Xavier Carter (2000) Doctoral Dissertation, (Pasadena, CA: Fuller Theological Seminary, 2000) 77
4. Oswald Chambers (1982) My Utmost Devotional Bible, (Nashville, Tennessee: Thomas Nelson, Inc., 1982) 22
5. Dr. Martin Luther King Jr., from a speech given in Birmingham, 1963.
6. Chambers, Ibid., 23
7. Dr. C.A.W. Clark (1982) from a sermon delivered at the Paradise Baptist Church, Los Angeles, CA, Subject is unknown.
8. Henry H. Mitchell, The Recovery of Preaching, Washington D.C. (1979) 56
9. Charles G. Adams, From a sermon entitled, "All Things are Yours" delivered to the graduating class of 1981; at Fuller Theological Seminary, Pasadena, CA